THE CIVIL WAR DIARIES OF Charles Kelly

THE CIVIL WAR DIARIES OF Charles Kelly

The 44th New York Volunteer Infantry in the War of the Rebellion

DON OWEN

By the Dock Publishing

First paperback edition October 2022

ISBN: 979-8-9870665-1-5

By the Dock Publishing
donowen9791@gmail.com
Don Owen
The Civil War Diaries of Charles Kelly

V.1.4

CONTENTS

Introduction

Charles Kelly

Charles Kelly was an officer in the Union Army during the War of the Rebellion, or what we now know as the Civil War. In the South, the war was commonly referred to as the War Between the States or the War of Northern Aggression. Charles mustered into the 44th Regiment, New York Volunteer Infantry, in the fall of 1862 with the rank of 2nd Lieutenant. He fought at Frederiksberg, Gettysburg and many lesser-known places. Wounded twice during the war, Charles mustered out of the army in October of 1864, with the rank of Brevet Captain.

Charles Kelly was the great-grandfather of my wife Gael. Charles left behind five volumes of leather-bound, hand-written diaries about 4 ¼" wide by 6 ½" high, in which he recorded his wartime experiences. The diaries date from October 6, 1862, to October 9, 1864. Some of the entries are in ink and some in pencil; in general, they are difficult to read. Gael and I have spent many hours transcribing the diaries verbatim into readable form.

This work is an attempt to follow Charles Kelly through his war years and, based on his diaries, to get a sense of what he experienced. I have also provided background into the broader scope of what Charles, together with millions of other Americans experienced before and during the time he served in Company C of the 44th New York Volunteer Infantry.

Note: When citing the diaries of Charles Kelly, I have maintained the spelling and punctuation as written in the diaries.

CHAPTER ONE

Torn Apart by War

From Glasgow to Harpers Ferry

2nd Lieutenant Charles Kelly climbed down from a railroad car about ten o'clock in the morning of October 12, 1862. He was a newly minted officer in the Union Army. Together with the rest of his Company, he was passing through Washington, the Capital of the Union, to join his Regiment, the 44th New York Volunteer Infantry. Both he and his men had a pleasant train ride on the short journey from Baltimore. They arrived in Washington at the New Jersey Avenue Station of the Baltimore & Ohio Railroad where they disembarked from the cars just a block north of the capital building.

Charles' long journey to Washington first began many years ago in Scotland. His parents, Neil Kelly and Mary Dougherty, were married in Glasgow, Scotland on May 7, 1830. Mary was born in Glasgow and was about 30 years old when she married Neil. Charles was born May 5, 1831, also in Glasgow. His mother Mary died soon after his birth.

Charles' father, Neil Kelly, was born in Donegal, Ireland, in the year 1800. He moved to Glasgow, Scotland, in 1820. In 1833, Neil married for a second time. His bride was Sarah McGill, born 1805, in Donegal, Ireland. Charles had four siblings from his father's second marriage.

In 1846, the Irish Famine was raging and working class Irish were pouring into Glasgow, where Charles lived. It was a time when Irish Catholics faced open discrimination in Protestant Scotland. The potato blight had reached Ireland in 1845, and within a few years a million people in Ireland died of starvation or related disease. Even more left Ireland. In Glasgow, with so many Irish seeking refuge, there were few prospects for an uneducated Irish Catholic like Neil Kelly. Neil made a courageous decision; he decided to take his family to America. He was not the only one; between 1845, and 1855, more than 1.5 million Irish immigrated to America. By 1914, the population of Ireland was half of what it had been in the 1840s.

In the fall of 1846, Neil Kelly and his family sailed to New York on the three-mast sailing ship *Pacific*. They traveled on the *Black Star Line* owned by Samuel Thompson. On the voyage, the Pacific carried 213 passengers along with a cargo of lumber. The trip from Liverpool to New York harbor took 34 days; the Kelly family arrived in New York harbor on September 19, 1846. After arriving, Charles' Father moved the family to Penn Yan, a small town in central New York and the County Seat of Yates County, New York. It was a good move. Many Irish immigrants, out of financial necessity, tended to settle near the port cities where they arrived, such as New York or Boston. Large numbers of poor Irish in concentrated areas reduced economic opportunities for Irish immigrants, and extended the years needed for them to join the economic mainstream. For Charles Kelly, there was abundant opportunity in the little town of Penn Yan.

Arrived.

Packet ship Victoria, Morgan, 28 days from London, with mdse to John Griswold. 70 steerage passengers.

Ship Sardinia, Crocker, Liverpool, 16th Aug. with mdse to Saml. Thompson, jun. 249 steerage passengers.

Br ship Macao, Scott, 48 days from Liverpool, with mdse, and 197 passengers, to Roche Brothers. On the Banks, spoke schr Cyrus, of Marblehead, with 11,500 fish, 4 months out.

Ship Pacific, Ludlam, 34 days from Liverpool, with mdse and 213 passengers, to Williams & Guion. No date, spoke British schr Catherine Elizabeth, loaded with lumber, bound to New York.

Notice of Arrival of the Ship Pacific with 213 passengers, 34 days from Liverpool. (New York Herald, September 19, 1846.) "Ludlam" refers to Joe Ludlam, Captain of the Pacific.

Like many immigrants, Charles was extremely ambitious and hardworking. The 1850 Yates County census shows Charles, at the age of 18, working as a blacksmith. Later, he learned the painting trade, but left that occupation to "read law" under the tutelage of A.V. Harpending, a respected attorney in Penn Yan. Reading law was an apprenticeship, and was at the time, a common path to becoming a lawyer.

Rather than continue in the legal profession Charles pursued a career in business. Perhaps this decision was prompted by A.V. Harpending leaving his law practice to become District Attorney for Yates County. Charles proved to be an astute businessman, and by the time he was 29 years old he owned *The Farmer's*

Saloon, which was an ale house as well as an eating establishment, and purchased the Yates County Brewery, both located in Penn Yan. He had also purchased empty property in Penn Yan, for future ventures. *The Penn Yan Gazette* and *Yates County Chronicle* both indicate that Charles was a respected and well-liked member of the community… Then the country was torn apart by war.

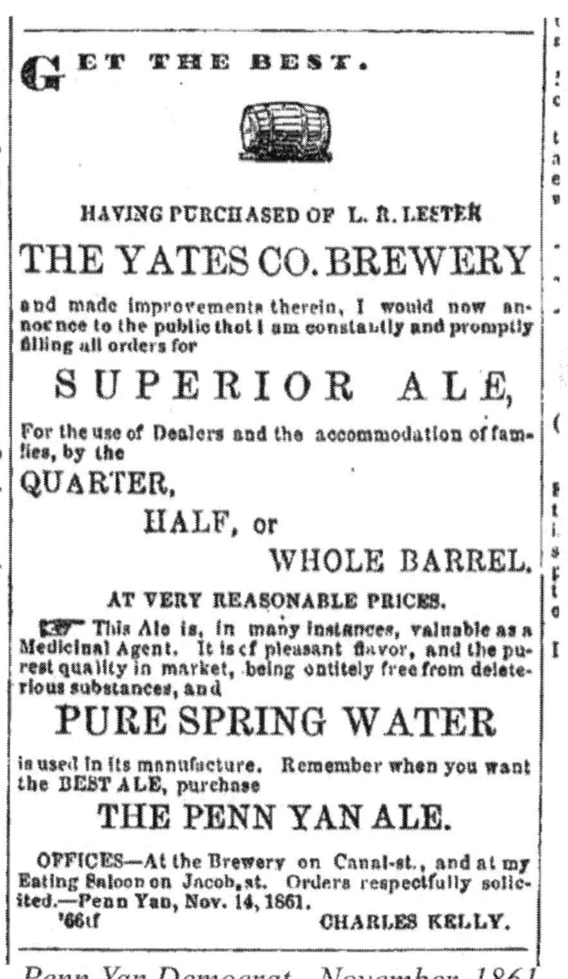

Penn Yan Democrat - November, 1861

This is an ad for the Yates Co. Brewery, owned by Charles Kelly, that appeared in the Penn Yan Democrat, in November of 1861, and also appeared in a number of other local newspapers prior to the time Charles left for the war.

Charles plunged into supporting the Union war effort with everything he had; he even opened a recruiting office in his alehouse.

One Penn Yan newspaper wrote on July 25, 1862,

> ***"It gives us pleasure to state that Charles Kelly of the village has been duly authorized to raise a Company of volunteers under the new levy and is now vigorously at work recruiting an Irish Company for the regiment in the District. The Irish are proverbially brave and loyal to the country of their adoption. Mr. Kelly will make an efficient and excellent officer and it is a gratifying fact that since last Wednesday morning, he recruited a number of vigorous men for his company. The patriotic Irishmen of the County will double step into line and enroll themselves under Captain Kelly until the company is filled up."***

The article is incorrect in referring to Charles as "Captain"; his rank at the beginning of his enlistment was 2nd Lieutenant. Bennett Munger would serve as Captain of the Company. Perhaps the reporter was a bit over enthusiastic for hometown Charles Kelly. Nevertheless, Charles did play a significant role in forming the new Company C of the 44th Regiment, New York Volunteer Infantry.

The Yates County Chronicle, a newspaper published in Penn Yan, wrote on October 2, 1862, *"No man has made greater sacrifices than Lieut. Charles Kelly, to go to the war. We predict that he will make a capital officer."*

The population of Penn Yan in 1860, was a little over twenty thousand.

Lieutenant Kelly's journey to Washington officially started at the Albany Barracks, in Albany, New York. The company arrived at the barracks on September 30, 1862, under the leadership of Captain Bennett Munger, where they began learning the rudiments of marching and being soldiers.

At the Albany barracks, some of the men had trouble adjusting to military life. On October 6, upon receiving thirteen dollars in advance pay for their first month of service, about a dozen of the company went down to Albany. All came back "***straight***" to the barracks but one, Private Peter Hibbard. When Private Hibbard did return, Charles wrote in his diary that he was as drunk as a fool and tried to strike Charles. Charles ***"took hold of him throwed him down and then called on the Boys and they take him to the quarters."***

In September of 1862, Captain Bennett Munger, who had been gathering and training recruits at Camp Swift near Geneva, New York, received orders to join his company to the rest of the regiment. They were to travel to Albany and from there to Washington to receive further orders. On October 9, after spending a few days at the barracks, the Company marched to the Albany docks on the Hudson River and boarded the paddle wheeler *New World* at nine p.m. to start their trip to Washington. The Company was a little less than 100 strong. In his diary, Charles reports that the men of Company C had a pleasant time on the boat ride to New York City.

The steamer *New World* was the largest steamship operating on the Hudson River between Albany and New York City. Later in the war, it was anchored at Fort Monroe at the tip of the Virginia Peninsula and used by the Union Army as a hospital ship. *(Hudson River Maritime Museum)*

The 44th NY Regiment originally formed about a year earlier at Albany, in October of 1861. The regiment began with a strength of 1,061 men, making up ten companies. By September of 1862, the regiment had lost 80% of its men due to battle casualties and disease. The 44th NY was reduced to about 200 muskets. Charles Kelly's company reinforced the regiment with a new company, Company C, Bennett Munger serving as Captain. What was left of the original Company C was dispersed to other companies. The men from the new Company C were predominately from Yates County, New York.

After arriving in New York City at about 8 a.m. on October 10, 1862, Company C disembarked and had a short march to the Jersey Ferry. The ferry took them to New Jersey where they loaded onto railroad cars for the ride to Philadelphia; arriving there about 1 p.m. The railroad through New Jersey ran parallel with the Delaware and Raritan Canal. Charles notes in his diary how level the country was and how poor the soil looked. Company C had a pleasant reception in Philadelphia; they were given dinner and a warm and friendly send-off by the Pennsylvania Relief Association of Philadelphia. Next stop Baltimore.

Company C arrived in Baltimore about half past two, on the morning of October 11. They slept in the railcars until daylight. With the arrival of morning, orders were given and the men marched to the union hall for breakfast. Charles Kelly was not pleased with the reception they received in Baltimore. He writes,

> ***"I think it is the most God forsaken city – I was ever in the boys got on quite a Drunk John McBride was left also Philip morse they went in to some drinking salon and was late for the cars Their is quite a contrast between the people of Philadelphia and the people of Baltimore I think the people of Philadelphia are the friendliest people in the world and the people of Baltimore are the meanest folks I ever came across in my life we tried to get rations for our company But we did not get it until it was to late for the train we had to stay over Night in Baltimore on the Clott farm at Night and it was quite cold for our Boys as it was the first time that the Boys slept without tents in the morning we had Breakfast at the union hall and started on the cars at 1/2 past ten o clock aboard but two men McBride and Morse"***

Baltimore Reception

There was a reason for the animosity from the people of Baltimore. It started at the very beginning of the war that would cost three quarters of a million American lives. We travel back about a year and a half to Fort Sumter, a fort built on an artificial island in Charleston Harbor, Charleston, South Carolina.

On Saturday April 13, 1861, shortly after 2 p.m., the Federal garrison at Fort Sumter surrendered to the forces of Confederate General P.T. Beauregard. Major Robert Anderson was allowed to strike the colors of his command and the next day, get aboard a ship for New York. Almost out of ammunition and food, the garrison at Fort Sumter had endured 34 hours of continuous bombardment before surrendering. Major Anderson had little choice. Years of neglect during the Administration of James Buchanan had left the Fort with little ability to defend itself. The War of the Rebellion had begun.

This picture was taken inside of Fort Sumter on April 15, 1861, one day after the evacuation of Federal forces. (Library of Congress)

On April 15, 1861, in response to the evacuation of Fort Sumter, Abraham Lincoln called for 75,000 volunteers to join the ranks of the Union Army. First priority was to defend Washington. The reality was that there were almost no troops in Washington and the city was practically defenseless. In all likelihood, a single Confederate Regiment from Richmond, less than a hundred miles away, could have captured the city.

After his call for volunteers, Lincoln spent several anxious days waiting for troops to arrive and reinforce the Capital. There was one problem; volunteers coming in by rail from the northern States had to pass through Baltimore, Maryland to get to Washington.

Maryland was a severely divided state. It was a slave holding state and in the recent presidential election Abraham Lincoln received only 2.5 % of the votes cast from Maryland. There was a lot of resentment when Lincoln called for troops to crush the rebellion, and support in Maryland for secession was high. Two days after Lincoln's call, the State of Virginia seceded from the Union. Many in Maryland wanted to follow Virginia's example.

On April 18, 1861, less than a week after the surrender at Fort Sumter, 460 newly mustered Pennsylvania state militia volunteers arrived at Fort McHenry in Baltimore,[1] on their way to Washington.

When the volunteers arrived in Baltimore they were mostly unarmed or without ammunition. Even so, many in Maryland considered these men to be foreign invaders. As the new recruits prepared to march from Fort McHenry and board railcars for the trip to Washington, a crowd of 700 southern sympathizers attempted to stop them from reaching the railroad depot. Local police were able to force passage for the men to Camden Street Station of the *Baltimore and Ohio Railroad.* Insults, stones and bricks were thrown, but the soldiers made it to Camden Station, loaded onto railcars, and continued their journey. They were the first troops to arrive for the defense of Washington.

---

[1] Forty-seven years earlier, Fort McHenry, with a garrison of about 1,000 men, stopped a force of 5,000 British soldiers and sailors from invading Baltimore. It happened in September of 1814. Just days earlier the British had burned the Presidential Mansion, The Capital Building, and many other government buildings in Washington. Fort McHenry was attacked but held. The British defeat at Baltimore was pivotal to ending the War of 1812. The battle at Baltimore inspired Francis Scott Key to write the lyrics to the *Star Spangled Banner.*

Washington was completely unprepared for war. No provision had been made for feeding or housing troops in the Capital. When the Pennsylvania volunteers arrived, they camped in the House wing of the Capitol building.

The next day, April 19, 1861, the 6th Massachusetts Militia arrived in Baltimore from Philadelphia, on their way to Washington. They had started from Boston on April 17. Their train pulled into the Philadelphia, Wilmington and Baltimore Railroad Depot, also called the President Street Station.

It was common at that time for cities to forbid construction of railroad lines through a city. Rail cars arriving at President Street Station that were bound for Washington were uncoupled from their locomotives and pulled by horses along rails built into Pratt Street to the B&O Railroad's Camden Street Station. From there the cars were attached to engines and began the thirty-mile trip to Washington.

As the 6th Massachusetts travelled the ten-block journey via horse drawn railcars, a mob attacked the last of the cars and blocked the route. With little other choice, those who had not yet reached Camden Station, a group of about 240 soldiers, left the train cars and began marching. Soon the mob began breaking store windows and attacking the rear of the marching column with bricks, pistols and paving stones. In response, several soldiers fired into the mob. A riot ensued.

Eventually the Baltimore Police were able to separate the mob from the soldiers and get the remaining soldiers to the rail station. The 6th Massachusetts had to leave behind much of their equipment including their marching band's instruments. Four soldiers of the 6th Massachusetts were killed and 36 were wounded. About a dozen civilians were killed. Later, the crowd destroyed the office of a German language newspaper that supported the Union cause.

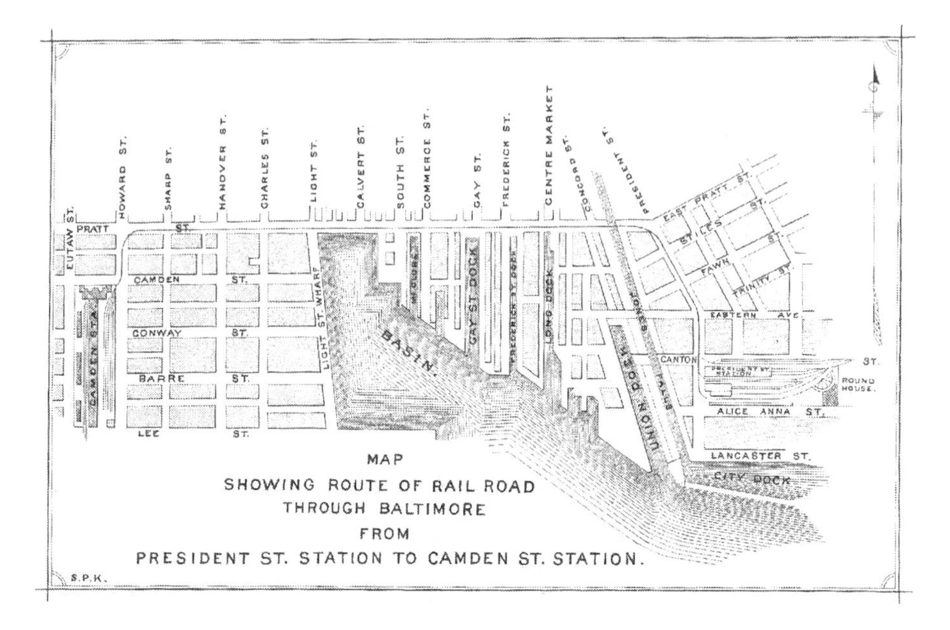

This map shows the President Street Station on the right, and the path taken to get to Camden Station for the ride to Washington. (Library of Congress)

A few hours after leaving Baltimore the 6th Massachusetts arrived in Washington. They were the second group of troops to arrive for the defense of the city. More were coming. The fortification of Washington had begun. By July there were 60,000 troops defending the city and Lincoln could begin to breathe easier.

Longtime Senate doorkeeper Isaac Bassett described the arrival of the 6th Massachusetts,

> ***"The Sixth Regiment of Massachusetts, nine hundred strong, under the command of Col. Jones, were attacked in Baltimore on their way to Washington. . . . On arriving here these were marched into the Capitol and immediately occupied the Senate Chamber. . . . The col. made the Vice President's Room his headquarters. They looked tired I saw blood running down their faces. Their clothes were full of dust. Everything was done that could be for their comfort."***

Three days after the riots, Baltimore sent a delegation of citizens to Abraham Lincoln to protest the "pollution" of their city, but returned to Baltimore empty handed. Soon after, railroad tracks coming into Baltimore were torn up, bridges were wrecked, and telegraph lines were cut. A year and a half later, when Charles Kelly with Company C passed through Baltimore, violence had been stopped, but the angry sentiment remained.

The Capital Building was undergoing a massive renovation during much of the war. This photo shows construction of the Capital dome in 1861. Early in the war, the Capital Building was used to house troops, and after the Battle of 1st Manassas was used as a hospital. (Library of Congress)

Lincoln had to maintain a delicate balance with Maryland. He simply could not afford Maryland seceding from the Union. Washington was located squarely between Maryland and Virginia; if Maryland declared for the South the entire Federal Capital would be surrounded by hostile territory.

On May 6, 1861, as tensions mounted, Federal troops occupied Baltimore and declared martial law. Shortly thereafter, President Lincoln had the mayor, police chief, the entire Board of Police, and the city council of Baltimore imprisoned without charges. He also ordered the arrest of a sitting U.S. Congressman from Baltimore.

The Governor of Maryland and others, implored President Lincoln to stop sending troops through Maryland. Lincoln later replied,

> ***"I have no desire to invade the South, but I must have troops to defend this Capitol. Geographically it lies surrounded by the soil of Maryland, and mathematically the necessity exists that they should come over her territory. Our men are not moles, and can't dig under the earth; they are not birds, and can't fly through the air. There is no way but to march across, and that they must do."***

On June 4, 1861, Roger Taney, then Chief Justice of the United States Supreme Court, a native of Maryland, and member of a wealthy slave-holding family, ruled that the President's actions were unconstitutional. Lincoln ignored the ruling. More arrests followed. On September 17, twenty-seven of Maryland's state legislators were arrested. This amounted to one third of Maryland's General Assembly. No further debate on secession occurred in the Maryland State Legislature.

In a letter written about two years later, Lincoln wrote a fascinating explanation of how he understood his duty to uphold the constitution. He wrote,

> ***"Was it possible to lose the nation, and yet preserve the constitution? By general law life and limb must be protected; yet often a limb must be amputated to save a life; but a life is never wisely given to save a limb. I felt that measures, otherwise unconstitutional, might become lawful, by becoming indispensable to the preservation of the constitution, through the preservation of the nation. Right or wrong, I assumed this ground, and now avow it. I could not feel that, to the best of my ability, I had even tried to preserve the constitution, if, to save slavery, or any minor matter, I should permit the wreck of government, country, and Constitution all together.***
>
> ***Executive Mansion, Washington,***
> ***April 4, 1864.***
> ***A.G. Hodges, Esq, Frankfort, Ky."***

Right or wrong, these are dangerous words from the President of a democracy, and yet they give us a glimpse into the mind of a remarkable man, carrying a burden that is difficult to comprehend.

Election of 1860

Lincoln was making bold moves with limited political support. When he was elected in 1860, there were no less than four political parties seeking to put their candidate into the White House. The primary point of contention was slavery. The Southern Democrats wanted no restriction on slavery regardless of what state was involved. They nominated John Breckinridge for their candidate. The Democratic Party nominated Stephen Douglas. He advocated "popular sovereignty", which meant that each new state added to the Union could choose what the status of slavery would be in that state. Members of the Constitutional Union Party refused to join either side. They wanted a compromise based on the constitution. What that compromise might look like was unclear. Then there was the Republican Party. The election of 1860, was the Republican Party's first attempt to put a Republican in the White House, Abraham Lincoln was their candidate. Their platform was that they would not interfere with slavery in the South, but opposed extension of slavery into any new states. Southern Democrats knew if this happened, as new states were added to the country, southern political power would be diluted, and they would eventually be at the mercy of the North.

Abraham Lincoln won the election of 1860, with 180 out of 303 electoral votes. He had 39.8% of the popular vote. Between the time of the election and Lincoln's inauguration seven states, all of whom had voted for Breckinridge, declared their independence from the Union. The then sitting President, James Buchanan, did nothing. Buchanan left office with the nation in chaos. He would let Lincoln deal with the mess.

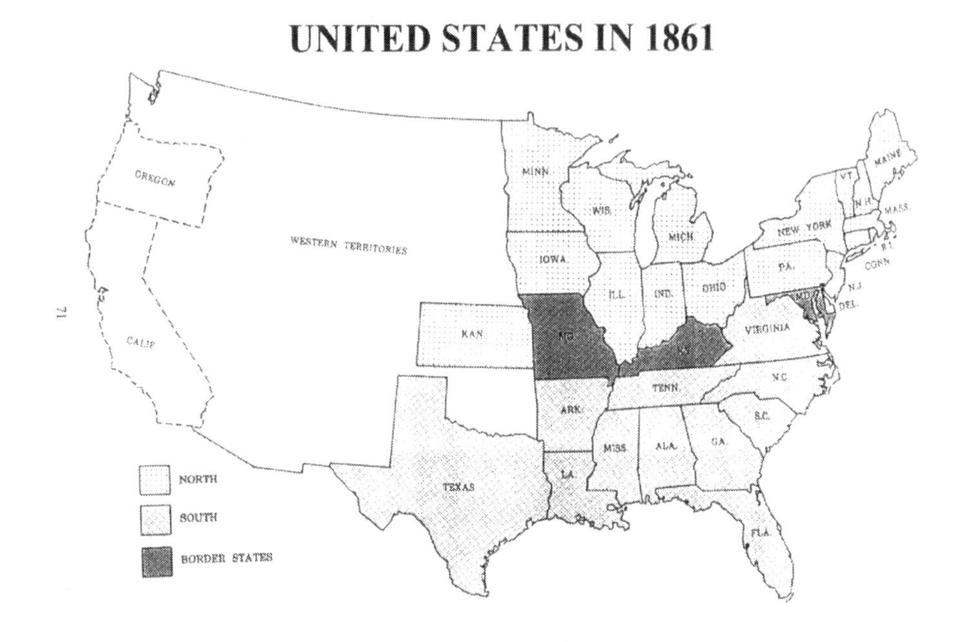

In 1861, The United States was a divided nation, split over the issue of slavery. This map illustrates the importance that future western states would play in the balance of power and the fate of the nation. (Map is courtesy of the Army University Press)

A Brief Stay in the Capital

The first order of business for 2nd Lieutenant Charles Kelly after arriving in Washington was to accompany Captain Munger to Army Headquarters and find the current location of their regiment so they could arrange transportation to join them. They learned that the 44th New York was camped with the rest of the 5th Corps, commanded by General Fitz John Porter, about two miles from Sharpsburg. A train would take them to Harpers Ferry, and they would travel by foot from there. Company C started loading onto the train to Harpers Ferry that afternoon about half past five. The train did not get going until after midnight. Charles was learning that waiting was a big part of the life of a soldier.

To get to Harpers Ferry, they had to retrace their journey toward Baltimore until they reached Relay House[2], about seven miles southwest of Baltimore, and from there head west. They arrived at Relay House sometime early in the morning of October 13, 1862.

After arriving at Relay, the company spent the remainder of the night in their railcars. That morning, an engine came along and started them once again on their journey to Harpers Ferry. By evening the company had arrived at Sandy Hook, a mile east of Harpers Ferry, and they were told that their regiment was about four miles away. They had another night of sleeping in the railcars.

THE RELAY HOUSE, WASHINGTON JUNCTION, NOW OCCUPIED BY THE FEDERAL VOLUNTEERS.

The Relay House is shown just to the right of the rail depot. (Harper's Weekly)

[2] Relay House was originally a relay station used for changing horses that pulled horse drawn rail cars. The first successful steam engine in the U.S., the Tom Thumb, ran from Baltimore to the Relay House on August 28, 1830. By 1850, the Relay House was the second busiest stop on the B&O line between Baltimore and Wheeling, Virginia.

CHAPTER TWO

❖

The Army of the Potomac

Life of a Soldier

About 3 o'clock in the afternoon of October 14, Company C arrived at the camp of General George Morrell's Division, a part of the 5th Corps. The 5th Corps was part of the Army of the Potomac, commanded by George McClellan. The entire 5th Corps was camped here.

The 5th Corps, at that time, was commanded by General Fitz John Porter. The 44th NY was part of the 5th Corps 1st Division, Third Brigade. The Third Brigade, commanded by Colonel Stockton, at the time had six regiments, one of which was the 44th NY, commanded by Colonel James Rice.

Order of Battle

Order of Battle refers to the organization, command structure, and strength of the various units that make up an army. The Union Army was organized into companies and regiments. A company had no more than a hundred men; often, after being in the field for a time, much less. Companies were named with the letters A through K. The letter "J" was not used. Each company was commanded by a Captain, a 1st Lieutenant, and a 2nd Lieutenant, in addition to non-commissioned officers such as sergeants and corporals.

Ten companies would form a regiment, which had up to a thousand men. Disease, combat, and desertion would rapidly reduce this number. If a regiment had only four to eight companies, it was called a battalion rather than a regiment. A colonel with his staff commanded a regiment.

A group of four infantry regiments formed a brigade. A brigade was commanded by a brigadier general (one star) aided by his staff.

Specialized units such as artillery batteries or cavalry troops were grouped into separate companies each commanded by a captain.

Three to five brigades formed a division, commanded by a major general (two stars). A full division could have as many as 12,000 soldiers.

Two to three divisions formed a corps. A major general usually commanded a corps. It could contain as many as 36,000 soldiers.

An Army, commanded by a lieutenant or major general, usually consisted of three or more corps, up to 80,000 men. All of these troop numbers and various ranks in command could change as the fortunes of war waxed and waned.

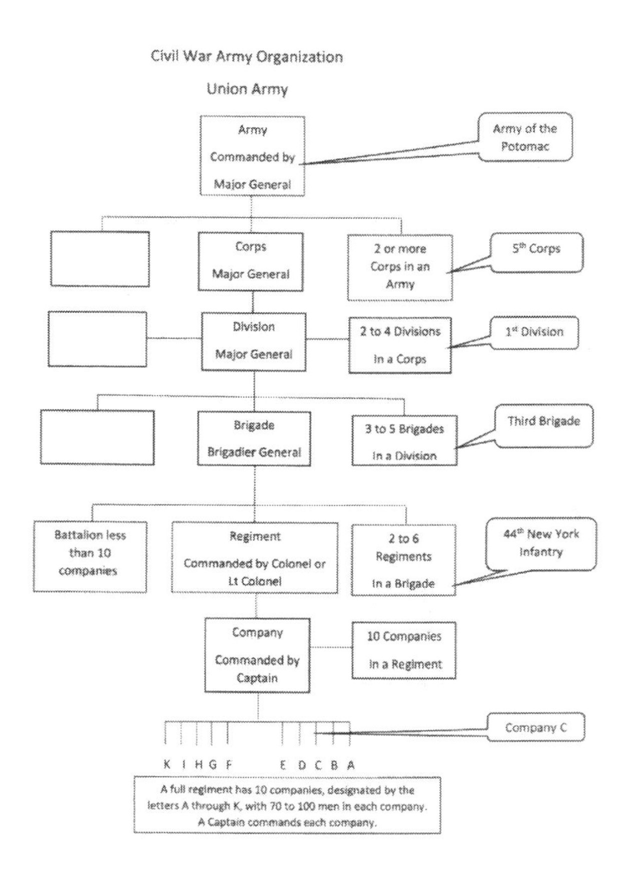

Charles Kelly was in Company C of the 44th New York Infantry Regiment. The regiment was part of the Third Brigade of the 1st Division, 5th Corps, of the Army of the Potomac.

Camp Life

Upon arriving at the camp of the 5th Corps, which covered about 300 acres, Charles noted that the soil was sand and clay. There were two or three log houses in sight but they were ***"of the poor kind and the chimneys are built on the outside of the houses".***

They were two miles from the small town of Sharpsburg near where Antietam Creek joins the Potomac River. A month earlier, just a short distance away, one of the most horrific battles of the war took place.

Despite the carnage still evident around Sharpsburg, Charles was enamored by the beauty of the place:

> ***"The country around harpersferry is the most sublime I ever beheld. How grand it is to look on the works of nature. They are so much grandeur than the works of art. Those high mountains looming up toward the skys the darkest of them 600 feet above the level of the bed of the rivers."***

The day after arriving at the camp, October 15, 1862, Charles reports that Company C,

> ***"tried their hand at drill today. We went then went on Battalion drill at 2 O'clock and at 4 we had dress parade. I made quite a mistake at the last maned drill."***

Charles, along with the rest of C Company, was learning the craft of being a soldier. The inexperience and lack of training of Company C was very evident to the rest of the regiment, and the new company received a less than cordial reception from the battle hardened veterans who made up the 44th NY. It would take a couple of months, and trial in the bloody battle of Fredericksburg, for Company C to be fully integrated into the 44th NY Volunteers.

The next day Charles awoke at 6 a.m. It was cold and foggy. Charles writes,

> ***"I slept quite comfortable last night for the first time in a month we had Breakfast at about 9 O'clock we had a Real camp meal Pilot Bread and smoked ham and good coffee after breakfast we went to cleaning up***

> ***our street and tents I went into the woods with 2 of our Boys to make Brooms we can hear the Booming of the cannon for the last hour and the officers and old soldiers say that they are fighting about 15 miles from here"***

Constant rumors traveling through an army camp were as old as armies themselves. That same day Charles writes,

> ***"some of the officers think that we are going into winter quarters while others think that we are going to advance right away By going up on the hill we can see the Rebels jackets Planely By the naked eye"***

Two days later Charles was already getting accustomed to a soldier's life. He writes,

> ***"I woke this morning with a very Bad cold and felt quite sick a soldiers life is not the Best life in the world But I think that after awhile I will like it first rate we had no Battalion drill to day But the company Drilled by themselves and we had a good Drill to we have not a very good tent for the officers but we expect one from harpersferry in a few days it is now evening and it is getting very cold this evening"***

On Saturday October 18, Charles was up at 6 a.m. He reports that he felt very bad but improved when the sun came out about 8 o'clock. After Company drill, the officers were required to study *Hardee's Tactics,* ***"a lesson every day"***. On Saturday evenings, they would recite what they had learned to Colonel Rice.

Rifle and Light Infantry Tactics; for Exercise and Maneuvers of Troops when acting as Light Infantry or Riflemen, was written by William J. Hardee in 1855. It was the standard manual for commissioned officers of both the Union and the Confederacy to instruct their commands. As Charles studied this work to learn the soldier's craft, William Hardee was serving as a Lieutenant General in the Confederate Army.

Food

Another adjustment to camp life was the food. Hardtack was a staple for both Federal and Confederate soldiers and sailors throughout the war. Hardtack, also called pilot bread, made from flour, water, and a little bit of salt, if kept dry, would last for decades. At the beginning of the war, hardtack stored during the Mexican/ American War (1846-1848), was shipped to both Union and Confederate soldiers. Packed in crates, hardtack came in 3 inch by 3 inch perforated squares about 3/8" thick. Soldiers found it more palatable if soaked in coffee or stew.

Federal soldiers were issued rations that were uncooked. When in camp, the official US ration per man for each day was 20 ounces of fresh or salt beef, or 12 ounces of pork or bacon, 18 ounces of flour or 20 ounces of corn meal or bread if available. Official rations also contained 1.6 ounces of rice or .64 ounces of beans or 1.5 ounces of dried potatoes. They were also issued 1.6 ounces of coffee or .24 ounces of tea, 2.4 ounces of sugar, .54 ounces of salt, and .32 gill of vinegar. A gill was about a half cup. When preparing for a march or battle, each soldier would be issued three days of uncooked rations. Official US marching rations per day would consist of 16 ounces of hardtack, 12 ounces of salt pork or 4 ounces of fresh meat, 1 ounce of coffee, 3 ounces of sugar, and salt. As can be imagined, these official quantities, developed by Commissary officers far from the realities of the march or the battlefield, were often only a dream in the mind of a hungry soldier.

High-ranking officers had cooks, but most soldiers were expected to prepare their own meals. When staying at a camp for a period of time Charles would often join with other officers and hire a cook to prepare their food. Usually, soldiers gathered in small groups in the evening to prepare their food. These groups were called "messes", others in your mess were called "messmates".

Food for soldiers during the Civil War was not high quality and lacked nutritional value. Confederate soldiers were often lacking in food especially as the war dragged on. Union troops were usually well fed but the food quality was not much better than what the Confederate soldiers were eating.

On the evening of October 16, Charles reports, ***"just ate my dinner it consisted of Bread Water and sugar"***. The menu must have seemed a bit sparse for a man who just a short time ago owned a saloon and eating establishment, and a brewery.

Soldiers learned to make do with what they had. Following is a recipe for Camp Soup that soldiers sometimes used when they were not on the march and had time to cook.

Camp Soup

8 oz. salt pork (washed)
2 oz. rice
5 hardtack
1 tsp sugar
¼ tsp pepper
water

Boil pork for twenty minutes. Drain water. Add 5 cups of water. Add rice. Add any vegetables you might have. Simmer for one hour over fire. Add crumbled hardtack. Cook for 10 minutes. Add pepper and sugar. Enjoy!

Coffee

Coffee was a beverage that soldiers on both sides craved. Raw green coffee beans were issued to Federal soldiers who roasted them in a pan over an open fire. Sometimes they would receive beans that were already roasted. Imports being abundant in the North, every Union soldier was allotted 36 pounds of coffee per year. The coffee was brewed in little pots called muckets.

In the last half of 1863, the U.S. Christian Commission (U.S.C.C.) began to operate coffee wagons at Union Army camps; the wagons were based on a design patented by John Dunton in March of 1863. The coffee wagon could produce as many as 108 gallons of hot coffee an hour.

The blockade of southern ports by Union Naval forces made coffee rare in Confederate armies. For the average Confederate soldier coffee became almost non-existent in the later years of the war.

In an *American Battlefield Trust* article, Ashley Webb tells of one Confederate soldier who received steady rations up until the summer of 1863. He remarked, ***"our shortness of rations began, and continued rather to intensify until the end. For one period of about two months, it consisted of only one small loaf of baker's bread and a gill (1/4 pint) of sorghum syrup daily."*** Another wrote, ***"We are reduced to quarter rations and no coffee. And nobody can soldier without coffee."***

Confederate soldiers frequently used coffee substitutes, such as chicory or roasted acorns, to make a hot drink. During the war coffee became a valuable commodity that Union soldiers could trade for tobacco or other scarce goods.

Company E Arrives

The 44th NY was joined by an additional 101 men on October 23, 1862. These men formed a new company, Company E, to replenish losses from battle and disease. These men were a group of faculty, students, and alumni of New York State's Normal School of Albany.

One soldier from the new Company E, not long after joining the remnants of the 44th Regiment in October of 1862, gives a description in the *Albany Statesman* of what he found there:

> ***"The 44th Regiment, to which we are connected, and which one year ago last Wednesday, left your city 1040 strong, today when drawn up in company front, the largest Co. did not cover our center and the remaining companies decreased in a fearful ratio, one numbering only 9 men. I do not wish to convey the idea that the remainder have been killed by the bullet, but those not killed are either wounded or prostrated by disease at home. Such is the fortune of war." From the Normal School Company, Antietam Ford, Md., Oct 24th 1862***

Disease was overpowering and devastating to both sides throughout the Civil War. Sleeping on the ground in all weather, as Charles Kelly and countless others often did, combined with poor quality and sometimes nonexistent tents, coats, and shoes all played a role. Charles often woke soaking wet from a leaking tent or shelter. In addition, poor quality diet and bad sanitation kept immune systems struggling to maintain health. If you were a Federal soldier, you were often hungry. If you were a Confederate soldier, you were sometimes near starvation. There were three times as many deaths due to disease in the ranks of the Confederate Army compared to the Federal Army. Overall, a soldier in the War of the Rebellion had a one-in-five chance of dying from disease. Pneumonia, typhoid, dysentery, malaria, tuberculosis, all took their toll. Two thirds of all deaths in the war were from disease.

Private Martin Stewart enrolled in the 44th NY Regiment, Company C, on August 2, 1861. He died of disease June 8, 1862, in the hospital at Fort Wood, New York Harbor. He was 23 years old. Fort Wood is now known as Bedloe's Island, home of the Statue of Liberty. (Library of Congress)

A Soldier's Life

By October 26, 1862, Charles was learning what it meant to be a soldier in the Union Army. He writes,

> *"I awoke this morning at 6 o'clock. The weather looks like rain and sure enough it is beginning to come down. Our Regt to go out on Pickets all day. Our orders are to go we don't know where. The orders are to have 3 days rations cooked and in our haversacks and 60 Rounds of cartridges in the men's boxes. The probability is that we will march in the morning into Virginia... Our tent leaks like a riddle. A soldier has just been brought in from his post. He had dropped down insencable one of the men came to our tent inquiring for a doctor just put up our rations for the officers and are already for a march."*

October 27, 1862;

> *"last Night was the most chilly rainy I ever experienced in my Life the officers went to Bed about 10 o'clock the rain came down in torrents and our tent was not the best I wrapt myself up in my blanket and poncho I then thought that I would get a little sleep I woke in about ½ hour felt something cold at my back I put my hand there to find out what it was I found that I was lying in the water I thought such things would never do so I moved my quarters very quick I rested some better during the night. This morning it was very cold and windy and the Boys felt down in the mouth. I did pity the old soldiers some of them without shoes or stocking others without any overcoats- But The Regt Rec'd some clothes to day But not half enough to keep them warm some of our company Rec'd some shirts and drawers and I Recd an overcoat and a pair of stockings we expect to go every moment the Boys are cooking their Rations as fast as they can I am just going to see some of the Boys that is in the hospital I did not go the hospital The Bugal sounded and I had to come Back to camp in double quick time. The Lieut and myself went through with the Days parade firstrate I was appointed officer of the day to see that the Lights were put out in camp & the taps."*

In spite of poor food, cold nights, washing in Antietam Creek, and disease that was common in camp, Charles Kelly seemed to take to camp life. He deeply appreciated the natural beauty around him.

> ***"Antietam Oct 29th, 1862; this is a Beautiful day it looks like spring if I was in penn yan I should almost say it was spring I slept quite comfortable Last Night I was out with the company Drilling with their arms and they done first rate I am now writing on a hill overlooking the Patomac there is a horse down below insight it is a Beautiful afternoon and I enjoy it greatly I tell you the Patomac is about a ¼ of a mile from where I am sitting in the afternoon we had a fine Drill the Night is Beautiful and mild the orderly is making out the muster role for pay."***

The next day Charles would be leaving camp life and experiencing life on the march.

CHAPTER THREE

On the March

A Soldier's Burden

Being on the march was no easy task for a soldier. The Federal soldier's load weighed around forty-five pounds. His musket and bayonet alone weighed 14 pounds. In addition he was equipped with a cartridge box with strap that contained forty rounds of ammunition for his rifle, and a cap box for percussion caps.

He would have a knapsack, with straps for carrying on the back, and a haversack, containing his food larder, carried on a shoulder strap. A haversack would carry about half of a modern paper grocery bag. Designed to hold three days' rations of biscuit (hardtack) and bacon, and small bags called poke sacks which held coffee, sugar, salt, rice, and other dry goods, the haversack was often all that stood between a soldier eating and going hungry on a multi-day march.

A soldier might carry somewhere between three to eight days' rations; when his haversack was full he used his knapsack to carry additional hardtack and other foodstuffs. He also carried a canteen, a blanket, an overcoat, a half shelter, a rubberized ground cloth and spare sox. Charles Kelly had a rubberized poncho that he mentions often as being his prime protection from the rain, when the wagon with the officers' tent fell behind the company's camp for the night. Veterans of long marches, to eliminate the six-pounds of the knapsack, would sometimes roll up their rubberized ground cloth, blanket, and half tent, to make a roll carried over the shoulder. Extra clothing such as socks would be wrapped up in the roll. They left empty knapsacks lying on the side of the road.

A soldier carried his own mess gear, which might include a cup, knife, fork, spoon, and skillet. He also carried small amounts of personal gear which varied greatly but might include such things as a sewing kit, razor, letters, paper, pencil, or a Bible. Charles Kelly carried a small leather-bound blank book in which he made his diary entries.

Clothes and Shoes

The annual allocation for clothes issued to an infantry soldier was two caps, one hat, two dress coats, three pair of trousers, three flannel shirts, three flannel drawers, and four pair of stockings. A soldier might also be issued a great coat, a woolen blanket, a waterproof or rubberized blanket, perhaps a pair of gaiters for protecting the ankles, and a flannel sack coat for use on non-combat work duty. He could draw from his regiment's Quartermaster a pair of trousers or a new coat, or more stockings when needed but if he exceeded his annual allotment without good justification, the cost came out of his pay. Many times a soldier would need socks, or a warm coat, but none were available.

Then of course, there were shoes. Shoes, or lack thereof, was often a problem for soldiers on the march. Charles Kelly mentions some of his men lacking shoes during a long march on a number of occasions. Lack of shoes was a constant problem in the Confederate army.

By far the most common shoe worn by Federal infantry during the war was the Brogan, sometimes referred to as the Jefferson Bootee. The Brogan was an ankle high work shoe with rawhide laces and a short heel. The soles had one or two layers of leather, and the heels attached to the sole with hand set square nails. "Brogan" comes from a Gaelic term meaning "little shoe".

A pair of Civil War era Brogans with rawhide laces and sewn soles. Note the lack of metal eyelets for the laces. Metal eyelets did not become common until after the war.

Before the war, almost all army shoes were made at the Susquehanna Arsenal where pieces were cut out and then sent to small contractors for sewing, on a piecework basis. Army shoes were improved by direction of Jefferson Davis, U.S. Secretary of War under Franklin Pierce. After his post as Secretary of War, beginning in 1857, Jefferson Davis was a U.S. senator from Mississippi. When Mississippi seceded from the Union, he resigned. In January of 1861, a month after leaving the Senate, he was chosen to be president of the newly formed Confederate States of America.

The war created tremendous demand for shoes and rapid advances in machinery, especially machines capable of sewing the upper portion of the shoe to the sole, made possible production on a large scale. Making a pair of shoes with a right and left shoe became the norm. Using wooden pegs to fasten the soles to the uppers was replaced by sewn shoes, which were greatly preferred by the army. The Federal army would pay $1.80 to $2.00 per pair for sewn shoes but would pay only $1.25 per pair for pegged shoes. The Model 1859 cavalry boot, worn by officers, cavalry troopers, and artillery units, was 14 inches high and cost the Federal army $3.25 per pair for sewn boots and $2.50 for pegged boots.

Though the Federal army purchased over six million pairs of Brogans during the war, shoes were often lacking in the Federal ranks. On a number of occasions, Charles Kelly notes that his men lacked shoes and suffered greatly on long marches. Part of the problem was the short life of these shoes when subjected to heavy use, sometimes marches over twenty miles a day on a sustained basis. The Federal army allocated four pair of shoes per infantry soldier per year, but this proved to be insufficient in harsh, muddy, winter conditions. Another factor was that the tremendous need for shoes furnished the opportunity for some shoe manufacturers to sell shoddy products to the military that would literally dissolve after three or four weeks of hard use.

Weapons

It was not until October 28, 1862, more than a week after arriving at the camp of the 44th NY, that the men of C Company received their muskets. A year earlier, the original 44th NY, received new Springfield Pattern 1861 rifled-muskets as they travelled from Albany and passed through New York City on their way to Washington.

The United States Armory and Arsenal, in Springfield Massachusetts, made the Springfield muskets for the Federal Army. The 44th NY was fortunate to get the Springfield rifles this early in the war. The Springfield Armory in late 1861was just beginning to ramp up production of the Pattern 1861 musket to satisfy the tremendous demand. A year after the original regiment received their weapons new Company C soldiers received the same rifle, to ensure compatibility of ammunition with the muskets first issued to the 44th NY.

Demand grew so quickly throughout the Union Army for these weapons that the Springfield Armory opened up their patterns to about twenty private manufacturers, such as the *Colt's Patent Firearms Manufacturing Company.* In mid-1861, Colt worked together with the Springfield Armory and developed improvements to the weapon, emphasizing interchangeable parts as demanded by the Springfield Armory, and ease of manufacture. The rifles manufactured by Colt were called "Colt Special" rifled-muskets. Most of the improvements developed by Colt were incorporated into the Pattern 1863 Springfield rifled-musket, a musket very similar to the Pattern 1861. The Springfield Armory produced over 250,000 Pattern 1861 muskets, and private contractors made an additional ¾ of a million during the war. The cost for a musket was about $15.

The Springfield rifled-musket had a 40-inch long barrel and weighed about nine pounds. It shot a .58 caliber projectile (.58 inch diameter) and had an effective range of 200 to 400 yards. Expert marksmen could extend this range out to 500 yards. It used a percussion cap, which was a small sealed copper capsule filled with fulminate of mercury that would ignite when struck by the musket's hammer, and ignite the powder charge. The percussion cap musket was far more reliable and weather resistant than the flintlock musket. A soldier could load and fire up to three rounds per minute. When in battle a more realistic rate might be two rounds per minute.

The projectile for this rifle was the minie ball, a type of bullet designed by Claude Minié, and improved upon by Captain James Burton, an armorer at the Harpers Ferry Armory. Rifling refers to spiral grooves cut into the inside of a gun barrel, which caused the bullet to spin. This increased a bullets stability and range. Claude Minié invented a conical shaped bullet with a hollow base that would slightly expand at the base when a powder charge ignited. This forced the base of the bullet to engage with the spiral grooves in the barrel and spin as it was driven out by the powder charge. This bullet could penetrate 6 inches into a pine log at 500 yards.

The minie ball came wrapped in thin paper, together with a premeasured charge of black powder, to form a cartridge. To load the Springfield musket, the soldier would tear off the top of the paper, usually with his teeth, pour the powder down the barrel of the musket, place the ball and paper wrapping in the barrel and tamp into place with his ramrod. He then placed a percussion cap in the breach of the musket, and was ready to fire.

Springfield versus Enfield Muskets

Most Union Army soldiers preferred Springfield muskets to all others. They were the most widely used musket by the North during the war. There were numerous exceptions however, including the muskets used by the 54th Massachusetts Infantry Regiment. The 54th Massachusetts was the second Black American Regiment formed in the Federal Army. This regiment participated in many battles and won fame for their actions at the Battle of Fort Wagner, which took place outside of Charlestown, South Carolina. Sergeant William Carney of the 54th Massachusetts was the first Black American to receive the Medal of Honor for his actions at Fort Wagner. The 54th Mass. was armed with the Enfield Pattern 1853 rifled-musket, a weapon very similar to the Springfield musket. Some believed the Enfield musket to be superior to the Springfield musket.

The Enfield rifled-musket was the second most widely used musket during the war. It propelled a .577 caliber minie ball. If the paper wrapping of the Springfield rifle cartridge was pulled back it could be used in the Enfield rifle, very handy when all you had was captured ammunition. Used by both sides, it was the preferred rifle of the Confederate Army. The Enfield had a more elaborate sighting mechanism than the Springfield, which if used properly, extended the range of the weapon. Made in England, the South imported about 900,000 of these rifles during the war. Many were purchased from private contractors and gunrunners; the Enfield was used in every major engagement of the war.

At the beginning of the war, almost 70% of Confederate soldiers were armed with smooth bore muskets, as opposed to rifled muskets. By the end of the war, the vast majority of Confederate soldiers used rifled muskets, mostly the Enfield Pattern 1853. There were many exceptions, such as cavalry troopers and other specialized troops, but a common soldier from either side most likely carried a Springfield or an Enfield.

Colonel Joshua Chamberlain, who achieved fame for his stalwart defense of the Union left flank at Little Round Top on the second day of battle at Gettysburg, made an interesting comment about Enfield rifles. In his report of the battle, he noted that during lulls in the struggle, his men used the opportunity to remove wounded and gather ammunition from the cartridge-boxes of the fallen and ***"even to secure better muskets than the Enfields, which we found did not stand service well."***

As late as the battle at Gettysburg, some Federal regiments were still armed with smoothbore muskets. In the after battle report of Lieutenant Colonel Leonard Carpenter, 4th Ohio Infantry, written July 6, 1863, which was three days after the final assault on Cemetery Hill, the Colonel wrote; ***"We were armed on going into the fight with the smooth-bore muskets, but these were exchanged for good Springfield rifles that we captured from the enemy."***

During the war, both the North and South underused the Springfield and Enfield rifle's capabilities due to lack of marksmanship training. Most soldiers were not trained to estimate ranges or to properly adjust their sights to account for the "rainbow-like" trajectory of the large caliber conical projectile that these weapons sent hurling toward the enemy. Many Civil War soldiers did not fire a cartridge until their first engagement.

The Springfield and Enfield rifles foreshadowed a change in the practice of war. The rifling of these weapons, together with the minie ball, greatly extended the range and killing power available to a common soldier. The massive minie ball used by these weapons, which weighed over an ounce, inflicted horrific damage, shattering bones and cutting blood vessels as it passed through a body. Fatal wounds and amputations were greatly increased compared to previous wars. If you were hit in the arm or leg by a minie ball the limb was probably going to be amputated in an attempt to save your life. Some would survive the procedure; some, such as Stonewall Jackson, died not long after.

High-ranking military commanders looked back to the wars of Napoleon, with massed squares and gallant cavalry charges, to develop tactics they refused to believe were now outdated and nearly suicidal. For example, at the Battle of Salamanca (July of 1812), in central Spain, the Earl of Wellington, soon to be the Duke of Wellington, faced off against Napoleon's Marshal Auguste Marmont. Each side had about 50,000 men armed with smooth bore muskets. The British muskets were nicknamed "Brown Bess". They had a bore of .76 inches, which is equivalent to a 12-gauge shotgun, and fired a round ball. The effective range of these weapons was about 40 yards, sometimes up to a hundred yards. The French had similar weapons.

At Salamanca, Marshal Marmont was defeated and eventually driven from the Spanish Peninsula. Afterward, Napoleon's inspector general noted that 3,000 cartridges were expended for each man disabled; some estimated the number to be 10,000 cartridges. The reality was that beyond fifty yards the smoothbore muskets used by both sides were not effective. This made it possible to approach a massed line of men to a distance such that a final charge with cavalry or infantry with fixed bayonets just might be successful.

It was a hard lesson for military leaders to realize that such tactics were no longer effective. Frontal assaults on massed infantry and infantry entrenched in even rough fortifications now did not work. Tens of thousands of soldiers at Malvern Hill, Fredericksburg, Gettysburg, and countless other places, died proving this to be the case. The accuracy, range, and power of the new weapons, even though their full capabilities were often underused, allowed the common soldier to kill and maim at a significant distance. The cavalry charge became a massacre of riders and horses. Even artillery, which once could be placed at a range of four or five hundred yards to fire on enemy formations with impunity, now had to be much further away. The men who were actually doing the fighting quickly learned to send out as many as half their formation to form a skirmish line at least 400 yards in advance. Skirmishers did not stand in long rows but hid behind whatever cover they could find and fired independently of high command.

In response to rifled muskets and minie balls the Civil War devolved into trench warfare and protracted sieges. The advantage had shifted to the defense. Fifty years later, armies had even more powerful weapons such as modern artillery and machine guns, but the lesson of the dead at Fredericksburg and Gettysburg was ignored in the fields of France. In World War I, frontal assaults on entrenched infantry continued. Millions died because military leaders refused to see that the world had changed.

There was one great irony concerning the rifled muskets used by both sides. Much better weapons were available. One example is the Spencer repeating rifle. The Spencer was a lever-action repeating rifle designed by Christopher Spencer. It used breach loading brass cartridges that were weatherproof and would not fall apart when wet or mistreated.

Sometimes whole wagon loads of Springfield or Enfield paper cartridges were ruined by moisture. A six-mule wagon, loaded with paper wrapped cartridges for the single shot Springfield musket would hold twenty boxes of ammunition with each box containing 1,000 cartridges; a significant loss if the cargo became soaked. This did not happen with brass cartridges.

The Spencer repeating rifle held seven rounds of ammunition and could fire twenty rounds per minute. The short-barreled version of the rifle called a Spencer Carbine was a favorite of the Union Cavalry, but did not come into production until late in 1863. Prior to receiving carbines, the Federal cavalry was among the first to receive Spencer repeating rifles. In July of 1863, recently promoted General George Armstrong Custer, always seeking combat and glory, used Spencer repeating rifles to good effect when he charged at the front of his four cavalry regiments straight into Jeb Stuart's 6,000-man cavalry troop near Gettysburg. Jeb Stuart was seeking to position his cavalry behind the Federal line on Cemetery Ridge, hoping to attack the blue clad soldiers as they were driven back by Longstreet's charge on the afternoon of July 3, 1863. The Yankees were not driven back, and somehow Custer survived long enough for General Gregg to send in more troopers, which convinced Jeb Stuart to withdraw, and abandon the mission.

Any soldier who could get his hands on a Spencer would do so, but for a Union infantry soldier the Spencer cost about three months wages. Many soldiers who used a Spencer said they owed their lives to this weapon. Lack of copper made the South unable to manufacture brass cartridges for this and other brass cartridge weapons, and captured Spencers had limited use to them.

After the Battle of Gettysburg Abraham Lincoln attended a demonstration of the Spencer repeating rifle. He was deeply impressed with the weapon. Lincoln ordered General James Wolfe Ripley, Chief of Ordinance for the U.S. Army Ordnance Department, to adopt the Spencer for production. Ripley ignored the order. Use of rifled muskets continued. Ripley believed use of the repeating rifle would cause immense waste of ammunition and that Army Ordinance would not be able to keep up with demand for cartridges. Later that year Lincoln fired Ripley.

Pistols

Charles Kelly did not carry a rifle. Union Officers carried a pistol and a sword. Charles' pistol was probably a Colt Army Model 1860 Revolver. *Colt's Patent Firearms Manufacturing Company* made more than 100,000 of these pistols during the war. The pistol had an eight inch long rifled barrel and weighed 2 lbs. 11 oz. Made from tool steel rather than iron, these pistols were lighter than previous revolvers. The effective range was 50 to 75 yards. The cost for a Colt revolver was about twenty dollars.

This pistol propelled a .44 caliber conical bullet. To load the revolver you rotated the six-chambered revolving cylinder and inserted a paper wrapped powder charge with bullet down the front of each cylinder. You then pushed the cartridge into position in each cylinder with the rack and pinion loading lever that was built into the pistol. You then loaded a percussion cap into the back of each cylinder. You were now ready to fire six shots. When paper wrapped cartridges were not available you could load each cylinder with a powder charge, wad, and round bullet, all tamped into place with the loading lever.

On occasion, the flash from a cartridge firing in these revolvers would set off all the other rounds in the cylinder. This would destroy the pistol and could severely injure the user's hand.

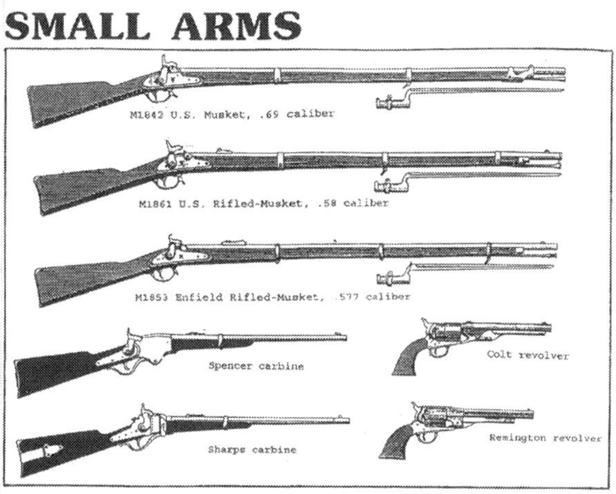

SMALL ARMS

M1842 U.S. Musket, .69 caliber
M1861 U.S. Rifled-Musket, .58 caliber
M1853 Enfield Rifled-Musket, .577 caliber
Spencer carbine
Colt revolver
Sharps carbine
Remington revolver

From Chancellorsville, Staff Ride Briefing Book
(U.S. Army Center of Military History)

Swords

Charles Kelly carried a Pattern 1850 Infantry Officer sword, manufactured by *Horstmann & Sons* of Philadelphia, Pennsylvania. Officers were expected to buy their own swords. Swords were no longer a useful weapon in war, especially for infantry, but were a symbol of leadership and authority. In the chaos and carnage of battle, you followed the man with the raised sword.

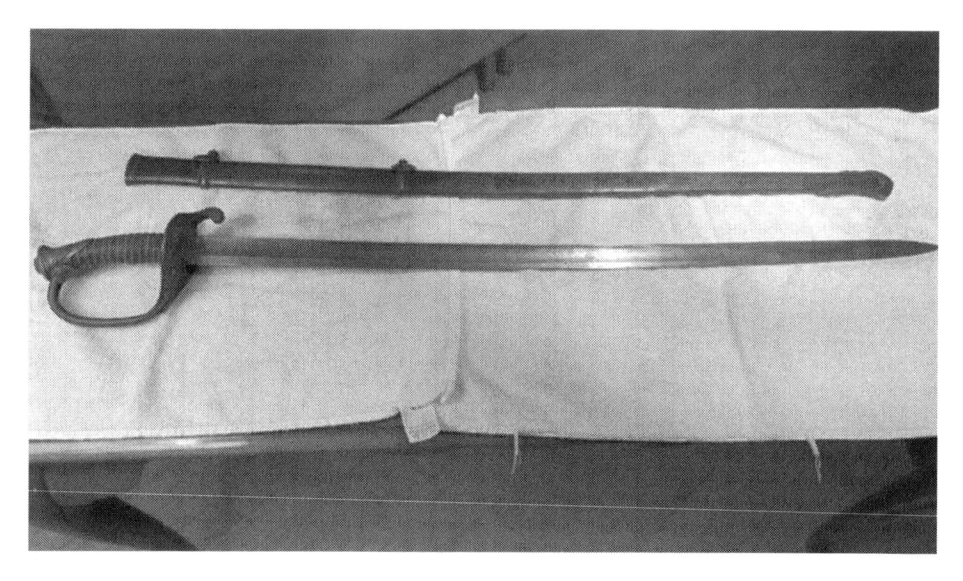

This sword belonged to Charles Kelly and was carried by him throughout his time with the 44th New York Infantry Regiment.

March to Warrenton

On October 30, 1862, the 44th NY, together with the entire 5th Corps, was on the march. They struck their tents and started for Harpers Ferry about 7 p.m., marched 6 miles, and camped for the night in a wheat field.

Charles writes,

> ***"I rested as well as could be expected   I layed down and put my poncho under me with nothing But my overcoat on and slept quite comfortable … we arrived at our present camp about ½ past 10 o'clock at Night the Boys thought it was very Rough to carry such a big Load***

> *and some of them came very near given out the capt had to carry some of the Boys guns."*

Charles had a rubberized poncho which protected him through many a cold, wet night. The march continued and for some in Company C the going was hard. The brigade marched through Harpers Ferry about 2 p.m. October 31, and spent the night 6 miles to the south. The next morning the resiliency and optimism of Charles shines through,

> ***"Nov. 1st 1862 6 miles south of harpersferry***
>
> ***I feel first rate to day and a Beautiful day it is I think it will Be quite warm & we expect to march to Leesburgh this day it is 18 miles from there I slept quite comfortable last Night But along toward morning I felt some cold. Breakfast consisted of coffee cold ham and soft bread...the Boys are nearly out of provisions they having no haversacks to carry their provisions in we are incamp in a wheat field..."***

It is odd that the men of Company C had not yet received their haversacks. Army Commissary Regulations dictated that each enlisted man would receive a knapsack with straps, a haversack with straps, and a canteen with straps.

Marching rations were a stripped down version of camp rations. A typical three-day marching ration might include 30 ounces of salt pork, 30 pieces of hardtack, 6 ounces of green coffee beans, and 7 ounces of sugar. Sometimes the salted meat given to the soldiers was past its prime, so they nicknamed it "salt horse". When available, for three days of rations, the soldier might be issued four pounds of beef instead of salt pork, and a little over three pounds of flour or corn meal instead of hardtack. As previously noted, ordinance regulations called for supplementing these rations with small amounts of beans or peas, rice, and ½ ounce of salt per day. Enlisted men were also entitled to receive ½ ounce of soap per day and a candle that was shared with other enlisted men.

The precise calculations of rations for each man were not always realized. A soldiers rations might have been shipped to the wrong location, or be sitting in a railcar turned on its side by enemy forces. The rations might be in a six-mule wagon stuck up to its axles in mud, miles away, or the wagon, along with dozens of others, might have been looted and burned by Jeb Stuart's 1st Virginia Calvary.

Soldiers Dumplings

½ pound flour
½ teaspoon salt
½ teaspoon pepper
10 tablespoons water

Use fork to stir dry ingredients, add water and mix. Knead dough for 5 minutes. Roll out and cut into 16 pieces. Sprinkle with flour. Boil for ten minutes.

"Nov. 2, 6 miles from harpersferry

It is now 7 o'clock and all is Bustle in camp Bugle has just sounded and we must Be off we are incamp about 6 miles south of harpersferry we are on the march in the Valley of Virginia and its a very hot day and the Boys talk of given out our first march without a Rest was 4 miles the country which we are marching through is a Beautiful farming country it is Valley in the Mountains of Virginia the Blue Ridge is on the Right of us and over the Ridge lies the shanendoah Valley we are traveling on a Big Road to go up on to the Blue Ridge to do picket duty when we got up there we found the 14th Infantry Regiment and we relieved them the Reg't left our Brigade when we turned to go up on the Blue Ridge we traveled up a hill about 2 miles long the Reg't camp at the top of the mountain & the Right of it went on Picket the Reg't that was here said that there was a camp of Rebles about 3 miles from out camp"

The 44th NY, ordered on picket duty, now detached from the rest of the Brigade, and marched 15 miles, most of it uphill, on Sunday, November 2. They camped in a cleared field on the crest of the Blue Ridge Mountains. Establishing a picket line down the western slope of the Blue Ridge served the vital function of guarding one of the numerous mountain passes while the rest of the 5th Corps continued on their journey southward. One observer remarked on the beauty of the country that could be seen from the crest of the Blue Ridge; ***"Well, if the world was made in six days I have seen one dammed big day's work"***

"Nov 3rd camp 16 miles south of harpers ferry on the Blue Ridge

We are about six miles from Smokey Vale the Boys felt quite smart this morning the Night was very cold on the top of the mountain I feel a little stiff after the march yesterday the company officers went to a farm house for some Breakfast it consisted of hotcake coffee and Bacon it is 4 miles to the Shenandoah River lying to the west of our camp half of our company is on picket duty to day and the other half goes out to Night and I am in the command of the Reserve at the headquarters."

Picket duty consisted of a company, traveling four or five miles, or more, beyond the main body of troops to act as an early warning in case the enemy approached. The picket detail usually took enough rations to last three days, after which they were relieved.

"Nov. 4th camp 18 miles from harpersferry south of that place

I slept quite comfortable Last Night the capt went out on Picket with the Boys he came in this morning for some Breakfast I then went down to see him he has good quarters, in an old home the home must have Been Built in the days of Noah he must have settled on this mountain the Boys are stealing the farmers poor hens eggs sheep cattle hogs are all coming in to camp By the Boys our wagon has just come up on the mountain top and the Boys will have something to eat some of them are out of Hardtack they will get their rations I expect this afternoon the Boys came in from picket to Night the Rebles are about 4 miles south from here the union forces had a turn with the Rebles to night at snickers gap and our forces got here just in time to stop them coming through the gap."

The 5th Corps together with most of the Army of the Potomac, about 90,000 men, was now marching south along the eastern side of the Blue Ridge Mountains. Just a few miles away, on the western side of the Blue Ridge Mountains in the Shenandoah Valley was Robert Lee's Army of Northern Virginia.

The ***"turn with the Rebles"*** that Charles refers to in his diary, was not an attempt by Lee to attack through Snicker's Gap and engage the far superior numbers of McClellan's Army. Lee had sent General Jeb Stuart, Lee's commander of cavalry, with about a thousand cavalry troopers and some horse artillery through Snicker's Gap to delay the forward elements of the Union Army. On November 2, Stuart attacked Union forces near the village of Unison. Not knowing how large a force they had encountered, the Union troops advanced slowly. Stuart withdrew, fighting each step of the way. He managed to hold the Union Army at bay until the night of November 3, and then crossed back over the Blue Ridge Mountains at Ashby's Gap. The result was that Lee gained enough time to reach Culpeper and get his Army between Richmond and the Army of the Potomac.

To Lincoln, this looked like another opportunity lost by McClellan; perhaps it was the small action at Unison that made Lincoln decide this would be McClellan's last lost opportunity. General McClellan had a long history of strained dealings with Lincoln and to understand why, we must go back to a small river southwest of Washington called Bull Run. Bull Run flowed near the town of Manassas, about 32 miles from Washington.

CHAPTER FOUR

❖

The Rise and Fall and Rise and Fall of General McClellan

The Battle of 1st Manassas (1st Bull Run)

It was July of 1861. Three months had passed since the evacuation of Fort Sumter. Lincoln wanted his army to march against Richmond, the capital of the Confederacy, only 100 miles south of Washington. Lincoln believed the fall of Richmond would lead to the collapse of the rebellion. In his eyes the longer it took to mount an assault on Richmond the more difficult it would be to end the war. His General, Brigadier General Irwin McDowell, told Lincoln that the Army was untrained and not ready for an assault on the South. Lincoln replied; ***"You are green, it is true; but they are green also; you are green alike."***

After a number of delays, and still under pressure, General McDowell led 18,000 poorly trained troops about 30 miles to the southwest of Washington and crossed the small river of Bull Run. There they engaged the Confederate forces, entrenched between Gainesville and Centreville on the Warrenton Turnpike. It was July 21, 1861. The Southern forces were led by General P.T. Beauregard. At first things went well for the Union even though McDowell's orders were poorly executed. Nevertheless, in all the chaos, Beauregard's generals regrouped their shaky men. Many rallied around the Brigade of Confederate General Thomas Jackson who, it was said, stood his ground like a stone wall. Thomas Jackson was forever after known as Stonewall Jackson.

Late in the afternoon, Confederate reinforcements under Col. Jubal Early extended the Confederate line and Jackson's men advanced. This forced a withdrawal of the Federal center that quickly spread to the flanks. Virginia cavalry under Col. James "Jeb" Stuart arrived on the field and charged into the ranks of the Federal infantry. The Federals retreated. Then Gen. Joseph Johnston of the Confederate army arrived from the Shenandoah Valley by rail with 10,000 men.

The South launched a strong counter-attack and McDowell's green troops broke under fire. The newspapers reported that some ran all the way back to Washington. It was a disaster for Lincoln's army.

The Army of the Potomac

After the 1st Battle of Bull Run, or as it was called in the South the Battle of 1st Manassas, Lincoln removed McDowell and put George McClellan in charge of the Federal Army. He was 34 years old. McClellan had an impressive resume. He was a graduate of West Point, and before the war, a railroad executive. His troops had been victorious in the first land conflict of the war on June 3, 1861, at the minor Battle of Philippi, in western Virginia. McClellan was a tireless worker, and soon after taking command, he oversaw the construction of 48 forts and strong points around Washington. He was exceptionally gifted in the art of organizing and training an army. In a few months, the Army of the Potomac was a well-trained and well-organized fighting force. On November 1, the aging Winfield Scott retired and George McClellan became general in chief of all Union Armies.

One thing McClellan was not good at, at least as far as Lincoln was concerned, was aggressively taking the fight to the enemy. By the winter of 1861, Lincoln, under great political pressure, was becoming more and more frustrated with McClellan's failure to launch an offensive. In December of 1861, and January of 1862, while McClellan was recovering from typhoid fever, Lincoln began meeting with Cabinet members and generals in an attempt to get the Army to act.

He told the generals ***"If General McClellan does not want to use the army, I would like to borrow it for a time."***

McClellan deeply resented interference in his command believing that Lincoln was not qualified to judge his actions. In fact, McClellan believed that no one was qualified to make military judgments, or any other kind of judgements, about his actions. Lincoln grew weary of McClellan's promises to begin a campaign and on March 8, 1862, Lincoln reorganized the Army and relieved McClellan of his post as General in Chief of the Union Armies. McClellan, given command of the Army of the Potomac, received orders to attack Richmond. To save his job, with resentment of Lincoln growing, McClellan finally acted.

The Peninsula Campaign

McClellan's newest plan was to transport the Army of the Potomac by steamer from Alexandrea to Fort Monroe. Fort Monroe, located at the tip of the Virginia Peninsula where the York River and James River flow into Chesapeake Bay, was the largest stone fort ever constructed in the United States. It is now part of Hampton, Virginia. In 1862, Fort Monroe was under control of Federal forces and thus ensured a secure supply line. From Fort Monroe, McClellan planned to march his army up the peninsula to Richmond. Lincoln hated this plan. It removed the Army of the Potomac from between Washington and Richmond, thus inviting an attack on the nation's Capital. After months of haggling with McClellan, Lincoln finally gave his approval.

On March 17, 1862, the Peninsula Campaign began. It involved 389 ships moving 121,500 men, 44 artillery batteries, 11,500 wagons, and 15,000 horses. The 44th NY along with the rest of the 5th Corps was part of this force. Once they arrived at Fort Monroe, relatively small Confederate forces and extraordinarily heavy rains continually delayed McClellan's march to Richmond. When McClellan's army first arrived on the Peninsula, there were only 11,000 men to stand in his way to the rebel capital. McClellan believed the number to be 100,000. When McClellan reached General Johnston's line of defenses anchored at Yorktown, and extending across the peninsula, McClellan ordered his army to dig in and prepare for a long siege. McClellan was constantly overestimating the strength of Confederate forces to his front, and to Lincoln's frustration, constantly calling for more troops, supplies and equipment.

On May 4, after a month's preparation to besiege the city, Union forces realized that General Johnston had just abandoned Yorktown to prepare positions at Williamsburg. Charles Kelly's regiment was the first Union force to occupy Yorktown (the very place that General Charles Cornwallis had surrendered to George Washington in 1781). McClellan resumed the march toward Richmond, and for now, the 44th NY was left to garrison Yorktown. They were not there for long. They would soon be in the thick of gory battles at places they had never heard of like Mechanicville, Gaines' Mill, White Oak Swamp, Turkey Bend and Malvern Hill. As McClellan resumed his march, escaping slaves flooded into Yorktown seeking food and freedom.

General McClellan's Army of the Potomac was again stopped at Williamsburg. There they met the rearguard of the Confederate Army under command of

General James Longstreet. The main body of Joe Johnston's southern Army was moving toward Richmond, just fifty miles away. At Williamsburg on May 5, 1862, McClellan reported an army of 100,000 in his path; the actual numbers were 41,000 Federal forces engaged against 32,000 Confederate forces. When it came to how large a force he was facing, McClellan was not good at counting. At the end of the day 4,000 men, north and south, lay dead and wounded. For the Union, seven Medals of Honor were earned. The battle was inconclusive.

That evening and the next day while McClellan prepared for yet another siege, Joe Johnston withdrew Longstreet from Williamsburg. Johnston had not won the battle at Williamsburg but he had gained precious time for his army to reach Richmond. It would take two weeks for the Army of the Potomac to catch up.

Out of frustration, Abraham Lincoln paid a visit to Fort Monroe on May 6, 1862. McClellan was not present. Lincoln pulled rank on the local commander of Fort Monroe, 78 year old John Wool, a very capable commander, and ordered him to assault Norfolk, Virginia. Norfolk was about four miles by water from Fort Monroe, just across the mouth of the James River. General Wool landed 6,000 troops on Willoughby Spit on May 8, and Federal forces occupied Norfolk on May 10, 1862, without firing a shot. The Federal occupation of Norfolk put Gosport Shipyard into the hands of the Union and eliminated the base of operations for the Confederate ironclad CSS Virginia. Norfolk remained in Federal hands for the rest of the war.

Meanwhile, McClellan was expecting reinforcements from a large Union Army that had been chasing Stonewall Jackson in the Shenandoah Valley. On May 25th Stonewall Jackson soundly defeated Federal forces at the 1st Battle of Winchester. Concerned about the safety of Washington, Lincoln recalled forces from the Shenandoah Valley back to Fredericksburg. There would be no reinforcement of the Army of the Potomac.

By the end of May, McClellan's Army had advanced to within five or six miles of Richmond. Confederate General Joe Johnston saw but one weakness in the superior force before him. Part of McClellan's Army was now north of the Chickahominy River and part was south of the river. Johnston planned to wait for a heavy rain to make it almost impossible for one part of the Federal army to reinforce the other, and then attack.

Still, believing his Army to be outnumbered two to one, McClellan maneuvered for what everyone knew was a coming battle. The night of May 30, both Federal and Confederate armies suffered through a horrendous thunderstorm that washed out bridges, flooded the Chickahominy River, and turned roads to soup. Artillery sank in the roads like doomed ships; gunners worked in mud up to the waste trying to free their field pieces. Wagons had mud up to their axels. While camped at Gaines' Mill, Sargeant Henry Howlett of Company C, 44th NY, was killed by lightning.

Sergeant Henry Howlett, Company C, 44th NY Infantry Volunteers was killed by lightning at Gaines' Mill, May 30, 1862 (Library of Congress)

The next day, Confederate forces attacked the Union forces south of the Chickahominy River at Seven Pines, also known as Fair Oaks. During the bloody battle, just as the Federal position neared collapse, reinforcements arrived. The Union position stabilized. General Joe Johnston, commander of the Confederate forces, was seriously wounded. Rebel forces attacked again the next day with little success. Both sides claimed victory.

To replace Joe Johnston, Robert E. Lee was appointed Commander of the Army of Northern Virginia. McClellan now faced a brilliant and determined adversary whose aggression knew few limits.

After the Battle of Seven Pines, McClellan's Army of the Potomac sat within 6 miles of Richmond. Federal soldiers reported that they could hear church bells ringing in the city; it would have been a devastating blow to morale if they had realized the march to Richmond was over. Seven Pines had shaken George McClellan. The Union army would get no closer to Richmond during this campaign.

While McClellan waited for the roads to dry Lee reorganized his forces. He knew that McClellan was bringing up his siege guns from Williamsburg and that Confederate forces were not strong enough to withstand a protracted siege of Richmond. Lee sent word to Stonewall Jackson, in the Shenandoah Valley, to return as quickly as possible.

The Seven Days Battles

On June 26, Lee saw his chance and took a huge gamble. He left 20,000 troops south of the Chickahominy to stand in front of 70,000 Federal troops, and attacked Fitz John Porter's 5th Corps, which was more or less isolated north of the Chickahominy. Between June 26, and July 2, Lee fought a series of aggressive bloody battles knows as The Seven Days Battles. It started at Mechanicsville. Gaines' Mill was next. Then Lee attacked the Union rear guard at Savage Station. McClellan wired Secretary of War Edwin Stanton that he was attacked by greatly superior numbers and was afraid to reinforce north of the river and afraid to advance south of the river.

By the end of June, McClellan had had enough. On the night of the battle at Gaines' Mill, McClellan began to withdraw his forces to Harrison's Landing on the James River, with Robert Lee hot on his tails. At Harrison's Landing, McClellan's troops would be under the protection of Union gunboats stationed on the James

River. Some of McClellan's generals such as Phil Kearny, protested to the point of insubordination, claiming they could take Richmond with two divisions.

On July 1, 1862, as the Federal Army withdrew, Lee concentrated his forces and attacked at Malvern Hill. During the battle, Lieutenant Colonel Rice of the 44th NY could be heard shouting ***"Men we are Christians and we can die."*** A soldier from Company "H" remarked, ***"I don't see what the Hell is the use of his saying that for we are dying fast enough."*** Indeed, on that day, the 44th NY suffered 99 casualties out of the 225 men engaged at Malvern Hill. After the battle, Lt. Colonel Rice reported that there were only 98 muskets left in the entire 44th NY.

However, Lee had made a serious mistake at Malvern Hill. He had launched a frontal attack with 30,000 Confederate troops into positions that 27,000 Federal troops had fortified with artillery and trenches. Lee's Army suffered 5,600 casualties compared to Union casualties of 2,100. The Union Army had not budged. For now, Lee's attempt to crush the Army of the Potomac was over. In the months to follow, it does not appear that Robert Lee remembered the lesson of Malvern Hill.

It was not until July 2 the 44th NY realized the Federal Army was withdrawing from the march on Richmond. Captain Eugene Nash of the 44th NY wrote in his history of the Regiment that ***"no army every experienced greater humiliation."***

In the end, the "butcher's bill" on both sides of the Seven Days Battles was horrendous: 16,000 casualties for the North and 20,000 for the South. For the entire Peninsula Campaign, casualties were 23,900 Federal troops and 29,600 Confederate troops. McClellan commanded the largest Army ever assembled in North America, but in the end had little to show for it but bloodshed.

McClellan's retreat after the Seven Days Battles crushed Northern morale. So many men, so much equipment, so much hope placed into the hands of George McClellan. Morale in the Confederate States of America skyrocketed.

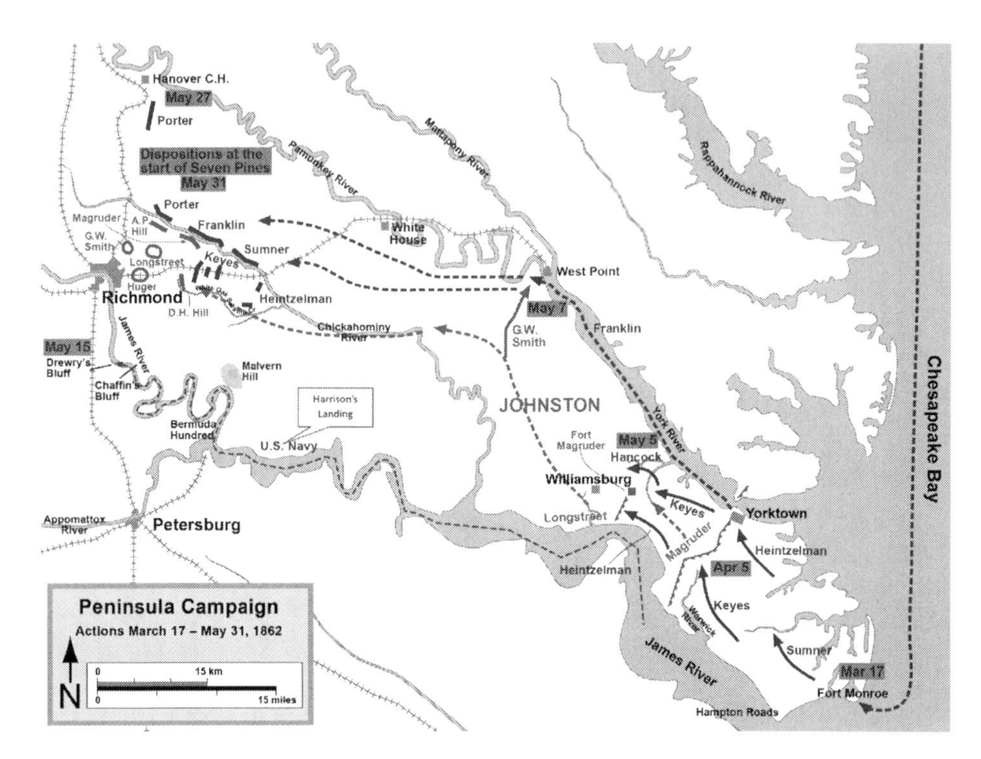

This map illustrates the campaign of General McClellan on the Virginia Peninsula. I have pointed out the location of Harrison's Landing, a few miles to the southeast of Malvern Hill. Harrison's Landing is where McClellan withdrew to the protection of Union gunboats on the James River. Norfolk Virginia is south of Fort Monroe, across the mouth of the James River. This map is courtesy of "Map by Hal Jespersen, www.cwmaps.com".

CHAPTER FIVE

❖

Protecting His Homeland

General Robert Lee and General James Pope

After the Seven Days Battles, early in July of 1862, Robert Lee had difficult decisions to make. McClellan was camped with as many as 140,000 troops just 25 miles from Richmond on the banks of the James River at Harrison's Landing. His Army could emerge from the protection of the gunboats at any time and threaten Richmond. Union General John Pope, one of the most disliked officers in the North or South, had 56,000 men in the field near Manassas, Virginia. Union General Irvin McDowell had 11,500 men at Falmouth, just north of Fredericksburg, Virginia. Pope and McDowell were less than a hundred miles from Richmond. Union General Ambrose Burnside had 12,000 men mysteriously waiting on transport steamers at Fort Monroe. They might appear almost anywhere without warning. Lee knew that if all of these forces were effectively combined, and used against him, he could not hold Richmond.

Lee also had a bigger objective. At no time did the South want to conquer and hold northern territory. What the South wanted was recognition of the Confederate States of America. The South wanted acknowledgement of the right to establish their independence from the North, to remove Federal troops from their home ground, and to end the war.

The basis of this demand for independence was the deeply rooted belief throughout the South, and a good deal of the North, that the "white race" was superior to the "black race" and that subjugation of Black Americans as property, to use as slave-owners saw fit, was natural and lawful. Southern leaders saw ample support for this position in the Declaration of Independence and in the United States Constitution. Southern leaders believed that the society they built was for the benefit of and the protection of *"the people"* which did not include Black Americans.

The 1857 ruling of the Supreme Court, in Dred Scott v. Sanford, as far as they were concerned, settled the issue once and for all. Five of the nine Supreme Court justices who heard the case were members of slave holding families. Chief Justice Robert Taney wrote for the majority opinion that slaves were property; He wrote,

> ***"They had for more than a century before been regarded as beings of an inferior order, and altogether unfit to associate with the white race, either in social or political relations; and so far inferior, that they had no rights which the white man was bound to respect".***

In the Dred Scott decision the Court ruled Black Americans could never be citizens, had no right to sue in Federal Court, and that the Missouri Compromise of 1820 was unconstitutional. The Missouri Compromise, which had helped to hold the Union together up to this point, declared all territories west of Missouri and North of Latitude 36 degrees 30 minutes, to be forever free of slavery. New states meant new Senators and Congressmen. Whether a new state was a slave holding state or an anti-slavery state meant political and economic power for whichever side prevailed.

The Dred Scott ruling opened many old wounds in Congress. With the growing intolerance of slavery in the North, culminating in the election of Abraham Lincoln, Southern leaders felt that their economy, their way of life, and the fundamental beliefs they held about their place in the world, were under existential threat.

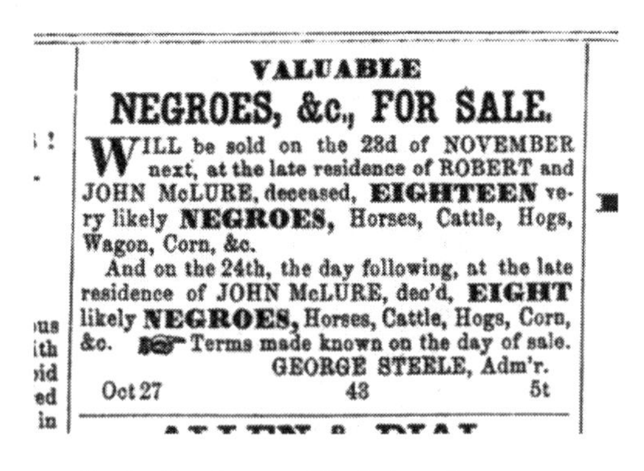

VALUABLE

NEGROES, &c., FOR SALE.

WILL be sold on the 28d of NOVEMBER next, at the late residence of ROBERT and JOHN McLURE, deceased, EIGHTEEN very likely NEGROES, Horses, Cattle, Hogs, Wagon, Corn, &c.

And on the 24th, the day following, at the late residence of JOHN McLURE, dec'd, EIGHT likely NEGROES, Horses, Cattle, Hogs, Corn, &c. ☞ Terms made known on the day of sale.

GEORGE STEELE, Adm'r.

Oct 27 48 5t

In the South, most Black Americans were considered property, to use as best benefited their owners.

In 1860, about 9 million people lived in the 11 states that would form the Confederate States of America. Of these about 3.5 million were slaves. This left about 5.5 million white Southerners. Of this number, a little over 316,000 Southerners were slave holders, but the number was much greater if you consider that this number represents only the heads of slave holding families. Regardless of how the count is made, the majority of Southern whites did not have a direct stake in the slavery issue. What they did have a stake in was the worldview that their race was superior to the race of the slaves that made up such a large part of the Confederate States. This view, combined with the belief that loyalty should always be first to one's state, and only then to the Country at large, formed the basis of support from common people of the South for the rebellion.

Robert Lee believed that if he could take the war from Virginia to the Northern states, and let the people of the North feel the horrible cost of war, that northern support for the war would collapse. A just peace could be negotiated, and the Confederate States of America would be recognized, and allowed to pursue their way of life without northern interference. He knew his army was outnumbered at least three to one but also knew a decisive series of victories would open the door to English and French support, and weaken the will of the North to continue the fight.

Abraham Lincoln also pondered what was to come after the Peninsula Campaign. He was adamant that the United States must remain intact at any cost. His every action was in pursuit of this objective. Lincoln visited George McClellan at Harrison's Landing in early July, and was not encouraged by what he found there. Rather than use the massive Union army to reverse the outcome of the Seven Days Battles, McClellan sat and waited for more reinforcements. What was more troubling, McClellan was now delving into politics. While Lincoln was at Harrison's Landing McClellan gave him a detailed written plan of what direction the entire nation should take, with subtle hints of his own central part.

Lincoln also knew that the current situation of having essentially four separate un-coordinated Union armies in the eastern theater alone was a recipe for disaster. After returning to Washington, under great political pressure, Lincoln filled McClellan's previous position of General-in-Chief of all the Union Armies that had been vacant since March. He appointed Maj. Gen. Henry Halleck to the position. Halleck proved to be another mistake. Lincoln would continue to hire and fire Army commanders until he found one that was as ruthless and as determined as he was to crush the armies of the South. For now, McClellan kept his job as Commander of the Army of the Potomac.

With the November elections approaching, Abraham Lincoln needed a victory. The country was still reeling from the failed Peninsula Campaign, Lincoln's support was eroding, and his armies were scattered and vulnerable to attack. Amidst all of this, Lincoln was looking for an opportunity to announce his Emancipation Proclamation, which would free all slaves held in enemy territory. Lincoln hoped this act would galvanize support for the war in the North. For now, this document would remain in Lincoln's pocket. Moreover, as Lincoln had feared, the bulk of the Union army positioned outside of the path between Washington and Richmond was an open invitation to an aggressive general like Robert Lee. On August 3, 1862, Lincoln ordered the Army of the Potomac to abandon the Virginia Peninsula and return home.

The survivors of the 44th NY, along with much of the Army of the Potomac made their way back down the Virginia Peninsula, through Williamsburg and Yorktown, and finally loaded onto steamers at Fort Monroe. The 44th NY arrived at Aquia Creek Landing about 8 a.m. August 20, 1862. Aquia Creek flows into the Potomac River about 15 miles from Fredericksburg and was a transportation hub and supply depot during much of the war. From Aquia Creek, the 44th NY took railcars to Falmouth just outside of Fredericksburg.

Robert Lee would not wait for the Army of the Potomac to rejoin Union General John Pope's newly formed Army of Virginia. Lee sent Stonewall Jackson to occupy the vital rail hub at Gordonsville, a junction of the Virginia Central Railroad, and a lifeline for Richmond. General Pope was advancing toward Gordonsville to relieve pressure on Federal forces withdrawing from the Virginia Peninsula. Stonewall Jackson arrived at Gordonsville July 19, with 14,000 men, and by July 27 was reinforced with an additional 10,000 men commanded by General A.P. Hill.

Cedar Mountain

When Lee learned that General Pope had ordered Union General Nathanial Banks to advance toward Gordonsville with a force of only 8,000 men, he saw his chance. Banks was near Cedar Mountain, just twenty miles north of Gordonsville when Lee ordered Jackson to attack. Time was critical; the Army of the Potomac would soon arrive from the Peninsula to reinforce Pope. Jackson attacked on August 9, 1862.

Jackson's attack was poorly coordinated and nearly failed. When the battle turned against him, he rallied his men as only Stonewall Jackson could. He bought enough time for General Hill to arrive and reinforce the attack. The Federal line was broken. In the Union retreat that followed both General Pope and General Banks were nearly captured. Jackson cut off the pursuit by moonlight around 10 p.m. when a division from General McDowell's Corps arrived to cover the retreat of Federal forces.

As Bank's Federal Army received reinforcements, Jackson withdrew to south of the Rapidan River. Banks did not pursue. Lee ordered General Longstreet to move to Gordonsville with ten Brigades, and General Hood to move to Hanover Junction. After confirming that McClellan was withdrawing from the Virginia Peninsula, Lee moved his headquarters to Gordonsville; he arrived on August 15, 1862.

General Halleck, as well as Abraham Lincoln, feared a concentrated attack on General Pope's forces before McClellan's troops arrived, and Lee very much wanted to accommodate them. Before Lee could act Pope withdrew his forces to north of the Rappahannock River and was ordered to hold that line until McClellan arrived with more men.

General Halleck had good reason to be cautious. Lee was preparing to attack Pope's Army entrenched north of the Rappahannock and in preparation sent General Jeb Stuart on a raid to cut off Pope's line of supply. Before dawn on August 22, Jeb Stuart took 1,500 cavalry and rode completely around the north end of Pope's forces, while at the same time Jackson and Longstreet faced off against Pope's Army from the south side of the Rappahannock.

Stuart's troopers passed over Waterloo Bridge, through the towns of Warrenton and Auburn Mills, and then turned south to follow the east bank of Cedar Run to Catlett's Station. They arrived around midnight during a terrific thunderstorm, in what Stuart described as ***"the darkest night I ever knew"***. They were just thirteen miles behind Pope's Army who were camped along the Rappahannock. At Catlett's Station, they drove off a small force guarding General Pope's Headquarters. During the heavy rain, Stuart sent men to destroy the nearby Orange and Alexandria Railroad Bridge that crossed Cedar Run, while the remainder of his troops looted Pope's headquarters. They gathered up the horses and mules, took prisoners, and cut telegraph lines. Most of the Federal soldiers escaped.

Catlett's Station, Virginia, August 1862, (Library of Congress)

While loading wagons with chests of papers containing Pope's orders and dispatches, all manner of food, clothing, and supplies, and $350,000 in Union greenbacks, Stuart's men discovered a prize that was most satisfying to Jeb Stuart, John Pope's hat, cloak and frock coat. Meanwhile Stuart's men who were sent to destroy the bridge over Cedar Run were frantically trying to set the bridge on fire during the heavy pouring rain. After this failed, they attacked the bridge with axes but were driven off by Federal soldiers from across the river. Unable to destroy the bridge, Stuart's troopers left before dawn and retraced their path back to Confederate lines. They arrived on the evening of August 23, 1862.

Although Stuart's raid of Catlett's Station failed in the attempt to destroy the bridge over Cedar Run, and thus sever the Orange and Alexandria rail line, General Lee gained something even more valuable from the raid. The dispatches and other documents that Stuart brought back reached Lee's headquarters on August 24. They gave Lee a clear picture of Pope's forces arrayed to his front, and showed him how quickly Pope was being reinforced by McClellan's troops arriving from the Peninsula. Lee now knew that it would be foolish to attack Pope's superior numbers sitting across the Rappahannock. Lee also knew he would not be able to hold his current position for long. Pope's Army was 75,000 strong and growing.

Rather than retreat toward Richmond, and try to hold off the inevitable siege, Lee did something that few commanders would have attempted. While facing a larger army, he split his force into two groups. General Longstreet with his four divisions was tasked with holding Pope's ten divisions sitting just across the Rappahannock River. At the same time, General Thomas "Stonewall" Jackson would take his army of 24,000 men, march around the north end of Pope's Army, continue up the eastern edge of the Bull Run Mountains to Salem, and pass through Thoroughfare Gap. From there they would head south through Gainesville and place themselves along the Orange and Alexandrea Railroad squarely between Pope's army and Washington. Jackson had ordered his men to leave their knapsacks and everything else except weapons for a forced march. Even though his troops looked worn and scraggly, many marching without shoes, Jackson had supreme confidence in his men's ability.

After Jackson was underway, Pope's scouts observed columns of Confederate's moving to the west but Pope assumed they were headed for the Shenandoah Valley. It was a big mistake.

Jackson Raids Manassas Junction

On the evening of August 26, 1862, after marching fifty-four miles in thirty-six hours with little food, Jackson's men emerged at Bristoe Station, located where Broad Run crosses the Orange and Alexandrea Railroad. There they tore up track and destroyed two Federal trains. While his men were engaged in the destruction Jackson learned that just up the rail line about five miles away, the massive Union Army supply depot at Manassas Junction was lightly guarded. Even though his men were exhausted and hungry he sent one of his trusted brigade commanders together with Jeb Stuart's cavalry to, if possible, capture the depot. In a night attack that lasted only minutes, Jackson's men overran the depot and captured 300 surprised Federal troops.

Some of Stonewall Jackson's handiwork. This photo was taken in August of 1862, near Manassas Junction. Note the initials "U.S.M.R.R.", on one of the cars, which stands for United States Military Railroad. The USMRR was a separate agency established by the U.S. War Department to operate trains and telegraph lines seized by the U.S. government for military use. (*The Photographic History of The Civil War in Ten Volumes: Volume Four, The Cavalry.* The Review of Reviews Co., New York. 1911. p. 96.)

Jackson left three brigades as a rear guard under Command of General Richard Ewell, and marched the rest of his army five miles to Manassas Junction early on August 27. There his hungry men found that Jackson had led them to what must have seemed like the Garden of Eden, straight out of the Bible. There were more than a hundred boxcars loaded with supplies and acre after acre of warehouses stuffed to the brim with every manner of food and equipment. Jackson attempted to restrain his men, but hunger and depravation won out. Jackson did order the destruction of most of the barrels of whiskey, wine, and brandy before his men got to them. His men fought off a Federal brigade coming from the east, and with the junction secured, all available wagons were filled with desperately needed medical and other supplies; everything else was left to his men.

Molasses, coffee, cigars, jackknives, writing paper, uniforms, shirts, pants, blankets, knapsacks, haversacks, new underwear, shoes, saddles, and an endless variety of delicacies such as ham, canned lobster, pickled oysters, tongue, candy, cakes, nuts, lemons, pickles, and mustard, were found in incredible abundance. What the men could not carry or eat, they burned.

By noon, it was over. With the railroad bridge at Bull Run engulfed in flames, Jackson knew his work at Manassas Junction was done. That evening General Ewell withdrew from Bristol Station after holding off Union troops in a brilliant series of maneuvers that lasted throughout the afternoon. He re-joined Jackson's main force at Manassas Junction. They were well aware that soon the entire Federal Army from both the east and west would be paying them a visit.

By the evening of August 27, Union General Pope was about five miles west of Manassas Junction. He ordered his scattered troops to converge at the junction around dawn of the next morning. He expected to attack Jackson with 60,000 Union troops coming from three different directions. Feeling he had Jackson trapped at Manassas Junction, Pope eagerly looked forward to the next morning. That night General Pope watched the sky to the east turn orange as the vast supply depot at Manassas Junction burned.

Around 9 p.m. that same evening, as Pope waited for his trap to close, Jackson's forces began heading north to find a safer place to wait for Longstreet to join them, and reform Lee's Army. His men took several different routes in the dark, partially because Jackson knew where he wanted them to go but was not quite sure how they should get there, and partially because coordinating such a movement in the dark was not Jackson's strong suit. By midnight, Manassas Junction was nearly empty. Oddly enough, the lack of coordination of Jackson's withdrawal ended up working to Jackson's advantage.

Pope had based his entire plan for defeating Jackson on Jackson staying put at Manassas Junction. He ignored reports that Longstreet was approaching with 25,000 Confederate troops by way of Thoroughfare Gap, thinking that first he would defeat Jackson and then turn on Longstreet. When Pope's poorly coordinated troops began arriving at Manassas Junction around noon the next morning they found nothing but acres of desolation. Jackson had not stayed put.

One of Pope's Staff Officers wrote,

> ***"On the railroad tracks and sidings stood the hot and smoking remains of what had recently been trains of cars laden with ordnance and commissary stores intended for our army. As far as the eye could reach, the plain was covered with boxes, barrels, cans, cooking utensils saddles, sabers, muskets, and military equipments generally; hard bread and corn pones, meat, salt, and fresh beans, blankets, clothes, shoes, and hats, from brand-new articles, just from the original packages, to the scarcely recognizable exuviae of the rebels, who had made use of the opportunity to renew their toilets."***

After arriving at the ruins of Manassas Junction, Pope frantically began redirecting his marching columns. There was one problem: Pope had no idea where Jackson was. Pope was flooded with reports of Jackson's men having passed through first one place and then another. Jackson's somewhat disorganized withdrawal over several routes from Manassas Junction had paid off.

At 2 p.m., Pope sent orders to General McDowell to pursue Jackson in the direction of Centreville. Before his orders could reach McDowell, Pope seems to have suddenly taken seriously the threat Longstreet posed coming through Thoroughfare Gap. He now decided to commit much of his Army to stopping Longstreet before Longstreet could meet up with Jackson. A couple of hours later Pope changed his plan again and decided that Jackson really was the big threat. He ordered his generals to abandon the pursuit of Longstreet and converge on Centreville.

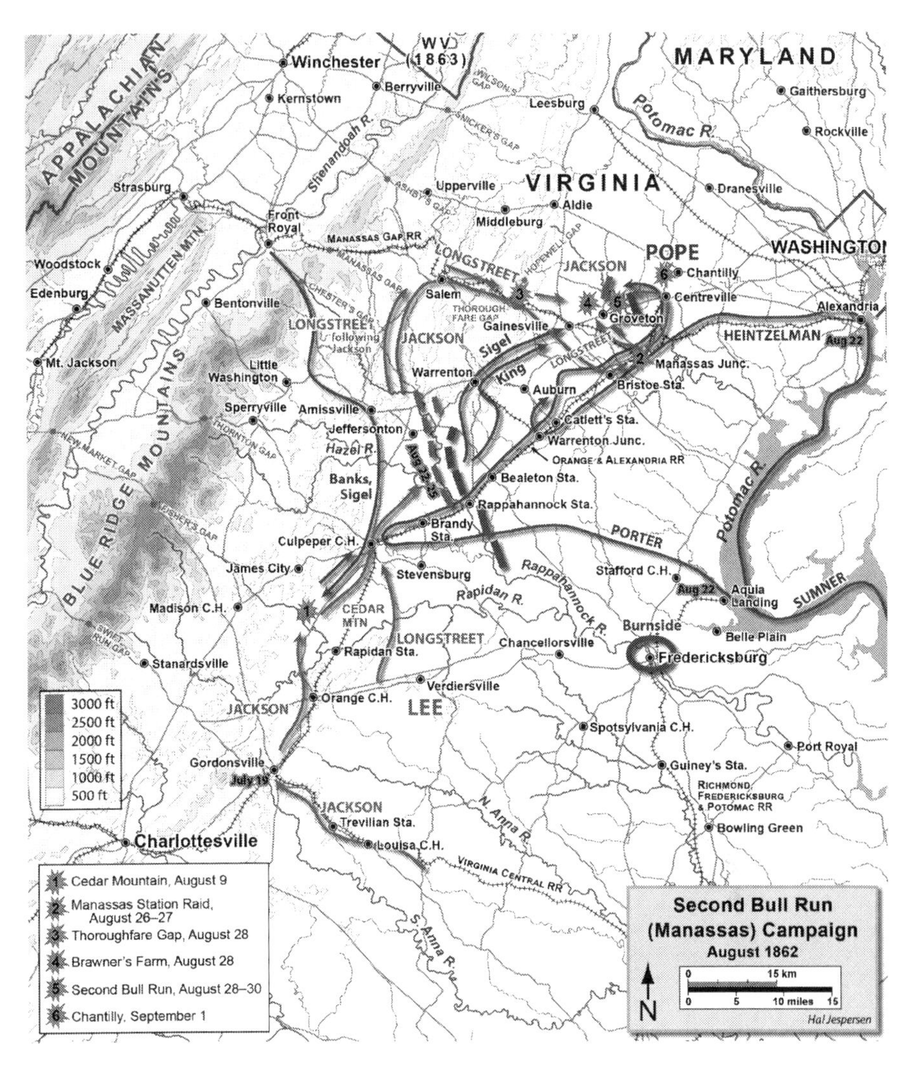

This map illustrates the route the 5th Corps took when they returned from the Peninsula campaign and the path of the various corps leading up to 2nd Manassas. The 44th NY is with General Porter's 5th Corps. Charles Kelly joined the 44th NY about six weeks after the battle of 2nd Manassas. This map is courtesy of "Map by Hal Jespersen, www.cwmaps.com".

2nd Manassas (2nd Bull Run)

That afternoon while marching on the Warrenton Turnpike toward Centreville, and indulging in a good deal of grumbling about the chaotic orders they were receiving, a number of Federal soldiers observed a lone rider on a rise that ran parallel to the road 1,000 yards to the north. He was riding back and forth and watching the Union columns pass by. Behind the lone rider was an unfinished railroad grading and beyond that, wooded hills. In those woods, between Sudley Springs and Groveton, were Jackson's 24,000 men, arrayed along a front that extended more than a mile. Union General Abner Doubleday later claimed that the rider they saw that afternoon was Stonewall Jackson. He could not convince anyone around him to be concerned.

It was near sunset just east of Gainesville, when Jackson attacked one of the Union columns marching to Centreville. Two hours of bloody fighting followed. Although greatly outnumbered the Federal troops proved as tough as anything Jackson could throw at them. Both sides suffered heavy losses. Union casualties were over 1,000. Jackson lost almost as great a number. Among the wounded were two of Jackson's highest-ranking lieutenants, General William Taliaferro, and perhaps Jackson's best commander, General Richard Ewell. Both would live to fight again but Ewell would lose a leg. Both sides withdrew after dark.

Jackson seemed satisfied with the day's work and expressed no worry over what the next day would bring. He had achieved his objective of getting Pope's attention away from General Longstreet, and now awaited the arrival of Longstreet, and his Army's Commander, Robert Lee.

The next morning, August 29, Pope was convinced that he had Jackson's army cornered. He planned on attacking both of Jackson's flanks, one at Sudley Springs and one northwest of Groveton.

General Jackson would have politely disagreed with General Pope's assessment of his position. He did not believe he was trapped. He had placed his men with care in an excellent defensive position along an unfinished railroad grade with Sudley Mountain (Stony Ridge) to his back. He intended no maneuvers, only to hold his position until Longstreet arrived. The armies would be fighting on the same ground the War of the Rebellion, or as the South called it, the War of Northern Aggression, had begun in earnest with the Battle of 1st Manassas (1st Bull Run), a little over a year ago.

General Pope's plan to spring his trap did not materialize as he had envisioned. Delayed by darkness and conflicting orders, many of his troops were not where he expected them to be. The confusion coming from his command over the past days now exacted its toll. Not sure where some of his men were, Pope sent out staff officers to find the commands of General McDowell and General Porter.

Despite the delay in concentrating his men, Pope decided to use the troops he had with him to launch a frontal assault on Jackson's position.

On August 29, 1862, Pope sent wave after wave of troops against the railroad grade only to be driven back. Many of the assaults were nearly successful especially near Sudley Springs but Jackson's men held. Unknown to Pope, at about 10 o'clock that morning Longstreet's men began to arrive and position themselves on Jackson's right.

Pope continued his assaults throughout the day, putting intense pressure on Jackson's men. Casualties on both sides were high. Part of Jackson's line was near collapse. Later that day, Lee arrived with Longstreet's Corps. Lee suggested to Longstreet that he send some of his troops forward to relieve pressure on Jackson; Longstreet said he was not ready. All of his troops had not yet arrived, and most troubling of all, there were two Federal divisions under General Porter coming up on his flank from the South.

Outnumbered three to one, Jackson's men survived the long bloody day and, withdrew after dark to the woods behind their lines for a night's rest. Pope took the withdrawal to mean that Jackson was beaten and in full retreat.

Pope was pleased with the day's work in spite of numerous missteps. In his mind, the biggest problem had been the failure of General Porter to obey orders. As Porter came up from Manassas Junction, Pope commanded Porter to attack Jackson's right flank. Porter sent word to Pope that Longstreet stood in his way with a force three times larger than his own. Pope did not believe him. Again, at around 4:30 p.m., he ordered Porter to advance against Jackson's right. Again, Porter insisted that he had half the rebel army to his front. It was too late in the day to force the issue. Pope gave up and moved Porter's two divisions to his main line in parallel with the Warrenton Turnpike. He prepared to finish Jackson's army once and for all, the next morning.

The morning of August 30 found General Longstreet's troops arrayed between the railroad grade and Manassas Gap Railroad at an almost 90-degree angle to Jackson's troops. The two Confederate armies formed a giant jaw ready to clamp down on Pope's Army. At the hinge of the jaw, Longstreet had positioned his artillery, which overlooked the entire line of battle.

Oblivious to the danger he was in, and refusing to listen to General Porter, Pope still believed that Jackson was retreating, and gleefully prepared to crush the rebel army. He formed three massive lines of troops to make a frontal assault on Jackson. It took until 3 p.m. that afternoon to get everyone in place, and then he attacked. The first line hit Jackson's weary troops with a vengeance. Time after time, the Federal troops faltered, and then rose again to attack Jackson's position along the railroad grade. Jackson's troops held.

Longstreet watched the battle for an hour from his position at the hinge of the jaw. He knew that Porter was now to his front and that his flank was secure. He now waited only for Pope to commit his reserves before closing the jaw. It was then he received word that Jackson had asked for assistance, something that Jackson had never done before. With Lee's blessing, about 3 p.m., Longstreet opened up on the Federal line with artillery. Instantly the Federal troops knew they were in trouble. Around four p.m., Longstreet advanced with 25,000 infantry. The Federal lines gave way. Jackson advanced his troops on the north side of the turnpike while Longstreet advanced along the south side. The jaw was closing. Pope must have felt that the hammer of God had come down on his men.

After marching for two days without food, along with the rest of the 5th Corps, the 44th NY joined the attack on Jackson at 3 p.m., just as the Federal attack was getting underway. Under command of General Butterfield, the 44th NY entered the battle with 12 officers and 148 men. In a short time, half of the officers were wounded or taken prisoner, and 65 of the enlisted men were killed or wounded. General Sykes, then Commander of the 2nd Division, 5th Corps, later wrote in his report of the battle that ***"Butterfield's attack was gallantly made and gallantly maintained until his troops were torn to pieces."***

After an initial rout, and the efforts of many brave men to form a rear guard, Pope restored order to his Army and retreated beyond Bull Run, through Centreville, to inside the defenses of Washington. The Battle of 2nd Manassas (2nd Bull Run) was over.

The night of August 30, as the rest of the Federal Army retreated to Centreville, the 44th helped to guard the retreat. When their turn came to withdraw, the bridge over Bull Run had already been destroyed. The brigade had to wade across the waist deep muddy waters of Bull Run. They arrived at Centreville on August 31, wet, tired, and hungry, and got their first meal in three days.

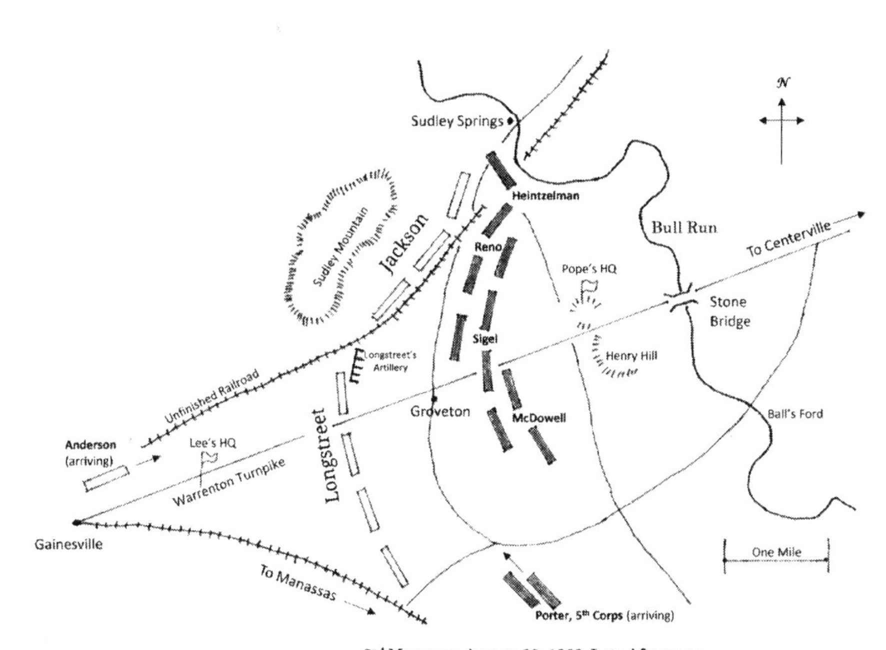

2nd Manassas August 29, 1862, Late Afternoon

On the afternoon of August 29, as General Porter approached the battlefield he was ordered by General Pope to attack Jackson's right flank. General Pope did not realize that Longstreet's entire Corps had arrived and was now between Jackson and Porter's 5th Corps. Twice Porter protested the order to attack a force three times his size but General Pope did not believe what Porter was telling him. General Porter refused to attack and General Pope refused to acknowledge that Longstreet was on his left flank. Longstreet held off putting his Corps into the fight until the following day when Porter was no longer on his right flank but directly to the front of Jackson. On August 30, Pope's army was routed, with heavy casualties, and chased back to Centerville. The 44th NY, part of General Porter's 5th Corps, was one of many Federal regiments nearly destroyed that day. The remnants of the 44th NY helped to form a rear guard allowing Pope's main force to escape across the stone bridge that crossed Bull Run.

In the aftermath of 2nd Manassas, Abraham Lincoln, and the rest of the North were greatly disheartened. Lincoln's General in Chief of all Union armies, General Halleck, had proved to be useless. For example, looking for reinforcements, just three days before 2nd Manassas, General Pope had complained to Halleck that he was not being kept up to date about the movements of General McClellan and the Army of the Potomac. Halleck responded, ***"Just think of the immense amount of telegraphing I have to do and then say whether I can be expected to give you any details as to the movements of others, even when I know them."***

Then there was George McClellan. McClellan had returned from Harrison's Landing on August 22, 1862. Since arriving, he had done everything he could to avoid sending his troops to Pope's aid. On August 10th he had written his wife ***"I have a strong idea that Pope will be thrashed during the coming week—& very badly whipped he will be & ought to be—such a villain as he is ought to bring defeat upon any cause that employs him."*** When Lincoln asked for McClellan's advice regarding Lee's incursion into eastern Virginia he told Lincoln to concentrate all his troops in Washington and ***"leave Pope to get out of his scrape"*** as best he could.

As for General Pope, he was relieved of command and sent into political oblivion to serve in Minnesota. He remained stationed there for the rest of the war. One military historian describes Pope's brief period of command as follows:

> ***"The braggart who had begun his campaign with insolent reflections ... had been kicked, cuffed, hustled about, knocked down, run over, and trodden upon as rarely happens in the history of war. His communications had been cut; his headquarters pillaged; a corps had marched into his rear, and had encamped at its ease upon the railroad by which he received his supplies; he had been beaten or foiled in every attempt he had made to 'bag' those defiant intruders; and, in the end, he was glad to find a refuge in the entrenchments of Washington."***

From his post in Minnesota, Pope bombarded Halleck with angry letters especially against General Porter. For now, Porter was safe under the political umbrella of his friend George McClellan. After McClellan was gone, on November 25, Porter was arrested and court martialed. On January 10, 1863, General Porter was found guilty of disobedience and misconduct at 2nd Manassas and dismissed from the Army. The North lost a valuable asset.

In Washington, after the debacle at 2nd Manassas, the infighting and witch-hunts rose to a level that was off the charts even for Washington. The Republicans demanded a new commander who was a strong abolitionist regardless of what other qualifications he may or may not have. Morale in the army sank to new lows. Elections were coming. Lincoln's cabinet members were having their own little war amongst themselves. Lincoln needed a victory if his Emancipation Proclamation, still unannounced, was to have a chance of uniting the North.

CHAPTER SIX

General McClellan Returns

Lincoln did not like McClellan but he recognized McClellan's genius for organization and logistics. With a sigh, Lincoln believed he must use what tools he had. On September 2, 1862, he appointed George McClellan to the somewhat ambiguous role of *"Commander of The Fortifications of Washington, and all the Troops for the Defense of the Capital"*. There was plenty of wiggle room in that title, enough to give Lincoln ample opportunity to deal with McClellan as he saw fit at a later time.

The Union army was jubilant and McClellan felt vindicated. In a remarkably short amount of time, McClellan restored order and morale to the broken Federal forces. Wanting to overcome talk of being too cautious, he set out from Washington with 87,000 men in pursuit of Robert Lee on September 5, 1862.

Lee Goes North

Lee's achievement since being given command of the Army of Northern Virginia was nothing but remarkable. A little over two months before 2nd Manassas he faced a far superior force positioned just five miles from his Capital. In that time, he had driven the Federal Army from his Capital all the way to the outskirts of the Federal Capital, demoralized and in disarray. His own forces had suffered greatly but remained intact.

Perhaps Lee's victory at 2nd Manassas, his second greatest victory of the war, caused him to overlook how fragile his army had become. Large numbers of casualties, loss of many skilled officers, lack of a dependable food supply, the effects of prolonged marches including many men lacking shoes, had all exacted a toll. Even so, Robert Lee believed that he was one great victory away from breaking the will of the North to continue the war.

"Headquarters Near Fredericktown, Md.,
September 8, 1862.

His Excellency Jefferson Davis, President of the Confederate States, Richmond, Va.: Mr. President,--

The present position of affairs, in my opinion, places it in the power of the government of the Confederate States to propose with propriety to that of the United States the recognition of our independence. For more than a year both sections of the country have been devastated by hostilities which have brought sorrow and suffering upon thousands of homes, without advancing the objects which our enemies proposed to themselves in beginning the contest. Such a proposition, coming from us at this time, could in no way be regarded as suing for peace; but, being made when it is in our power to inflict injury upon our adversary, would show conclusively to the world that our sole object is the establishment of our independence and the attainment of an honorable peace. The rejection of this offer would prove to the country that the responsibility of the continuance of the war does not rest upon us, but that the party in power in the United States elect to prosecute it for purposes of their own. The proposal of peace would enable the people of the United States to determine at their coming elections whether they will support those who favor a prolongation of the war, or those who wish to bring it to a termination, which can but be productive of good to both parties without affecting the honor of either.

I have the honor to be, with great respect, your obedient servant,
R. E. Lee, General."

After a few days' rest for his men, Lee left the battlefield at Manassas on September 3, and started marching north. From September 4, to 6, Lee's Army crossed the Potomac River at three different fords. They were now in Maryland, a divided state but still in the Union. On September 9, Lee's Army concentrated at the town of Frederick, Maryland.

While at Frederick, Lee issued Special Order No. 191, a detailed plan that again divided his Army into several parts. General Jackson would attack Harpers Ferry from three different directions and secure Lee's line of supply from the

Shenandoah Valley. Once Harpers Ferry was secure, Jackson would rejoin Lee's main body of troops at Boonsboro. From there they would occupy Harrisburg, Pennsylvania, and destroy the bridge over the Susquehanna River to protect their flank.

Lee knew that splitting up his forces deep in enemy territory was a big risk. Lee also now knew that General McClellan was again commanding the Federal forces that would be pursuing him. He said of McClellan, ***"He is an able general but a very cautious one."*** Lee believed the Federal Army was demoralized and in disarray and it would take three or four weeks for the North to reorganize. He did not expect effective action against his army before then; and by then he would be over the Susquehanna River.

Lee misjudged the condition of his enemy's army. The Federal Army was receiving regular rations, they had a commander that they loved, and morale quickly recovered from the debacle of 2nd Manassas. In addition, while in Frederick, the fates dealt Lee a nasty blow. Someone had used a copy of Special Order No. 191 to wrap two (or three) cigars and put the package inside of an envelope. The envelope became lost while Lee's Army was at Frederick. McClellan's Army passed through Frederick in pursuit of Lee, and on September 13, Corporal Barton Mitchell of the 27th Indiana Volunteers discovered the envelope laying on the ground. The envelope quickly made it up the chain of command, cigars and all, to the hands of General McClellan. Corporal Mitchell probably wished that he had kept the cigars.

McClellan was ecstatic. At least for the time being, the doubts and fears that constantly haunted him disappeared. He would force Turner's Gap at South Mountain, an extension of the Blue Ridge Mountains, and destroy the Confederate forces of Longstreet and A.P. Hill at Boonsboro. At the same time, he would send 18,000 men under command of General Franklin through Crampton's Gap, six miles south of Turner's Gap, and relieve the 12,000 Union troops at Harpers Ferry. McClellan himself would march with 70,000 men through Turner's Gap.

Battle of South Mountain

McClellan attacked the much smaller Confederate force at Turner's Gap, and just to the South, Fox's Gap, on September 14. A desperate battle ensued and the Confederate position was near collapse when General Longstreet arrived with reinforcements. The rebels managed to hold the Gap until nightfall. Longstreet reported to General Lee that the Gap could not be held past daylight of the next morning. To the south, less than 1,000 Confederate troops holding Crampton's Gap had no chance against the 18,000 Federal troops commanded by General Franklin. A short battle at Crampton's Gap was followed by Confederate troops retreating down the west side of South Mountain. Federal troops did not vigorously pursue the retreating troops and the gray coats were able to reform their line.

That evening, with the might of the Union Army almost on top of him, Lee realized that he had divided his Army once too often. He knew his invasion of the North was over, and his entire Army was in grave danger. There would be no occupation of Philadelphia or Baltimore or Washington. He had reached too far. By then he also knew of McClellan's discovery of the lost order; it was time to return to Virginia. He ordered Jackson and the two other wings of the attack on Harpers Ferry to withdraw and join his army near the little town of Sharpsburg, which had nearby fords crossing the Potomac. However, that evening Lee learned from Stonewall Jackson that all three of Jackson's columns were in place in the heights around Harpers Ferry and at first light planned to bombard the Federal garrison, now trapped in a fishbowl, into submission.

Lee withdrew from South Mountain that night, leaving behind 2,325 dead, wounded, and captured. He could not afford to lose a single one of them. One of his accomplished Generals, Samuel Garland Jr., lay dead at Fox's Gap.

The next morning, September 15, the Federal garrison at Harpers Ferry withstood the bombardment of Jackson's three-pronged assault for one hour and then surrendered. Jackson took 12,500 prisoners, and captured over ten thousand small arms, 73 cannon, and a large quantity of food and other supplies. He then left one division commanded by General Hill in charge of Harpers Ferry and started with five divisions on the short march north to meet Lee at Sharpsburg.

Lee's army reached Sharpsburg on September 15, and was joined by Jackson that afternoon. His army deployed along a ridge just west of the little town, with both flanks protected by a bend in the Potomac River. They prepared to meet the pursuing Federal Army. Even though his invasion plan had failed, Lee would not go meekly back into Virginia.

Antietam Creek (Sharpsburg)

McClellan's troops arrived near Sharpsburg on that same evening and deployed on a ridge opposite the Confederate position with a small river called Antietam Creek between them. McClellan had reported his victory at South Mountain in glowing terms to just about anyone who would listen. Lincoln responded, ***"God bless you and all with you. Destroy the rebel army if possible."*** After arriving at Sharpsburg, McClellan wanted time to study the terrain and make his plans for attack. He also awaited the remainder of his army to arrive and considered it too late in the day for an attack on September 15.

On September 16, the two armies traded long-range artillery shells while McClellan waited for the fog sitting over the little valley to burn off. It was mid-morning before McClellan could see the latest Confederate positions and complete his plans. By the time he was ready, he again considered it too late for an attack. It could wait until the next morning.

On September 17, McClellan attacked. What followed was twelve hours of mayhem and bloodshed. Lee's position was nearly overrun several times. Fortunately for Lee, many of the Federal assaults were disjointed and confused. McClellan's refusal to send in his reserve of 20,000 men hampered the Federal attack; in contrast, Lee had no reserve. That afternoon, A. P. Hill arrived from Harpers Ferry and stopped the collapse of Lee's right. By nightfall, the Confederate position was still intact.

As the sun rose the next morning, Lee prepared to defend against another Federal assault that never came. McClellan still believed that Lee had more than 100,000 men hidden in reserve waiting to destroy his army. He wired Halleck for reinforcements. A truce was arranged so both sides could to tend to their dead and dying. Union casualties were over 12,400. Confederate casualties were about 10,300. Each side lost three generals. The battle at Antietam Creek (Sharpsburg) is considered the bloodiest single day in America's history.

That evening, as McClellan waited for reinforcements, Lee's Army burned small fires all along their position so they would appear to be bedding down for the night. In the dark they began a retreat across the Potomac. One story says that General Lee sat on his horse all night and watched as his army crossed the ford across the Potomac near Shepherdstown. As the last of his men passed, he was heard to say ***"Thank God."*** His men sought much needed rest in the hills beyond. After crossing the Potomac Lee left two brigades of infantry, reduced to the size of a small regiment, but supported by artillery, on the bluffs above the south side of the river.

On the evening of September 19, McClellan sent the First and Second Brigades of the 1st Division, 5th Corps, to cross the ford. They were able to capture four pieces of artillery and drive Lee's rear guard back. The next morning McClellan sent the entire 2nd Division and the remaining brigade from the 1st Division to support the foothold across the Potomac.

That morning while McClellan's men were crossing the ford, Lee counterattacked the two Federal Brigades already on the south side and drove them back to the river. Some units crossing the river, including the 44th NY, were still in the river when ordered back to the Federal side.

One tragedy among countless others in the whole grisly Antietam campaign occurred at this time when the newly formed 118th Pennsylvania Infantry Regiment, a regiment in the First Brigade, 1st Division, 5th Corps, attempted to hold the bluffs above the ford while the main body of Federal troops withdrew back to the north side of the Potomac. Colonel Provost, in command of the 118th, had received instructions to withdraw but the orders had not come down through the proper chain of command. He refused to retreat. This was the regiment's first battle. As Confederate General Hill's troops counterattacked the Pennsylvanians the green Federal troops discovered that more than a quarter of the Enfield rifles they had been issued were defective and would not fire. Desperate attempts were made to get their weapons to work. Colonel Provost was wounded while his remaining officers led a desperate bayonet charge that promptly failed. The regiment was routed. Some tried to escape by climbing down the bluffs while under fire. Some fell to their death on the rocks below. Some drowned and some were shot while trying to cross the Potomac. Some were killed by Federal artillery from across the river that was meant to support their withdrawal. 431 men of the 118th Pennsylvania made it back to the Union side. They had started the day with seven hundred.

Lee moved his Army to Martinsburg, and one week later, they rested near Winchester in the Shenandoah Valley. At that point, his army was 36,400 strong. McClellan's army was 97,400 strong, but McClellan considered Lee too strong to advance against. McClellan reoccupied Harpers Ferry and stationed the 5th Corps on the Sharpsburg side of the Potomac to guard the ford.

CHAPTER SEVEN

Lincoln Proclaims Emancipation (For Some)

In the nation's capital, Lincoln felt he could wait no longer. On September 22, 1862, he made public his Emancipation Proclamation, to go into effect January 1, 1863. After the debacle at 2nd Manassas Lincoln needed a victory on the battlefield before announcing his Proclamation. He could not afford that the announcement appear as an act of weakness. Lincoln felt that if he squinted hard enough, he could look upon the battle at Antietam as a victory. It would have to do.

The document Lincoln made public promised much but did little. Only those slaves where Lincoln could not make their freedom a fact were freed. All others remained bound by the iron chains of slavery. Yet this small document had more effect on the outcome of the war than all the blood that soaked the ground at Manassas and Antietam. As Shelby Foote wrote, ***"the container was greater than the thing contained."***

The Emancipation Proclamation changed the perception of the war. Time and time again Lincoln had said that the North fought to preserve the Union. If that required keeping slavery then so be it; if it required abolishing slavery for all of time, that is what he would do; if it required keeping slavery in some areas and abolishing it in others, that is what he would do. All of that was different now. The war was now a war to both preserve the Union and abolish slavery. There was no middle ground. The two things had become inseparable.

Abroad, those political leaders in England and France who wanted to intervene on the side of the South lost the support of their people to do so. They could not be perceived as perpetuating slavery. The possibility of recognition of the Southern States as an independent nation faded away. Although he did not fully realize it, Robert Lee's vision of getting support from Europe, and forcing a settlement with the North that would allow the Confederate States of America to live in peace, was now impossible.

The leaders of the Southern Confederacy believed that they were a superior race to that of their slaves. They believed that it was the natural order for Black Americans to serve them. They saw the society they had built, based on the Bible, the Declaration of Independence, and the United States Constitution, a society created for their own benefit, their own pursuit of happiness; no one had a right to question the beliefs that they had built their culture upon. When the Declaration of Independence spoke of ***"We the people"***, it referred only to white Americans.

Even the vast majority of Southern whites who did not own slaves had their values and their place in the world assaulted by this document. The United States of America - or even the Confederate States of America - was not their country. Virginia, North Carolina, or Mississippi was their country. Those from the north coming onto their land were foreign invaders. They had no right to impose their values on the South, and must be driven out.

The Emancipation Proclamation was a knife, thrust at the heart of who Southern leaders and much of the Southern white population believed they were. They had no choice but to fight. Now they could not stop until they achieved independence from the North, or the South lay in ruin. What's more, they saw the language of the Proclamation as open license for their slaves, who were a third of the population of the South, to murder them in their beds. Their lives and the lives of their families were believed to be in mortal danger as never before. No longer would gallant cavalry charges, and brilliant military maneuvers be enough to preserve their cause. No longer could they place their hope in intervention from other nations on their behalf. It was now a war of grinding attrition. It would last until one side or the other bled dry. For the North, this meant losing the will to fight and allowing the South to go their way, for the South this meant destruction of the society they had built.

An Auction House for slaves in Atlanta Georgia, 1864
(Library of Congress)

Lincoln understood these things and he understood that George McClellan was not the military leader he needed to accomplish what was necessary. Lincoln visited McClellan at Sharpsburg in the first week of October 1862; he reviewed the troops and visited the battlefields at Antietam and South Mountain. His final attempts to get McClellan to pursue Lee into the Shenandoah Valley were met with the usual excuses; when McClellan asked for more cavalry horses because his were tired out, Lincoln wanted to know exactly what his horses had been doing lately to get tired out. At that time, McClellan had over 38,000 horses and mules in his command. Later Lincoln noted, ***"General McClellan and myself are to be photographed if we can be still long enough."*** Lincoln felt General McClellan should have no problem.

Nevertheless, while reviewing the army camped at Antietam Creek, Lincoln noted how devoted the army was to McClellan, how they were inspired by his presence, how the Army of the Potomac was a thing that McClellan had created. While walking the heights above Sharpsburg Lincoln asked of a friend, O.M. Hatch, who had travelled with Lincoln, what he saw. The friend responded ***"Why Mr. Lincoln this is the Army of the Potomac."*** Lincoln replied ***"No, Hatch no. This is General McClellan's bodyguard."***

George McClellan's days as Commander were numbered, but his separation from the Army of the Potomac was a delicate matter.

Lincoln with McClellan and other Officers at Sharpsburg after the Battle of Antietam. (Library of Congress)

After the November elections, Lincoln felt he could now remove General McClellan. McClellan received orders late on November 7, 1862, to turn over Command of the Army of the Potomac to Major General Ambrose Burnside.

CHAPTER EIGHT

March to Warrenton

We now return to the story of Charles Kelly as his regiment, along with much of the Army of the Potomac, marches south along the eastern slope of the Blue Ridge Mountains and then east to Warrenton. As noted in his diaries, Charles learned of the Army's new commander, General Ambrose Burnside, and the removal of General George McClellan, on November 9, 1862. Charles saw General McClellan as he passed by the troops waving goodbye from his big charger on November 10, hat in hand, bowing to the troops and receiving cheers all the way.

> ***"Nov. 5th***
>
> ***This is a plesent day to Be in this mountain top the Boys are having a fine time foraging through the country they are taking every thing they can lay their hands on in the shape of provisions the order has just come in to camp ordering us to our Brigade the Brigade is 5 miles from here and we are going to it to Night the drum is Beating to fall in for march the Reg't got to Snickers Gap about 8 o'clock and we start the march at five o'clock in the morning."***

Having served their turn at picket duty, the 44th NY descended from the crest of the Blue Ridge Mountains and rejoined their brigade at Snicker's Gap where they spent the night. ***"Foraging"*** was common with both Federal and Confederate troops and could be devastating to a farmer. Sometimes thousands of men, having little to eat but hardtack and salt pork would pass through a region and strip it bare of crops, farm animals, and fence rails for firewood. The farmers had no way to resist except by attempting to hide their harvested crops and farm animals. Sometimes they were successful, sometimes not. Crops almost ripe in the field had little chance to survive. The 5th Corps considered themselves to be in enemy territory and whatever they could find they helped themselves to.

Bruce Catton recounts in his book, Mr. Lincoln's Army, that Union General Phil Kearny once told Lincoln, ***"If you really want to capture Richmond, just put a hen house and a peach orchard on the far side and the New Jersey brigade on this side---they'll get through all the fortifications of Richmond to get the hens and the peaches."***

"Nov. 6th

This day is warm and fine the Boys are feeling first rate to day we started on our march feeling quite smart to day we are in the enemy country the people Look downcast we are having a Long march this day we passed through Middleburg in Virginia the second cavalry passed through this Village on Saturday Last we incamped about 18 miles from Snickers Gap this Night the country Looks fine around here But the Buildings are horrible to look upon there seams a class of Ignorant peoples Living here there is now and then a good Building appears in sight which does a fellow good to Look upon we had a Long march to day the sun was shining like a summers day at the North. I had a cold time to Night the wagons did not come up with our baggage so that we had to Lay out on the ground and it was very cold."

'Nov. 7th

We are traveling about southwest I should think the intention of our General is to Beet the Rebles in to Richmond we are having a race with them to see which shall get to gardens Vale first the that get there first is going to win the Race the weather is very cold this Morning here But we marching on for Richmond as the Boys say the day is getting colder and it has just commenced snowing very hard and the Brigade has just turned into the woods to camp for the day and it is snowing very hard one of our Boys has just gone out after something to eat. McBride has just come in with a whole sheep and we are going to have some for Dinner and save enough we had some soup that was good and I eat 2 quarts of it & got some of the meat to eat & some to I put in my haversack the order is to start in the morning at 4 o'clock it is

Bitter cold night for me to tent out of Doors but soldiers can stand anything that can be stood and I must go to Bed I shall sleep more comfortable to Night than I have heretofore I have just drawn another Blanket from the Government which makes me quite an outfit we are within 5 miles of Bull Run that celebrated ground that has Been fought over 2 times.

Charles Kelly was exactly right. After the battle at Antietam, Lincoln had strongly suggested McClellan take advantage of the fact that his Army of the Potomac was closer to Richmond than Lee's Army of Northern Virginia. This may well be the reason that Lincoln journeyed to the Antietam battlefield in the first week of October, and met with McClellan. Lincoln believed a quick march on Richmond, with Lee's exhausted Army out of the way, could collapse the rebel Capital and end the war. However, getting a "quick march" out of McClellan was more than Lincoln was able to do. McClellan finally began to move his huge army on October 24, 1862, much too late to outmaneuver Robert Lee.

After leaving Snickers Gap, the 44th NY passed through Middleburg and New Baltimore. By November 9, they were two miles from Warrenton.

"Nov. 8th

We started on the march as usual the Morning was very cold the Reg't Passed a Railroad this morning it is called Orange & Alexander Road We also passed the Bull Run crossed a little stream about a rod wide the country is good for Virginia the old officers say it is the Best part of Virginia the Buildings look as usual if anything a Little Better But the inhabitants are all (?) to the backbone our Boys stand it first rate the Brigade is incamped for the Night on a sidehill about 2 miles from Warrenton theirs is about 3000 inhabitants in that place so I am informed I slept quite comfortable this Night Oh Dear me how tired I am this Evening the capt is officer of the day and he has just told the men to put out their fires the Night came around in about fifteen minutes and told the Boys again sargent ONeil did not put his out so the capt sent him to the Colonel and he told him to consider himself under arrest."

For his failure to obey the order of Captain Munger, Sergeant O'Neil was returned to the ranks. This meant that he was no longer a Sergeant but was reduced to the rank of Private.

A note on the railroad that the 44th NY passed on November 8, Charles got the name of the railroad wrong. They actually passed over the Manassas Gap Railroad. The Orange and Alexandria Railroad was twenty miles to the south. Common soldiers often had little information about exactly where they were and even less information about where they were going.

"Nov. 9

The Brigade started this morning at 5 o'clock on our way to Warrenton they marched about 2 miles and during the march sargent Donnell was ordered to draw the loads from some of the Guns when they stoped to Rest But instead of drawing the loads he shot one of the guns off and the Colonel inquired who done it when Being told ordered him under arrest and also another soldier By the name of Johnston we have got our stoping place for the Night it is in sight of Warrenton this is General Porter headquarters and the troops are coming in to this point from all quarters we expect to have a Battle in a few days the incamp to Night is that General McClelon is superseded by burnside and he is coming here to Morrow to Review the troops Before leaving for New Jersey"

"Nov 10

Slept quite comfortable last Night awoke this morning at the sound of the bugle warned the company to Be Ready for Review at 7 O'clock and we had to go out Before Breakfast and staid on the Review ground until 9 o'clock Before we was marched Back to our quarters I have seen McClellan for the first time the old soldiers seams to Like him very much and all the old officers to he is a small man with a large head and Round face he went through the Brigades with his hat Bowing the officers as he went on his way and the Boys give him 3 cheers & a (?)

I am officer of the day for the first time in my life the duties are not hard nor Laborious But one have to answer a good many questions in the course of the day I saw a man by the name of James Saams who

> ***formerly lived in Penn Yan he is in the Michigan Reg't as a teamster there is I should judge about 150,000 men within 5 Miles of here the camp Rumor is that the Rebles are in force about .5 miles from Warrenton.***

Lincoln breathed a sigh of relief that McClellan had gone without any great tumult among the Army. Burnside immediately set about reorganizing and making new plans. He formed the Army into three "grand divisions"; the right, commanded by General Sumner; the central; commanded by General Hooker, and left; commanded by General Franklin. Each grand division consisted of two corps. Burnside then headed for Fredericksburg, hoping to get between Lee and the rebel capital.

McClellan did everything with flair. Here he is saying goodbye to the troops at Warrenton. (Harpers Weekly)

"Nov. 11th

I had to get up last night at ½ past 2 o'clock to do a job for myself I having a small Turn of the Discentery it Being the second time I have had it since I have ben in the army the Reg't had Battalion Drill this forenoon and our company was split in two so as to form a 2 companies their Being only 9 companys in the Reg't one being on Detached service we had a fine Drill and I learned considerable many of the Evolutions sargent John O'Neil was Reduced to the Ranks for disobeying orders and a Corporal named Hobart was put under Arrest for not standing at attention in the Ranks... the capt of our company was with me and we had a fine chat about matters and things in General the capt and myself started for our own Brigade and when we got their the sargent told us that the Colonel wanted to see all the officers at his head quarters the capt and myself went there and found all the officers of the Reg't there the object of the visit was some instructions about a more Rigid Discipline in the Reg't the commander of the Different companys instructed their sergeants and Corporals in regard to the orders just rec'd the Railroad is opened to day for the first time Between Washington and Warrenton since the Rebles left the place Warrenton is a fine town for a Virginia Village but their seams to be that want of thrift which one sees in a Northern Village."

After General Burnside assumed command Charles reports that they remained in camp near Warrenton and fined tuned their skills at drill. Charles seemed to be able to maintain his health despite a poor diet, and sleeping on the ground, sometimes cold and wet for days at a time. He did have occasional bouts of sickness. Disease remained the number one killer of both Federal and Confederate troops. On Sunday November 16, the 5th Corps received orders to be ready to march at 5 o'clock the next morning.

Camburn's Picket Stew

Bacon, 2lbs or one ration per man
Hardtack, 3 per man
Cabbage
Potatoes
Water

Cut bacon up into cubes. Chop up cabbage. Break up hardtack, add pepper and salt. Stir continuously for 1 hour 40 minutes. If available add turnips, carrots, or onions.

CHAPTER NINE

Fredericksburg

March from Warrenton to Fredericksburg

"Monday, 17th Nov

We started this morning at 7 o'clock But we had our tents struck at 5 o'clock as we started this morning under gloomy circumstances 8 of our men were on the sick list John McBride is very sick the morning it has just commenced Raining and we have not started yet Hooker is commander of this corps now this corps is the center of the grand corps General Sumner is in command of the Right Wing General Franklin the Left Wing we are having a hard day of it we have just passed By the Junction warrenton it is called 9 miles from Warrenton we stoped at the Junction about a ½ an hour we traveled 6 miles south East from Warrenton we incamped for the Night about 7 o'clock and it was quite dark and it Rained very hard the Boys could not find any water nor wood for to cook their supper with and we could not find our tent oh didn't I swere some you Better Belive I did some."

"Tuesday Nov 18th

About 1 o'clock this morning the orders came that we get Ready to strike our tents about 5 o'clock we did so But did not march until after daylight quite a number of our men were sick this morning it was about 9 o'clock when we got on the Road… on our Journey to day we passed a home and they told us that the troops had Been passing on that Road since Saturday the Boys feels quite well all day and they have all come up to Night the officers feels quite smart Last night we had to sleep in the doctors tent Because the Doctor had taken our tent in a mistake we started about 9 o'clock on our march it is Raining very hard and has Been doing so since we started to strike our tents after striking our tents the Brigade waited from 6 o'clock until 9 o'clock it was Raining all the time on our Journey today we marched alongside another Brigade all going one way But where the Lord only knows...well we have just turned in to camp for the Night 9 miles North West of Fredericksburg it is still Raining and the road is ankle deep."

"Saturday Nov 22nd 1862

We got our Breakfast about 7 o'clock and the order came to strick tents and we done so the order then came to pitch tents again and I was mad you Better Believe we staid until about 3 o'clock when the order came again to strike tents for the third time well of course we had to obey orders and down went the tent then came the command to pitch tents But this time our wagons had gone about ½ mile from camp the Major sent the orderly to tell us that we would have to go to the Wagons and get our tents at Length we got our tent up for the Night John McLaughlin is very sick today we have a good many on the sick list just now Troops are continually passing by us towards Fredericksburg I think."

In Charles' diary entry of November 22, we again get a sense of the tumult and sometimes chaos associated with moving large numbers of men in a desired direction. In addition, we are reminded of the greatest enemy that soldiers faced, disease. Private John McLaughlin, mentioned in Charles diary as being very sick, was just a common soldier. In civilian life he was a house painter and after the war, a boatman. He was uncommon in that at the time of the march toward Fredericksburg he was 43 years old. On August 29, 1862, he had been discharged from the Army during the Battle of 2nd Manassas (Sharpsburg) for disability, probably sickness, as he is not listed among the wounded. That very same day he reenlisted! Both then and now, he recovered from his illness, and remained in the Army until September of 1864. He lived to be 82 years old.

"Nov 23rd Sunday

The order for marching came last Night about 9 o'clock to be in Readyness to march in the morning at 7 o'clock we struck our tents about 5 o'clock our Reg't is the Rear guard to day and it is the meanest Job I was ever in our company is in the rear of Reg't someone can never tell the sufferings of mankind as the sufferings of the soldiers that are atached to the army of the Union a person can't see it until he is a Rear guard just once.."

Being in the rear guard meant finding the soldiers, usually laying by the side of the road, who had collapsed during the march from sickness, or exhaustion, or both. Some of the men died, some were sent to hospital units, and some were forced back into the line of march.

"...it is a Beautiful morning to march we met an old Negro by the wayside I should think he must have been 80 years of age he made an Expression which I will always remember he said that the troops had been passing that way for the last 2 days and he guessed that we would get them this time But if we did not he begged on us for the Lord sake to give them up and go home"

The remarkable old man that made such an impact on Charles as the 44th NY marched by, just wanted the suffering to end. He may have arrived in this country chained to the hold of a slaver's ship, and sold in an auction, or maybe he had been born on a plantation and worked in the cotton fields until he was no longer able to work, and no longer had any value to his master. It did not matter. All he wanted now was for the suffering to end.

General Ambrose Burnside

When forward units of the Federal Army began to arrive at Falmouth, General Burnside had a shock. Pontoon boats were a key part of his plan to cross the Rappahannock, sweep aside the small Confederate force at Fredericksburg, and make a dash to Richmond. There was one problem: the pontoon boats he ordered had not arrived from Maryland.

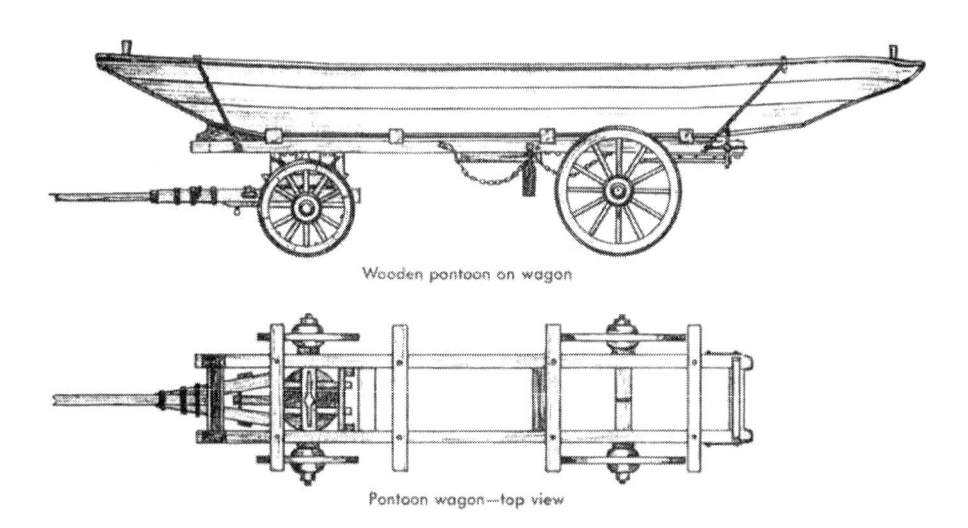

A typical Pontoon train consisted of some twenty to thirty pontoons on specially designed wagons. Each pontoon contained ropes, oars, hooks and other equipment. Timbers that were used for bridging (known as balks) and specially cut boards (chesses), which were laid upon the balks, were carried on an additional twenty wagons, which contained chains, cable, and anchors. Four wagon-loads of tools and two forge wagons completed the train. Courtesy of Staff Ride, Fredericksburg. (Army University Press)

The boats had left Maryland on November 12, but were delayed by extremely heavy rain and bureaucratic blunders. Burnside had relied on General Halleck, Burnside's commanding officer and General-in-Chief of the Union Army, to get the boats to Falmouth on time. Apparently, Halleck was no more competent now that he was at the time of 2nd Manassas.

General Edwin Sumner's troops began to arrive at Falmouth on November 17. Sumner, commander of Burnside's Right Grand Division, wanted to cross immediately when the number of rebel troops in Fredericksburg was around 500 men. Burnside said no, fearing Sumner might be cut off on the west side of the river. General James Longstreet's troops began to arrive on the heights west of Fredericksburg on the afternoon of November 21, and immediately establish a strong fortified position. B urnside's window of opportunity was now half closed, but he still outnumbered Longstreet three to one. The boats arrived November 25, ten days behind schedule.

General Burnside, who at times displayed a certain lack of creativity and adaptability, allowed the problem with the pontoons to bring his massive army to a halt. Burnside had moved too slowly to take Fredericksburg with minimal effort and now, rather than adapt and use the boats to attack Longstreet's much smaller force, he waited. Meanwhile, on November 29, Stonewall Jackson arrived to reinforce Longstreet. Burnside's window of opportunity slammed completely shut. The b oats s at, a long w ith t he r est o f B urnside's a rmy, u ntil D ecember 9 , w hen Burnside issued new orders. Meanwhile Charles wrote about the war, Thanksgiving Day, and being in camp.

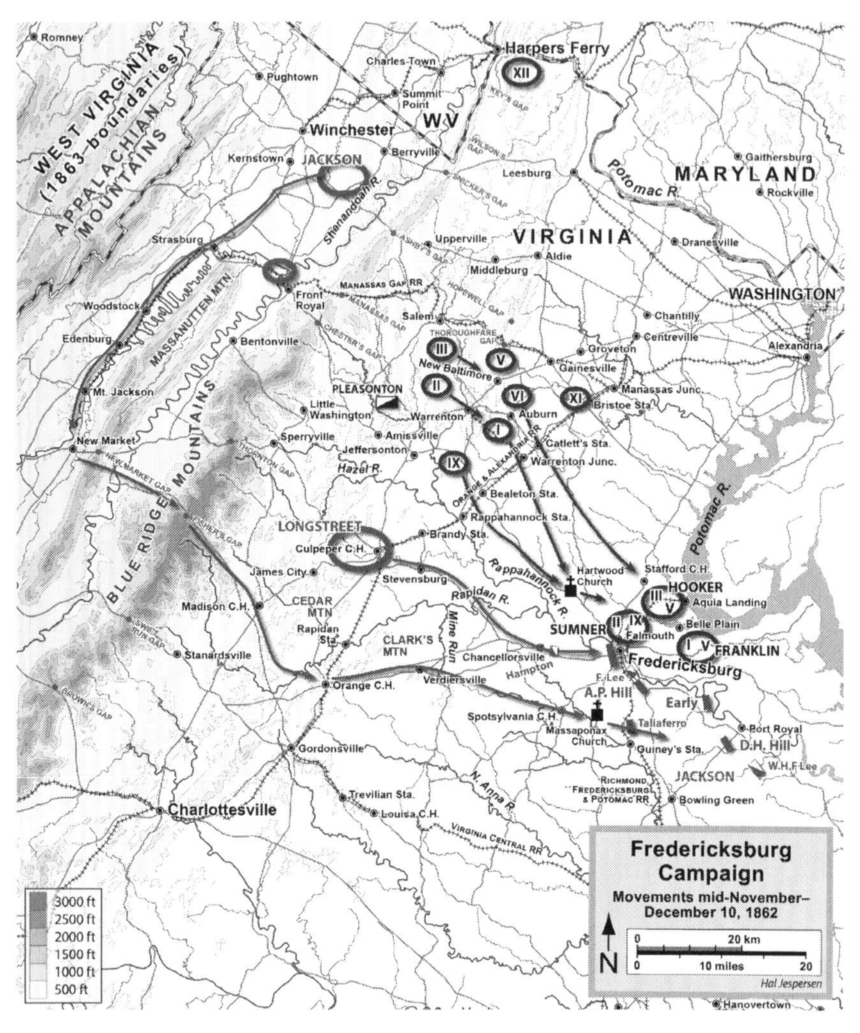

This map, courtesy of Hal Jespersen, shows the route to Fredericksburg taken by Longstreet, starting from Culpeper Court House, and Jackson starting from Winchester after the battle at Antietam. The Army of the Potomac is now commanded by General Burnside and divided into three "grand divisions" under command of Generals Hooker, Sumner, and Franklin. From Sharpsburg, Charles, with General Hooker's 5th Corps, marched by Harpers Ferry, passed Snicker's Gap, marched through Middleburg, crossed the Manassas Gap Railroad, passed through New Baltimore, and camped near Warrenton. From there they marched to Stoneman's Switch, just outside of Falmouth, and began to set up winter camp. "Map by Hal Jespersen, www.cwmaps.com".

"Thursday Nov 27

this is thanksgiving day in N.Y. the folks at home will be injoying themselves But we poor soldiers have to give thanks for what I don't know I gys for hard tack and coffie for we have nothing else to give thanks for the people at home Little know the hardships that the soldiers have to indure and if that was all it would Be nothing if the Leaders of this war was in ernest to put down the Rebelion But such is not the case in my own mind I think that it is prolonged for to make great men of some I think still further that the war could be closed in 90 days if they would take hold of it with a will John O'Neil is very sick today we have just John McLaughlin is getting better the company had no drill today the Reg't has been ingaged cleaning up their camp ground all day"

"Saturday Nov 29

...I am injoying a soldiers Night a Rest around a camp fire...if one of our Northern men should just sit one Night by a camp fire and hear a Relief guard talk they would be satisfied that there is little Patriotism in the army"

"Sunday Nov 30th

I was relieved this morning at 9 o'clock from guard duty – it was the coldest Night of the season Last Night nothing of unusual happened during the time I was on Duty I am all alone today the capt and 1 Lieut Being on Picket I recev'd a letter from Birtha to day"

"Tuesday Dec 2nd

The morning was very cold and the Night was the coldest night I ever experienced on guard Lieut Husted relieved me this morning and I have just made out my Report the day is fine and Looks like summer I made a discovery today I find that all the roads that surround our camp have been at one time cultivated for I have seen the corn Rows very distinctly and the growth of the Timber is I should think was about a foot through"

"Friday Dec 5th

The day is cold and it Looks like snow and sure Anough it is coming down the Wind is Blowing and the snow is flying it is a Bad day to Be on guard you Better Believe it was so cold that we had to get a pan of coals and put in our tent"

"Saturday Dec 6th

I waked up this morning it is cold as usual the officers are fixing up their tent for Winter quarters But I think it is all useless as we are going to move soon I rec'd a Letter from Dick Mahar to day and one from Mother the one from Mahar was Long as I might expect he has told me all the News from Penn Yan just what I wanted

Dick Mahar was the person to whom Charles Kelly rented his saloon in Penn Yan (*The Farmer's Saloon*) when he left to join the 44th NY. As far as letters from home, Charles is a good example; all soldiers want to hear the news and gossip from back home.

Almost daily now Charles talks about how cold and wet he is, especially when on guard duty.

"Sunday Dec 7th

The morning is clear and cold I have to go on guard today the weather is as cold this day as it is at the North at this time of the year their was a Death in our Regiment this morning... Harvey Ackley was in the hospital & so is John O'Neil we have a large tent fitted up for that purpose Ackley is feeling Better this morning O'Neils feet troubles him very much the Reg't is ordered out on Picket in the morning & I wont have to go But will have to come on guard the day after tomorrow"

"Monday Dec 8th

the day is very cold & the Boys have just started on Picket I have been relieved by Lieut Borne of Co. K this morning is cold and clear it was a Very cold Night was Last night the Reg't went out on Picket to day about six miles from here But I don't go with them as I was on guard yesterday Lieut Borne Relieved me we started our chimney to day But did not have time to finish it we tried it and it went first rate"

"Tuesday Dec 9 1862

I commenced work on chimney to and it is very cold for this country so the Boys say the Boys must have a cold time of it to day nothing of any importance happened today in camp today only that we Built our chimney we Expect to move tomorrow or Next Day"

Being warm at night in a winter camp required building a fireplace and chimney for your shelter. Old bricks, stones, and mud, were the primary components. Sometimes a chimney would be built with empty barrels lined with mud. Chimney fires were common. If there was an abandoned building nearby all of the bricks in the building would disappear unless some high ranking officer was using the building as his own shelter.

"Wednesday Dec 10th

The Night was very cold and slept colder last night than I have yet the Boys just came in from Picket feeling tired and hungry the capt thinks that our chimney is old Peaches the orders have come into camp that we must march in the morning it is to Bad to leave our chimney behind I feel bad over it our company Rec'd some clothing and they need them Badly some of them without shoes and we have just rec'd some more clothing for the Boys which will make the Boys laugh you Better Believe it now the weather is somewhat Milder than it has been for the Last Week or more"

"Dec 11th

This morning we started on the march at daylight the Roll opened about 10 minutes past 5 o'clock this morning and their was some Excitement Among the Boys they thought that we were going into Action the artillery began their march at five o'clock and it was kept up until about 2 o'clock in the after noon they then Rested until about 3 o'clock and the Roll opened again the News from the front this after noon is that we have fired Fredericksburg and then the new front that our forces have tried to Lay down the Pontoon Bridge but have failed at two different times we were laying in a field were I should thing there must have been 30000 men we Left Mapes Behind at our old camp this morning also Ackley and John O'Neil another of our men fell out sick just as we was going camp he has been sick some time the cannonading was splendid that is I thought so I thought at one time that we should Be in Fredericksburg to Night But we did not quite get there But I think will get there tomorrow the Wagons did not get up to our Reg't so that I have come without my Blankets to Night the weather was fine but oh dear me how muddy the mud was six inches deep the soil is clay in the Extreme The Army is in good condition at Present it is the intention of Burnside to drive the Rebels into Richmond and then take the city during the winter and if he does that one half of the army will be on the sick List for my part I wish that he would for I think it would Be Better for the country and for people"

That night the 44th NY camped on the elevated ridge overlooking Fredericksburg. The entire panorama of the battle to come was in view.

Fredericksburg was a fine-looking town of 5,000, located on the western bank of the Rappahannock River. If you traveled north from Fredericksburg for about fifty miles you would arrive in the Capital of the Union, Washington. If you travelled south for about fifty miles you would arrive in the Capital of the Confederacy, Richmond. On the east side of the river was a road running from the northwest to the southeast. Along this road, Falmouth, Virginia was just a couple of miles to the northwest of Fredericksburg. Falmouth was a major supply depot for the Federal Army. Sloping up from the road was a ridge called Stafford Heights that overlooked the river and Fredericksburg beyond.

George Washington grew up on the east side of the Rappahannock across from Fredericksburg, at a place called Ferry Farm, and John Paul Jones once lived in a house on Caroline Street in Fredericksburg. James Monroe, the fifth President of the United States, had a law office in the town for a number of years, on Charles Street. The history of this town was inseparable from the history of the nation.

On the west side of the river, after you passed through the town, there was a dry canal or ditch and beyond that a sunken road bordered by a stone wall. From there the ground rose rapidly to Marye's Heights, which overlooked Fredericksburg and the Rappahannock to the east.

Shortly after midnight, on the morning of December 11, hidden by the dark and the fog, Federal engineering units slid their pontoon boats down from the slopes of Stafford Heights with the objective of establishing three river crossings into Fredericksburg.

Confederate General William Barksdale, under command of James Longstreet had 1,800 rebel troops waiting to greet them. Barksdale's orders were to delay the crossing. The precision rifle fire from his men, entrenched among the buildings of Fredericksburg, inflicted heavy casualties on the engineers and drove them back time after time. Finally, Federal artillery opened up on the Confederate positions with 183 guns. Nine thousand shells were fired into the little town; still the engineers were unable to get their pontoon bridges across the river and into the city. The Federal artillery destroyed much of Fredericksburg. General Burnside then ordered two regiments to use pontoon boats to row across the river and secure landing zones. Why this was not an option two weeks earlier is a mystery. Fifteen minutes after Union troops arrived on the west bank of the Rappahannock, the engineers frantically resumed their work on the pontoons. In less than an hour the bridges were ready. It was the first opposed river crossing in American military history.

By five p.m. Federal infantry, after waiting all day for the bridges to be complete, began to cross. The engineers had established two pontoon bridges across the river on the north end of the town, one bridge at the south end of town near the city dock, and three bridges further south of the town. Rather than withdraw back to his lines, Barksdale defended the narrow alleys and brick houses of Fredericksburg for fifteen hours in the first urban combat of the war. Barksdale finally withdrew his troops late that night. With a small force, he had stopped the entire Federal Army for a day. On the evening of December 11, Federal troops sacked and destroyed the little town of Fredericksburg. Attempts were made by

Union Officers to stop the needless destruction but it continued throughout the next day. Lee considered the rampage to be an act of supreme barbarity.

Burnside wrote to General Halleck on December 9: ***"All orders have been issued to the several commanders of grand divisions and heads of departments for an attempt to cross the river on Thursday morning…I think now that the enemy will be more surprised by a crossing immediately on our front than in any other part of the river… we hope to succeed."***

Getting the drop on Robert Lee was something no Union general had managed up to that time. It is unclear, after his Army had sat for two weeks directly in front of Lee's Army, why Burnside thought he could pull off that trick now.

Lee would indeed be surprised, but only because he doubted that Burnside would be foolish enough to attempt such a feat. Lee wanted nothing more than for the Union General to make a frontal assault on his positions. He fervently hoped that was what Burnside would do, but remained doubtful that his own Army would be that lucky. He knew he was outnumbered and had positioned his Army with great care; the gray coats were arrayed along a seven-mile front with flanks protected by Massaponax Creek and the Rappahannock River. Divided into two corps, Lee's Army was commanded by James Longstreet directly west of the town and by Stonewall Jackson, to the south of the town.

Longstreet's corps was on the Confederate left, with infantry placed all along the sunken road, protected by the stone wall. Burnside had allowed Longstreet 20 days to prepare for the battle and Longstreet had used the time well. Longstreet placed six men for every yard of battle line facing the town. His infantry could fire a volley, then step back through three lines of troops to reload; at the same time the new front line would fire their volley. Longstreet's artillery was placed on Marye's Heights overlooking Fredericksburg, just behind and above his line of infantry. The heights were heavily wooded and provided excellent cover. There was about 800 yards of open ground between the town and the sunken road. Longstreet's concentration of troops would allow for a massive counterattack should the opportunity arise. As for his artillery, after the war Longstreet wrote in his book entitled *From Manassas to Appomattox*, ***"As I was inspecting my lines I found one gun not in position and asked General Alexander, Chief of Artillery, if it would not be well to place it in position and his reply was: 'We do not need it; our guns are so placed that we can rake the whole field as with a fine tooth comb. A chicken can't live on that field."***

Jackson's corps was a couple of miles to the south of Longstreet's position on Lee's right. He wanted to get at the invaders. His only hesitation was the massive number of Federal guns stationed on Stafford Heights, just across the river.

Field Artillery

Napoleon Bonaparte once said, "***God fights on the side with the best artillery***". The manufacturing might of the North tilted this balance to the side of the Federal Army. The north made more than a thousand new cannon during the war. Federal artillery units, called batteries, consisted of four or six guns (cannon), and were commanded by a captain. During transportation, each gun was attached to a limber and drawn by six horses. The limber chest carried 30 to 50 rounds of ammunition depending on the type of gun. A gun had eight crewmen and six drivers. Each gun also had at least one caisson, carrying spare ammunition, a spare wheel, and tools, also drawn by six horses. Each battery had a horse drawn forge and wagon for additional tools, horseshoes, and other supplies. A six-gun battery might exceed 100 officers and men, and 100 to 150 horses. *Staff Ride, Briefing Book*, from the U.S. Army Center of Military History, contains an excellent description of artillery and ammunition used during the war.

A trained team could un-limber a gun and start firing in about a minute. After firing two rounds per minute, they could limber up and be ready to move in three minutes.

Federal forces at the Battle of Hanover Court House captured this 12-pound howitzer on May 27, 1862, during the Peninsula Campaign. It is the first gun captured in the field by the Army of the Potomac. Note how the limber, when attached to the gun, forms a four wheeled vehicle that pivots in the middle. Six horses would pull the gun and limber. This gun appears to be a Model 1841 smooth bore howitzer, used by both sides in the war. (Library of Congress)

Artillery on the move. A drawing by Edwin Forbes made during the war, showing a gun and limber, with its six-horse team. (Library of Congress)

The war was a time of rapid innovation in artillery, as well as other weaponry. Although many different versions appeared, there were two basic types of field artillery, which refers to a cannon mounted on a two-wheel carriage for easy transportation. The first type, smooth bore cannon, were the bigger cousin of the old smoothbore muskets, and loaded from the muzzle or front end of the barrel.

The most common smoothbore was the 12-pound Napoleon. With a barrel weighing 1200 pounds, and a carriage weighing another 1200 pounds, the cast bronze cannon fired a 12-pound shell. Its maximum range was about 1600 yards but was most deadly at 250 yards or less. In the south, Napoleons were cast from iron when copper needed to make bronze metal ran short. During the war, firing canister, the Napoleon probably inflicted more casualties than all other artillery pieces combined.

The other type of artillery was the rifled cannon. There were a number of different kinds of rifled cannon used such as the 10-pound, 3.00-inch bore, Parrott Rifle. Its range was up to 1,800 yards, or a little over a mile. More accurate than smooth bore guns, and with a longer effective range, advances in steel, and in gun design greatly improved rifled cannon during the war.

Smoothbore cannon would often fire a spherical cannonball made of solid iron that would bounce across open ground killing infantry, horses and riders as it went. These guns could also fire a hollow cannonball filled with black powder called a shell. A fuse ignited by the detonation of the gun would explode the projectile sending shrapnel through the ranks of the enemy. Some shells, called spherical case shot, would contain gunpowder and iron balls intended to explode in all directions just before reaching the target. Finally, there was canister; tin cans with a wood base packed with as many as 49 iron or lead balls, deadly to infantry and cavalry at 200 yards. Rifled guns had their own versions of solid projectiles called bolts, rifled exploding shells, and rifled case shot.

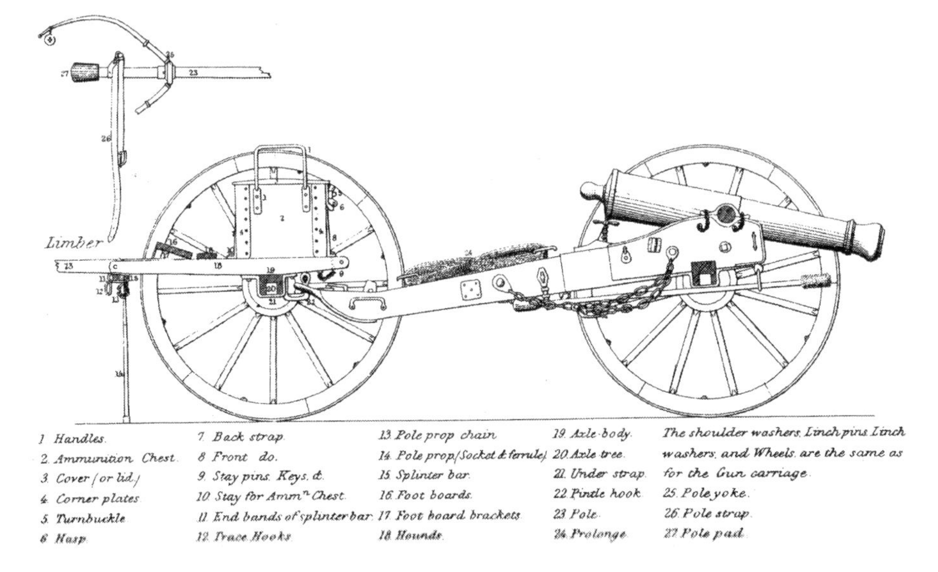

This illustration shows a limber on the left and a gun carriage with gun on the right. The limber was a two wheeled cart that would support the trail end of a gun carriage when being towed. The limber often carried a chest of ammunition; when full, for a twelve pound gun, the chest would weigh 650 pounds. A caisson was a two wheeled cart that carried two chests of ammunition and a spare wheel for the gun carriage. It also was attached to a limber for transportation. (Wm. H. French, Wm. F. Barry, and H.J. Hunt - Instruction for Field Artillery)

"Friday Dec 12th 1862

The morning is fine we camped Last Night in a piece of woods and night was very cold I did not sleep much But the ground was good for camping so that the Boys Passed a very good night the officers has no blankets so that we slept cold Last Night I slept about 6 hours during the night I cooked some coffie and McBride gave me some pork and I made out quite a Breakfast we started on our march and got about two miles from our Last night camping ground the day is the finest I ever seen for this time of the year we have just come to a stop I don't think we will cross the River today But we may we Rec'd our commissions the night Before Last and mine dates from the 9 of Oct and the capt from the 14th of the same and the first Lieut dates from the same time

Abener Stitler is in the 16 Michigan which is in our Brigade I have not seem him yet But George Woolkott has he deserted from the 33 Reg't when they were at Washington it Looks as if we were going to have good weather now the Boys are all sick of soldiering in our company we have about 8 or 10 men in ours who are deserting it this a term in the soldiering of Reproach of Lazyness or cowardice we are in camped in a Valley and Right over the Brow of the hill in the next Valley is Fredericksburg we have just started Back in the country to find a place to camp for the Night we marched about 1 mile from where we Lay all day our camping ground was situated in the woods"

Pontoon bridges just south of Fredericksburg. (Library of Congress)

CHAPTER TEN

The Stone Wall

"Saturday December 13th 1862

it was on an old camp ground the Land around here is all Been use by Troops the Night was cold But I slept warmer then I did the Night Before the army feels in fine spirits this morning the Bugle has just sound for the march I think we will have a fight to day the cannonading commenced this morning at 1/2 past 9 o,clock to our Left and is working to our Right there is a Balloon in the air to our Right the day is foggy and is getting warmer so that we will have a fine day the Balloon has come down and gone up Again"

Observation balloons had been used by the Union Army since the early days of the war. McClellan had used them extensively in the Peninsula campaign. At Fredericksburg, the balloon Eagle was piloted by Lieutenant Colonel William Teall. The Eagle was a one-man craft that rose up to about 900 feet in the air, and remain tethered there for observation of enemy positions. Most balloons were fitted with a telegraph wire going to the ground for instant reports of enemy movements. Special wagons were built to charge the balloons. These wagons would mix sulfuric acid with iron filings to generate hydrogen, which was used to fill and launch a balloon. Use of balloons by the Union Army went out of favor later in the war. The Confederate Army seldom used observation balloons.

The observation balloon Eagle during a storm. (Library of Congress)

"Saturday December 13th cont.

General Burnside is moving very conscientious and careful feeling his way a Little at a time he is Bound not to Be caught in a trap the News in camp yesterday was that Banks had arrived at Harrison Landing with 40,000 men if such is the fact the Rebbs are in a Bad Box our cook was in the city of Fredericksburg yesterday he says that the city is Badly damaged the houses are perferated with cannon balls the inhabitants have all left the city with the exceptions of 506 persons the homes are all open the furniture scattered around in the street the soldiers cooking chicken in the streets Barrells of flour lying open the soldiers helping themselves to every thing that they could Lay their hands it seems too Bad to see family Pictures and Letters handled of By the Rude soldiers and to hear them jesting over the Letters that they

> *had picked up from the different homes in their Rummaging through the city and the Boys have a fine time sitting by the camp fire and making comments over the manner of Wording and poor spelling when one stops and thinks what a dreadfull thing this war is and what a Large amount of Property is Distroyed and the property is nothing compared to the Loss of Human Life the wish of the army is that peace should be declared But they want it Declared in the right Way"*

Burnside attacked Lee's Army the morning of December 13, 1862. It was everything Lee had hoped. It started with Union General Franklin attacking Stonewall Jackson's position a couple of miles south of Fredericksburg. The morning was spent waiting for the dense fog to lift, and then a single Confederate gun manned by a very brave rebel officer stalled Franklin's attack. However, by early afternoon the Yankees were close to accomplishing a breakthrough. Unfortunately, Franklin's men lacked support and became stalled by Confederate counter attacks. They were driven back but managed to remain on the west side of the river, under protection of the Federal guns on Stafford Heights.

Two miles north, at the town of Fredericksburg, starting about noon, the Union forces began assaulting Longstreet's troops entrenched in the sunken road behind the stone wall at the base of Marye's Heights, just 800 yards west of town. Division after division rushed the rebel troops and were shot to pieces. Some made it within 150 feet of the stone wall. Before long, thousands of Union troops lay dead and dying in front of the rebel position; more men were ordered forward.

Charles writes,

> *the Bugle has just sounded for our Brigade the Expectation is that we get in to a fight we are Now crossing the River and getting in to the town it Looks hard to see those fine Buildings shattered with holes and the dead and wounded Lying in the street at every corner one turns on the dead and wounded are coming in from the field we are now Lying under cover of a Large house with a high Board fence the Brigade are all Lying on the ground expecting any moment to Be called into action oh my God if we have to go into it we might Lose half of our company*

The 44th NY had crossed the pontoon bridge on the south end of the city around three in the afternoon of December 13. From there they advanced through the city, and took cover in the ruined buildings on the west side of town where they awaited the orders they knew were to come. They were part of the Third Brigade commanded by Colonel T. Stockton, which was part of the 1st Division, under command of General Charles Griffin. The order to attack came that evening.

Charles describes the assault in his diary,

> ***"have just passed through most murderous that man ever passed through I was hit strong By a spent shell or a piece of shell it Brook one of my teeth filled my eyes with dirt and powder it nocked me down and stunned me for about ten minutes I got up and that I was not much hurt oh my God how the shell and Balls were flying and the Boys of our company were calling for help I mean those that were wounded I Recognized the Voice of A. Perry and I. Giddings Before I was wounded I saw the Col fall a Ball striking him on the arm our men had to charge the enemy around this house that I spoke of, going across the Railroad to the Right of where we Lay at the house we then took it up the hill charging on the enemy at Double quick time under the hotest fire that men ever passed through when I found the company they had got over the into a Little Ravine we Lay down there we then called the Roll and found that their was 16 of our men were missing and this morning I found 7 of them in the hospital"***

To recap Charles' description of the assault, the order came about 6:30 p.m., just before dark. It would be the last assault of the Federal Army at Fredericksburg. The 44th NY left the protection of the houses, and crossed over the Richmond, Fredericksburg, and Potomac Railroad, which was to their right. They continued across Frederick Street and turned left at the Fredericksburg fairgrounds, also known as Mercer Square. They charged up the slope toward the stone wall straight into thousands of rebel muskets and 37 rebel guns.

Charles Kelly was immediately knocked down and rendered unconscious by an exploding shell; Alexander Perry was hit, he would lose a leg; John Giddings was severely wounded but would survive. Fred Mitchell died of his wounds two weeks later. When Charles was able to get up he found his brigade in a small swale, hugging the ground, trying to get away from the death overhead. There are no better words than those Charles used to describe his experience: ***"have just passed through most murderous that man ever passed through".***

True to his word, Confederate General Alexander, Chief of Longstreet's Artillery, had ***"raked the whole field as with a fine tooth comb."***

The Stone Wall, at Fredericksburg. (Library of Congress)

On the night of December 13, Charles was told by his Captain to go to the rear and have his wounds dressed. Under cover of darkness about midnight, he left the regiment and made his way back to the town.

> ***"I Left the Boys Last Night at 12 o,clock to come to the Rear to have my eyes cleaned they having Been filled with dirt when I was struck in going to the city found some of our men helping others of the field one poor fellow Alexander Perry of our company Begging to be carried off the field the Boys answered in carrying Perry amid showers of bullets and canisters and shell also Ted Mitchell was Brought in By those that were Detailed for that purpose when I got in to city - which is about a mile from the front, soldiers were busy hunting for their friends and comrades that were missing I have one man wounded while hunting for his Brother that had fell early in the after noon he Belonged to the Irish Brigade But I was so blind that I could not help him so I Left him to his Fate he was an Irishman from N.Y. city when I got down to Fredericksbourgh the wounded were Being Brought in fast most every house was used for a hospital it was one of the hardest sights I ever Beheld in my life I went to our Division hospital and got some of the dirt out of my eyes the Doctor told me to stay in the hospital until morning I did so But oh Dear what groaning and moaning during the Night it was dreadful to hear it"***

The evening of the December 13, General Burnside, while having dinner with his officers, seeing his battle plan, not to mention his career and his place in history, sink into the bloody mud in front of the stone wall, announced that in the morning he would personally lead his troops in a mass assault on Marye's Heights. His officers talked him out of it.

Orders came down for the Third Brigade to stay where they were that night, less than a hundred yards from that awful stone wall, so they could make a new assault at first light. They spent the night and most of December 14 lying flat on the ground, in the mud, among eight thousand dead and dying Union soldiers.

On Sunday morning, December 14, after being treated for his wounds, Charles found it too dangerous to cross the ground from town back to his Company. He had to wait until dark. Charles remained in Fredericksburg for the rest of the day.

Captain Bennet Munger, Charles Kelly's immediate superior wrote of the wound Charles received at Fredericksburg,

> *"Lieut. Kelly now made his way to see us, but his face was all bloody and it was thought best for him to return to the city (about one mile) and have it dressed. He was probably knocked down by the bursting of a shell, as his face is powder burnt (they will knock a man down as quick as a thunderbolt) and was detained by the Doctor till morning and by rebel bullets until dark Sunday night, at which time he again joined us."*

On the morning of December 14, Charles writes,

> ***"Sunday morning Dec 14th 1862 Fredericksbourgh***
> *as soon as it was light the Doctor tended to my eyes and I started out in the streets and I came across a number of our Boys that had skulked when we went on to the field and I am sorry to say one or two of them were Irishmen But our capt and Lieut stood up like heroes to the work to day Just at sun down shipley our cook & myself started for the Reg't"*

Sergeant Robert Shipley, who Charles refers to as "our cook" went back to the lines with Charles as soon as it was dark on the evening of December 14. Sargeant Shipley would later be awarded the Congressional Medal of Honor for capturing the Colors of the 9th Virginia Infantry, at Five Forks Virginia. They rejoined the 44th NY without mishap:

> *"our Reg't and Brigade was drawn up in line of Battle But when we got their we found it was to be Relieved they had to stand there until about 10 o,clock before we could go and how the Boys felt I never seen any Body of men felt so nice as they did to Be Relieved from the position which they occupied for the last 20 hours"*

> *"we was then ordered to Return to the city we did so come onto the main street Bivouacked on the same street during the Night, slept quite comfortable myself not having slept the Night Before at all the Boys had it very hard the night that they staid on the front lines the whole Brigade done the same they all Laid in the mud the whole of this time and they could not go to get any water to Drink without (Monday*

Dec.15th 1862) Running a good chance to get hit Before they could get Back under the hill"

Returning to town late the night of December 14, the 44th NY slept in the streets of Fredericksburg, not knowing what to expect the next morning. It was better than clinging to the mud among the dead and dying, expecting at any moment to be hit by a minie ball or a shell fragment.

On Monday December 15, General Burnside arranged a truce with General Lee so the dead and dying could be removed from the field. Some of those still alive had laid in the mud for two days and two nights. The men assigned this task never forgot the things they witnessed while performing this duty. At the end of the day the gruesome work remained unfinished and would remain so for some time.

> *"their is any quantity of straglers going through the town trying to find their Regt we have staid in the street all day the Boys that skulked day Before yesterday are coming in this forenoon Just at Night we was ordered to fall in we moved about 1/4 mile up the street and was told that we might occupy the Buildings in the Rear for the night so here we are having a fine time in the cellar a Barrell for a writing table a good fire in the fireplace having Just eating a great meal of some flour that we found in the house that we are occupying for the night I think I can sleep to night some Being so comfortable*
>
> *I think to write home to night But I may not do so they have ordered all the sick and wounded to Be carried over the River to night it looks as if we are going to have a lively time in the morning if we were going to hold the city at all hazards there must have been a great loss of life in the last three days work on Both sides the Irish Brigade Lost heavily in the Saturdays fight perhaps half their number are kiled and wounded."*

What a relief for Charles and the rest of the 44th NY to get something to eat even if it was only flour. After the horrors of a night in front of the stone wall, the men had somewhere to sleep without fear of being killed or maimed at any moment. The night of the 15th Charles was sitting in front of a fire, in a cellar, writing letters on a wooden barrel. He looked forward to a good night's sleep. It was not to be. At 1 a.m., the morning of the December 16, the Brigade once again, was called to the front.

> *"I have just writen a Letter home to tell the folks that I am all right and well I Escaped Lucky when I think how many poor fellows are Lying on the field Dead and wounded while I am injoying the comforts of health the Rumor is that our forces lost in kiled and wounded 6,000 men But I think it is much Larger than that when I finished my letter I retired for the Night it Being Eleven oclock expecting to have a good Nights sleep but I was sadly Disappointed for at one oclock the Brigade was called out to go on to the front to Relieve Picket as I supposed but we got up to the front with now and then a Picket shot fired at us, (Tuesday Dec 16, 1862) and my God what a sight we Beheld Dead men lying as thick as one has seen stumps on a piece of Land that has not Been cleared off the muskets and cartrages Boxes napsacks blankets was scattered all around in the wild configuration and their not over ten Rods (about 160 feet) from us was the Reble's Pickets I then Began to think that our movements were only a front in order to withdraw our Pickets from the lines we were acting as the Rear guard of the Army But the men did not know it then as soon as the Pickets was Relieved one of our companys moved to the Right of us in order still more to Blind the Rebles the moon would now and then peep out from under a cloud to show the Rebles that we were all there on the lines Ready for the Renewal of the conflict in the morning shortly after Co. B moved to the Right of us our Maj. came along and told us to be Ready to move out By the Left flank and never saw men obey a command so quick in my life before the men were so still about it we then moved slowly down towards the city when we got to the point where we went into the fight on Saturday the Regt stoped and the Col called for six men and sargeant from our company to go to the front the capt sent them every thing seem in our favour it commenced Raining about this time we had to stop there until the Break of day and oh how many thoughtfull faces there were in the old 44 for that was all the troops that was left as Rear guard the other Regts left us when we went from the front and oh how anxious the officers and men were waiting for the Return of those six men and the sargent*

> *Just as day was dawning the order was given to fall in to go to the River I think I was the happy man in the world when we got down to its Banks the Regt marched up the opposite Bank Lighter than I have seen them for a Long time things Looked as we was going to our old camping ground to stop for the Night and sure enough we Land there through the mud and water about Noon and I never saw a tireder Lot of soldiers in my life But they were glad to get Back to their old camping ground in the after noon we put up our tent and it Began to Look like living once more I am so tired that I think of nothing more."*

As Charles relates in his diary, the Third Brigade, rousted out of bed at 1 a.m. on the morning of December 16, did not know that they were being sent to the front to put on a show for Longstreet's men and hide the withdrawal of the remaining right flank of the Federal army. Being the last man in a withdrawal before an enemy force can be tricky business. According to Charles, it got down to six men and a sergeant from the 44th NY, Company C, holding off the entirety of Longstreet's Corps. They all made it back across the pontoon bridge just as the day was dawning, and by noon were back in their old campground at Stoneman's Switch. Later that day, Confederate troops occupied Fredericksburg.

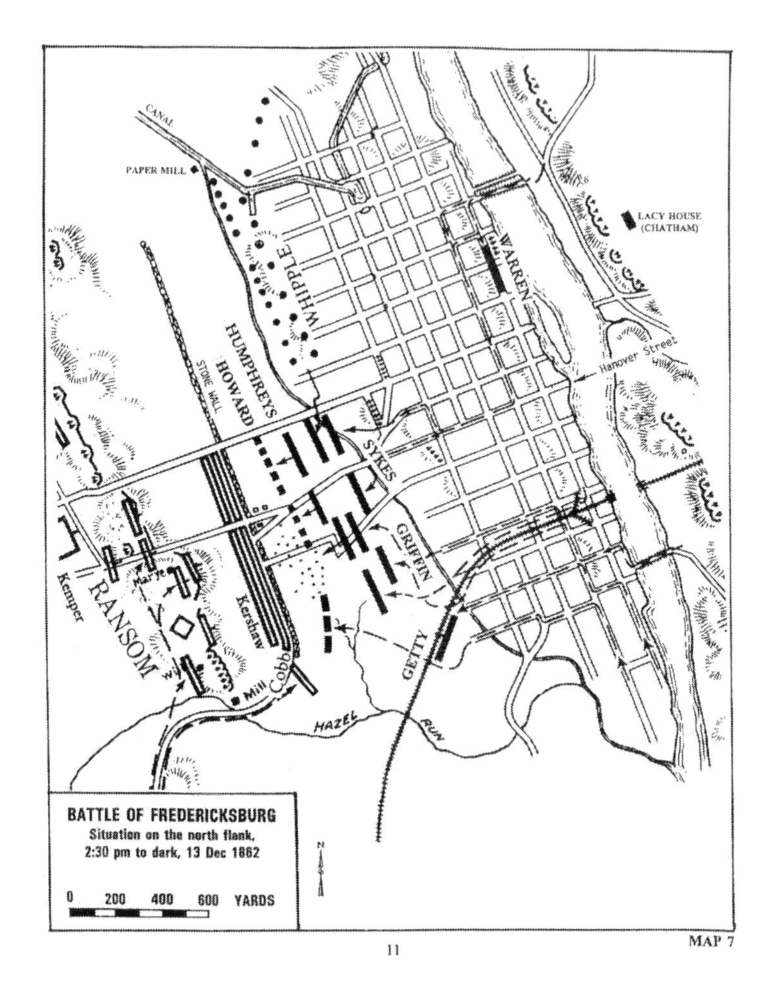

This map illustrates the battle just west of the town, on the afternoon of December 13. Charles, and the 44th NY, are with Griffin's 1st Division. They cross over the pontoon bridge on the south end of town about 3 p.m. They shelter in the city until 6:30 p.m., and then leave the houses, cross over the Richmond, Fredericksburg, and Potomac Railroad, and turn left into the rebel guns behind the Stone Wall.
(Army University Press)

CHAPTER ELEVEN

After Fredericksburg

Winter Camp

"Wednesday Dec 17th 1862

The day is quite warm But the Boys feel quite Blue I am completely wore out sore and stiff in the Joints the Regt is geting things straightened out to day some of our boys are coming in I mean those that skulked the day of the fight and we had quite a number of them the capt is about worn out with the Excitement John McBride has not come in yet I think he has been taken Prisoner their was 12 of our men wounded in the Saturdays fight I.W. Mandevale's father is here trying to get his son out of the Army But I think it no go we had no Dressparade to day on our color line their are some hospital tents But they are going to have them Removed By to morrow"

Private John McBride was among those who deserted Company C sometime during or in the days after the battle. It was not uncommon. There were at least fifteen men from the 44th NY who deserted during the war.

"Thursday Dec 18th 1862 Camp near Falmouth

I arose this morning feeling much Better than I have felt since the fight the Boys are geting up their tents in good style cuting Logs and fixing up generaly for the Winter But I think we wont stay here Long for it is my opinion that we are on the march as soon as we get reunited up some the weather is geting colder fast and we are going to have cold winter weather our Regt must have some Different tents from what they have got or all our men will Be sick we cannot turn out 30 men now for Drill such is a winter campaign if the army has to move

> ***around in Virginia this Winter their will be Little Army in the spring to do their fighting for them at the rate we are fighting the Rebles at present we cannot whip them in 20 years"***

After facing the Rebel Army at that stone wall outside Fredericksburg, the 44th NY, along with the rest of the Army of the Potomac now faced an even deadlier enemy: the rain and the cold of winter and the disease that followed.

Tents

Tents were vitally important to Charles Kelly, his Regiment, and indeed the entire Federal Army. Charles mentions them often in his diaries. Tents were the difference between a cold wet night and something better. The brutal truth of the war was that you did not get sick as often and you probably lived longer if you had a dry tent to sleep in at night. The story of Union Army Tents has been wonderfully told by John Billings in his book *Hardtack and Coffee*, published in 1887. I will relate some of the highlights.

Early in the war the Union Army supplied cone shaped tents called Sibley tents to the infantry. Henry Hopkins Sibley patented these tents in 1856. During the war, Henry served in the Confederate Army and held the rank of general.

When set up these tents were eighteen feet in diameter and twelve feet high. The tent came with a telescoping pole that fit into a tripod that supported the center. Twenty-four tent pegs held down the perimeter of the tent. The tent was designed to accommodate twelve men who would sleep in a wagon spoke type arrangement with their feet toward the center. The tripod could support a kettle hanging over a small fire pit in the center of the tent. The tent also came with a conical wood stove.

Interior of a Sibley Tent, Drawing by Charles Reed 9th Mass. Battery, Hardtack and Coffee by John Billings 1887. This drawing shows the stove which came with the tent, and shows the center tripod being used as a stand for muskets and other equipment.

There were a number of problems with the Sibley tent. The Sibley required transportation by wagon, and as Charles recounts in his diaries, the supply wagons were frequently not in the same place as the troops when they needed their tents. Charles and his regiment spent many a cold night in the rain because the supply wagons had not reached their location. The cone shaped stove was useless for cooking; if time allowed, soldiers would often build a small brick oven and use the cone shaped stove for the first section of a chimney. There usually was not enough stovepipe provided to reach the opening at the top of the tent, and the tent became as black as the inside of a chimney flue. Also, you can imagine the challenge that would present itself if you had just gotten off of guard duty at 2 a.m., and you had to make your way in the dark over eleven other sleeping men to reach your spot in the back of the tent. This could be more dangerous than guard duty. The Federal Army purchased about 12,700 Sibley Tents, mostly in 1861.

Another type of tent was the hospital tent, large enough to walk around in and accommodate 20 patients. They had vertical sides with sloped roofs, and were closed on the ends. If a larger tent was needed, these tents could be joined together at the ends. The Federal Army purchased about 25,000 of these tents during the war.

Wall tents were a smaller version of hospital tents, and were usually reserved for high-ranking officers. Back at Harrison's Landing during the Peninsula Campaign, General McClellan issued orders such that only generals, field officers and staff officers be given wall tents. Wall tents came in various sizes and were much preferred over the shelter tents given to the infantry. Many officers smuggled wall tents onto the supply wagons. When they could, lower ranking officers would share a wall tent with one or two other officers of similar rank. The Federal Army purchased over 70,000 wall tents during the war.

Company G, 71st New York Volunteers, in front of a Sibley Tent. (Library of Congress)

During the second year of the war, Sibley tents were largely phased out because they had to be transported by wagon everywhere they were needed, which could change on a daily basis. At first Sibley tents were replaced by the A or Wedge tent. Meant to accommodate four or five men, the wedge tent was six feet long, six feet high and had vertical supporting posts in the front and back. Both ends of the A frame or wedge configuration were closed in, with one end equipped with flaps that opened and closed.

By the end of 1861, the Federal Army was searching for a tent that would not require long trains of wagons for transport. They found their answer in what was called the shelter tent. Beginning in 1862, the most common tent for Federal infantry soldiers on the march was the shelter tent, often called by soldiers, the dog tent or half tent. These tents were the ancestor of the pup tent. The tents came in two separate halves. Each soldier was issued a half tent to carry in his knapsack, or wrap up with his rubber ground cloth and wool blanket to carry over his shoulder. When it came time for a soldier on the march to put up a tent for the night, or to get protection from the sun or rain, he would team up with one of his fellow soldiers and join two halves of a shelter tent together with buttons sewn on the tent. They would then stretch the tent over a rope or pole and secure the sides with tent pegs. The tent was open at both ends. In some cases, the soldiers would mount their bayonets onto their rifles, stick them into the ground, and then tie a rope between the two rifles to support the tent. These tents became very common. From 1861 through 1864, the Federal Army purchased over 2 million shelter tents.

Union soldiers with a shelter tent at a reserve picket station near Blackburn's Ford, Manassas, before the 2nd Battle of Manassas. (Library of Congress)

For winter camps, soldiers built log sides for their tents two or three feet high, sometimes higher, with the tents placed on top of the logs. Chinks between logs were filled with mud and clay as available. The tent would be warmer if they excavated down two or three feet, before building the log sides. If time and materials were available, they would install a floor made of boards. Sometimes three men would join together and use their extra half-tent to cover one end. Four men could fashion four half-tents to cover a branch framework with the ends covered by extra half-tents, or a rubber blanket. Walking through a winter camp one could see signs above many of these crude structures such as *Parker House*, *Hole in the Wall*, *Astor House*, or *Willard's Hotel.*

As previously noted, Charles Kelly talks of building a fireplace with a chimney for the officer's tent at Stoneman's Switch. Any abandoned houses in the vicinity would lose all of their bricks. Chimneys were common in winter camps, as were chimney fires.

Confederate infantry soldiers were not issued tents, although some Rebel units were issued canvas tarps with which they made lean-to shelters. As the war progressed it was very common for a Confederate camp to be filled with captured Federal tents as well as captured blankets, canteens, and haversacks. Rebel troops especially prized the Union rubber blankets and ponchos, which the Federal embargo made scarce in the south. They were ideal as a ground cloth or overhead shelter.

> ***"Friday Dec 19th 1862***
>
> ***the morning is cold and clear I am not feeling well this day the orders are from the Major that the officers go to studying hardies on military the capt went to see Fred Mitchell to day he is Down Near Falmouth in the hospital the capt thinks that they will not take of his Legg he came Back about 5 oclock in the after noon feeling sick and down in his mind I think he is Discouraged with his position in the Army we had Dress parade this after noon for the first time since the fight I have Rec'd no Letters from home in over one week Mandevale is here yet trying to get his son home the capt says that when he was down at the hospitals he saw some sights which he will never forget as Long as he lives"***

"Sunday 21st Dec 1862

we had inspection in the Reg't in the forenoon the capt went to see Fred Mitchell he thinks that his Legg will have to Be taken off the capt came Back sick and Broken Down in spirits he is quite sick to Night I hope that he wont Be sick Long Lieut James is under the weather he has Been sick quite a while he is sick of the service I Believe he would Like to go home"

Fred Mitchell died of his wounds on December 30. Meanwhile the aftermath of Fredericksburg was visibly weighing on Charles Kelly's captain, Bennett Munger. Any soldier who has been in combat can relate to the words, "*he saw some sights which he will never forget as long as he lives.*"

1st Lieutenant Elzor James of Company C, 44th NY Infantry was honorably discharged from the Army on January 31, 1863. The reason given was disability. In the week before Christmas Charles Kelly was appointed to the rank of 1st Lieutenant.

"Monday Dec 22nd 1862

the weather is very cold here to day and the men are making themselves as comfortable as they can do under the circumstances we are going to have a little more Drilling in the Reg't the officers have Recitation to night in the Maj. tent I passed through the Lesson firstrate we have another Lesson to morrow or day after the capt did not go on Dresprade this after noon our company is quite sickly H. Ackley is geting Better fast he is in the hospital at present camp near Falmouth"

"Dec 24th 1862

the day is plesant But cool Nothing of importance happened to day in our camp we have a New doctor in our Reg't and he is going to have things Different their is a good many sick in our Reg't from chronic Diarrhea which is pulling them Down them that are Looking so Bad Dirty are some of those that would be Dirty anywhere my day on guard Duty is about over this day is the worst part of my Duty in camp"

"Dec 25th

Christmas in old Va and a Blue day it is for me and the Boys feel Bad and blue for Christmas the capt and Lieut are quite sick and have Been sick for sometime the capt is trying to keep up all that he can it is a blue time for the Holiday."

Not a cheerful Christmas for Charles. Also, Charles Kelly's immediate superior, Captain Bennet Munger, would be plagued by headaches, sickness, and depression in the coming months.

"Saturday 28th

I am Busy in fixing my tent and have finely got through with it"

On Reconnaissance

"Monday 29th

went after wood this afternoon got a fine Load of hard wood this day the order was given to fall in to go on Pickets at noon the capt and Lieut Both sick so that I had to go out with the company on Duty well away we went and traveled 14 miles in the night it Being the coldest march we had yet 8 of our men fell out on the march one of them was Sargent we passed a church By the name of Heartwood Church the intention is to cross the river at Kelly's ford."

"Dec 30 Tuesday

we incamp in the woods over Night it was a cold Night in the morning we started for the ford Laid in the woods all day and Just at Night the order was given to Bivouac to the Night and Return in the morning"

"Jan 1st 1863

the weather is cold and clear it is a very Dull New Year for the Boys they are taken their Breakfast of hardtack and coffie and some of them has not even that for their Breakfast the Meal Being over the order was given to start for camp and away we went at quicktime we traveled to our camp without stoping But once on our way I was never so tired in my Life in fact I was completely worn out"

On New Year's Day, about 1 o'clock in the afternoon, the 44th NY returned along with the rest of the 1st Division from a reconnaissance march first to Hartwood Church and then to Richard's Ford, about two miles upstream from the point where the Rapidan River joined the Rappahannock River. Two brigades had crossed the Ford and the third Brigade, of which the 44th NY was part, remained on the north side of the river in reserve.

The cold and the rain and the physical exertion are wearing Charles down. He is exhausted. Remarkably, he has avoided much of the sickness, and even despair, that is common in his Regiment.

There was much more going on with the New Year's march than a mere reconnaissance, even though the officers of the 1st Division of Butterfield's 5th Corps were not aware of it. During the last week of December General Burnside had developed a new plan to flank General Lee who remained at Fredericksburg. Burnside's plan was to march the bulk of his army south along the Rappahannock River, six or seven miles from Fredericksburg, and cross with pontoon boats a short distance downstream from the town of Hayfield. After crossing, he would flank Lee's entire position.

At the same time he would feign an attack with 2,500 cavalry troops and the 1st Division of Butterfields 5th Corps. The infantry would cross at Richards Ford while 1,000 of his best cavalry continued upriver to Kelly's Ford. From there this cavalry troop would cross the Rapidan, continue south and cross the Virginia Central Railroad at Louisa Courthouse, cross the James River at Goochland, cross over the Richmond and Lynchburg Railroad, and continue on to Suffolk. The plan was that they would blow up the locks on the James River Canal, blow up the bridge on the Richmond and Lynchburg railroad, and destroy the bridge on the Richmond and Weldon Railroad. Along the way, they would wreak as much havoc as possible. At Suffolk, they would board steamers waiting to take them back to Aquia Creek. The whole purpose of the raid was to create a diversion for the main attack of the army.

By December 30, positions for artillery to protect the crossing of the Federal Army at Hayfield were prepared, the roads surveyed, and corduroy installed to support wagons and artillery. The main body of the Army received rations and ammunition and was ready to march.

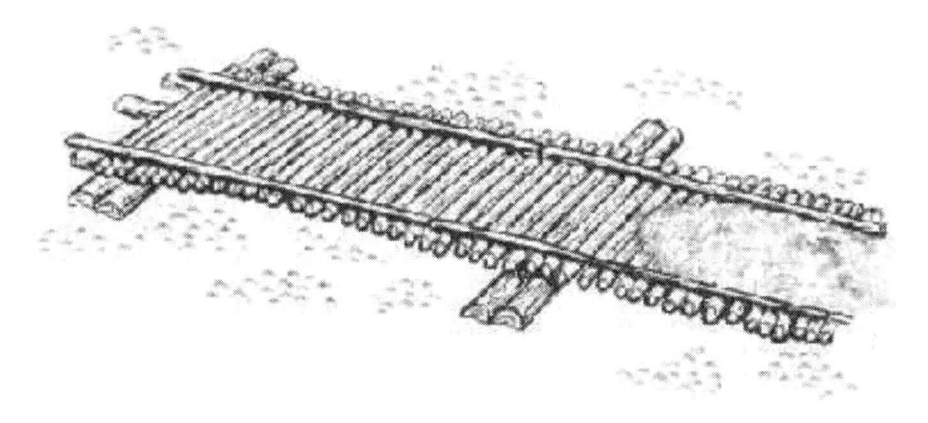

Corduroy reinforcement of roads was common in the wet, muddy, winter roads of the time. It was often the only way artillery and wagons could get over rain soaked roads or roads through swampy areas. (Forest Service of the United States Department of Agriculture)

If the Army's movement to the south was discovered prematurely, troops would be ready for a major assault from above Fredericksburg via the crossings already held. Elite cavalry troops were ready to cross at Kelly's Ford, the 1st Division was approaching Richards Ford...and then, sometime after 3:30 in the afternoon of December 30, General Burnside received a telegram from Abraham Lincoln.

> *"I have good reason for saying that you must not make a general movement without first letting me know of it".*

Good Reason

Ambrose Burnside was stunned. He had no idea what was behind this message. Full of anger and frustration, he sent a rider to recall the cavalry troopers, recalled the men at Richard's Ford, and cancelled orders for the bulk of the Army to march. He then travelled to Washington to meet with Lincoln and find out what "*good reason*" Lincoln had for the telegram.

Burnside met with Abraham Lincoln in Washington on the morning of January 1, 1863. It was the same day Lincoln would sign the Emancipation Proclamation. Lincoln told Burnside that some general officers in his command had called on him and told him that Burnside was planning a new major offensive. They believed that it would end in disaster. Burnside discussed his plan in detail with Lincoln and Lincoln brought in General Halleck and Edward Stanton, Secretary of War, to discuss the merits of the plan. It was the first they had heard of the plan or the visit from Burnside's officers. The political storm let loose after the battle of Fredericksburg was still raging in Washington, and Burnside got no clear direction from the meeting. He tried to discover who in his command had gone behind his back to the President, but Lincoln would not divulge the names of the two officers. Even General Halleck agreed with Burnside that whoever these officers were, that they should be arrested or dismissed from the Army.

Within a couple of days, Burnside's plans were circulating in the streets of Washington. His opportunity was gone. Lincoln was no stranger to the constant backbiting and intrigue among generals and politicians, and his actions seem odd. Burnside's plan was bold, and had a reasonable chance of success. The plan could have made a substantial impact on the war. This was just the kind of thing that Lincoln had spent months trying to get General McClellan to undertake. However, Lincoln's confidence in Burnside had been badly shaken by Fredericksburg, and Lincoln now believed that Burnside had little support from his generals. Burnside's command of the Army of the Potomac was drowning in the mire of Washington politics and the muck of dissent among his own generals.

"Jan 2nd 1863 (Thursday)

it is a fine day for this time of the year But oh how much I am used up after march the capt and Lieut are sick as yet nothing of importance happened in camp today"

At this point in Charles Kelly's diaries, there is a gap in entries until May 1, 1863.

Not long after the reconnaissance march north of the Rappahannock, Colonel James Rice, commander of the 44th NY, ordered construction of a chapel for his regiment camped at Stoneman's Switch. It was a log structure 16 feet wide and 32 feet long, big enough for about 160 men. Poles and rubberized blankets were used for a roof. Later, a canvas covering was found. This structure became a popular evening refuge for the men. When not being used for religious services, debates were held, musicians played, poetry was read, and a variety of other events were presented.

Corporal McKendree Shaw of company D wrote of the chapel, ***"I doubt there being any church in the Nation, that was the earthly channel of better spiritual influences, than was our log chapel, with its log seats, log fire place and hard-tack box for pulpit, during the winter of 1862-3."***

On January 16, the 44th NY received a new flag to replace their worn regimental battle flag. The old flag had 84 bullet holes, and shrapnel had broken the staff twice. Captain Eugene Nash, in his definitive history of the 44th NY writes that although he had been unable to verify the exact numbers, he was told that twelve men had died and eighteen men had been wounded carrying the colors of the 44th New York Infantry Regiment.

44th New York Infantry Battle Flag. (Library of Congress)

When not on duty during that long winter, the men would spend their time cooking meals, and writing letters to home. An empty hard-tack box made a serviceable desk to write on. Postage stamps stored in small envelopes often served the troops as money. The men enjoyed playing cards, cribbage, euchre, and checkers, but rarely chess. Some men spent their evenings alone, maybe smoking a pipe, but most sought out social interaction and conversation. Men of the same town or village would exchange gossip had from the latest letters from home. They would share letters about mutual acquaintances who had been married or signed up for some regiment, or been wounded and returned home. From some tents music could be heard, singing or violin or banjo. The men discovered that a bayonet, stuck in the ground, made a great candlestick holder that would light up a tent.

During the day, when the weather was good, some men enjoyed the growingly popular game of baseball. Still in its infancy, once everyone had found a set of rules they agreed on, many spirited games were played. A Massachusetts regiment once beat a New York regiment 62-20. Some men preferred to spend the daylight hours making pipes from the root of mountain laurel, or rings from dried horn.

Early in January, General Burnside received reports that Robert Lee had moved some of his troops from Fredericksburg to Tennessee and North Carolina. Burnside saw this as an opportunity to recover from the fiasco of Fredericksburg, and launch a new assault on Lee's Army. He planned to move General Franklin's and General Hooker's troops about a dozen miles north along the Rappahannock, cross at one of the many fords along the river, and then move south in order to assault Lee's flank, while at the same time renewing the attack on Lee's front at Fredericksburg. Once again many of Burnside's generals believed this operation would fail and did everything they could to undercut Burnside's authority.

The Mud March

The 44th NY struck tents at 10 a.m. on January 20, 1863. There was the usual chaos of getting tens of thousands of troops, tens of thousands of horses and mules, and hundreds of wagons and pieces of artillery moving in one direction. The 44th NY actually began marching around 4 p.m. Things seemed to be going as planned until it started to rain. The 44th NY marched for two miles and then camped in nearby woods. They experienced heavy rain all night. The morning of January 21, the rain was still coming down. Everything was soaked and the roads had turned into rivers. Wagons and artillery were soon stuck in mud up to the axels. Double-teams were hitched to wagons but the wagons would not budge. Hundreds of horses and mules died. Ropes were attached to cannon and pulled out of the mud by 150 men, only to become stuck again. Cavalry, infantry, artillery, all were stopped. Desertions reached an all-time high. The rain still came down. Burnside's columns covered two miles that day. All pretense of a surprise march on

Lee had been lost and Burnside surrendered to the weather. On January 22, Burnside ordered his army to return to their camps; the men had to build corduroy roads to get back. The 44th NY reached their camp at Stoneman's Switch about 3 p.m. on the 24th, they were covered in mud and completely exhausted. What came to be known as "The Mud March" was over.

On January 25, a day after the Mud March, General Burnside traveled to Washington and met with President Lincoln. Burnside demanded that Lincoln remove several high-ranking generals from command, chief among them Joseph Hooker and William Franklin, because of their constant attempts to undermine his authority and his command of the army. He believed they were responsible for the defeat at Fredericksburg. Burnside told President Lincoln that they must go or he must go. Lincoln's confidence in Burnside had been shaken at Fredericksburg, and the Mud March tipped the scale. Without consulting his cabinet, Lincoln removed Burnside from command of the Army of the Potomac and named General Joseph Hooker as his replacement.

For the next two months, the 44th NY, along with much of the Army of the Potomac, remained in their camps near Falmouth.

CHAPTER TWELVE

Chancellorsville

Joseph Hooker

Joseph Hooker, 48 years old, was now in command of the Army of the Potomac. He had served with distinction during the Peninsula Campaign, and had led the 1st Corps at South Mountain, where they defeated Longstreet's much smaller army. He was wounded, though not severely, at Antietam. During the Battle of Fredericksburg, he was in command of the 3rd and 5th Corps which formed the awkward Central Grand Division.

Joseph Hooker proved to be a gifted administrator. He was a meticulous planner, and when his Army marched, it did not result in mile-long columns of men colliding with mile-long wagon trains trying to use the same road. He streamlined the commissary system and greatly improved the diet of the Army of the Potomac. He ordered ovens built so that while in camp his men could have fresh bread. He improved camp sanitation, improved hospitals and the furlough system, and created *The Bureau of Military Information*, the first formal intelligence agency of the Union Army. He combined the Federal cavalry into a single corps making it much more effective in combating Jeb Stuart's Confederate cavalry, and increased officer training and drills throughout the Army.

On the darker side, Hooker was viciously critical of his superiors. Although often correct in his judgements, he seldom passed up a chance to undermine his commanding officers to the detriment of Army morale. For example, when he appeared before the Congressional Committee on the Conduct of the War in March of 1863, he was asked why the Peninsula Campaign failed; he replied, ***"I do not hesitate to say that it is to be attributed to the want of generalship on the part of our commander."*** Hooker was equally critical of General Burnside, and General Franklin, and testified in detail on why he believed the battle at Fredericksburg would have turned out differently if he had been making the decisions. He was full of bravado, loved whiskey and female companionship, and entertained often at his headquarters in order to build a network of loyal cronies within the Army. One officer described his headquarters at Falmouth as being a combination of a barroom and brothel. A few weeks after Hooker assumed command, he famously pronounced, ***"I have the finest army on the planet. I have the finest army the sun ever shone on... If the enemy does not run, God help them. May God have mercy on General Lee, for I will have none."*** His men called him Fighting Joe Hooker.

Abraham Lincoln was well aware of General Hooker's deficiencies. When he appointed Hooker to be in command of the Army of the Potomac he handed him an elegant letter that expressed the concerns, fears, and hopes Lincoln had for him:

> ***"Executive Mansion***
> ***Washington, January 26, 1863***
> ***Major General Hooker:***
> ***General.***
>
> *I have placed you at the head of the Army of the Potomac. Of course I have done this upon what appear to me to be sufficient reasons. And yet I think it best for you to know that there are some things in regard to which, I am not quite satisfied with you. I believe you to be a brave and a skillful soldier, which, of course, I like. I also believe you do not mix politics with your profession, in which you are right. You have confidence in yourself, which is a valuable, if not an indispensable quality. You are ambitious, which, within reasonable bounds, does good rather than harm. But I think that during Gen. Burnside's command of the Army, you have taken counsel of your ambition, and thwarted him as much as you could, in which you did a great wrong to the country, and to a most meritorious and honorable brother officer. I have heard, in such way as to believe it, of your recently saying that both the Army and the Government needed a Dictator. Of course it was not for this, but in spite of it, that I have given you the command. Only those generals who gain successes, can set up dictators. What I now ask of you is military success, and I will risk the dictatorship. The government will support you to the utmost of its ability, which is neither more nor less than it has done and will do for all commanders. I much fear that the spirit which you have aided to infuse into the Army, of criticizing their Commander, and withholding confidence from him, will now turn upon you. I shall assist you as far as I can, to put it down. Neither you, nor Napoleon, if*

he were alive again, could get any good out of an army, while such a spirit prevails in it.

And now, beware of rashness. Beware of rashness, but with energy, and sleepless vigilance, go forward, and give us victories.

Yours very truly
A. Lincoln"

Victories were just what Joseph Hooker intended to deliver. By late April he had finished what he believed was a perfect plan to crush Lee's Army. His plan was similar to General Burnside's plan that he had so vehemently criticized, and that had sunk into the mud of Virginia's winter roads. General Hooker planned to trap Lee's Army between Fredericksburg, and an army of 60,000 men coming from behind Lee's position. His men would cross the Rappahannock upstream of Fredericksburg, and flank Lee's Army. At the same time, 60,000 men would cross just below Fredericksburg where General Franklin had previously come close to breaking Lee's line, and attack Lee's front. In addition, General Hooker would send the newly organized and improved Union cavalry, with 11,500 troopers and 22 guns under command of General Stoneman, across Kelly's Ford and south to Gordonsville and then Hanover Junction, to destroy as much of Robert Lee's supply and communication lines as possible.

The Move to Chancellorsville

After a delay due to heavy rain, the march to flank Lee began at sunrise on April 27, 1862, when Generals Slocum (12th Corps), Howard (11th Corps) and Meade (5th Corps) started toward Kelley's Ford, which was 15 miles upstream of the junction of the Rapidan and Rappahannock. They could not cross at Banks Ford, five miles upstream from Falmouth, or U.S. Ford, 12 miles upstream from Falmouth, because rebel forces heavily defended these fords and recent rains had flooded the river. The Army would pass by Hartwood Church and Morrisville, and then south to Kelly's Ford. From there they would cross the Rapidan River at Ely's Ford or Germanna Ford and march to Chancellorsville.

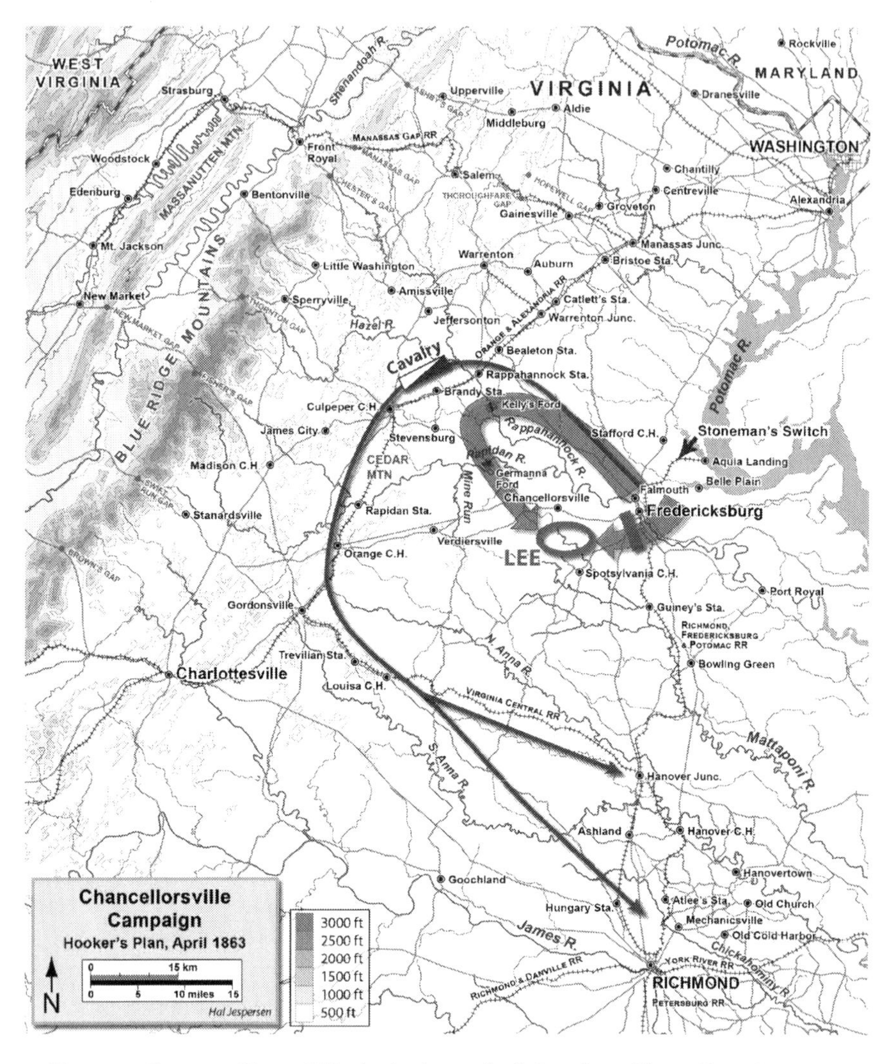

This map illustrates General Hooker's plan to flank Lee from Chancellorsville, attack him head on at Fredericksburg, and disrupt Lee's supply line from Richmond. I have pointed out the location of Stoneman's Switch, where the 44th NY spent the winter of 1862-1863. "Map by Hal Jespersen, www.cwmaps.com".

Charles Kelly and the 44th NY began the march from Stoneman's Switch about noon on April 27, with orders to carry eight days rations. They were able to cross the Rappahannock at Kelly's Ford on pontoon bridges. When they arrived at Ely's Ford to cross the Rapidan River, they hung their cartridge boxes on their bayonets and waded across the cold, chest deep water. They got across without incident and camped for the night. That day they marched 21 miles and crossed two rivers. The 44th NY reached Chancellorsville with the rest of the 5th Corps on April 30, around 11 a.m. General Slocum and General Howard joined them around 2 p.m.

Camp at Stoneman's Switch. Note the various types of tents; Sibley, wall and wedge tents. (Library of Congress)

Joseph Hooker's plan called for General Couch (2nd Corps) to start from Falmouth at dawn on the 29th, march the short distance to Banks Ford with pontoon boats in tow, and erect a secure line of supply across the Rappahannock as soon as General Slocum cleared the south side of the river of rebel forces. General Couch would leave behind General Gibbon's division at Falmouth, under watch of Lee's forces across the river at Fredericksburg, to aid in hiding the movement of the main army. Due to heavy rebel entrenchments at Banks Ford, General Couch crossed with pontoon bridges at U.S. Ford rather than Banks Ford, and arrived at Chancellorsville before nightfall.

Chancellorsville was not a village but a single large brick and timber house with a two-story veranda and a few out buildings. Its military value was that it was located at a junction of the Orange Turnpike Road and the Plank Road both leading east to Fredericksburg, and the River Road leading east to Bank's Ford. Chancellorsville sat in a clearing of about 100 acers in what was called the Wilderness. General Oliver Howard described the Wilderness as ***"stunted trees, such as scraggy oaks, bushy firs, cedars, and junipers, all entangled with a thick, almost impenetrable undergrowth, and crisscrossed with an abundance of wild vines."***

The execution of General Hooker's plan went remarkably well considering the number of troops involved. It was a brilliant achievement to get a large army behind Robert Lee with little or no resistance. The march had been exhausting for the men who were carrying fifty to sixty pounds of gear in what was increasingly hot weather. Many threw knapsacks, blankets and other gear on the side of the road, a common occurrence when the Union Army was on the march in summer months.

Joseph Hooker's generals were preparing to continue the march eastward a couple of hours after arriving in Chancellorsville when they received orders to remain in Chancellorsville until General Hooker got there. He arrived about 4:30 that afternoon.

Back at Fredericksburg, on the same day (April 30) General Sedgwick had built five pontoon bridges across the Rappahannock just south of Fredericksburg and crossed the river with the 1st, 3rd and 6th Corps, as planned. They crossed with minimal resistance. After crossing, the Federal troops immediately began constructing stout entrenchments on the south side of the river under protection of the guns on Stafford Heights. They expected an attack from Marye's Heights, where Robert Lee was carefully watching the development from his headquarters.

Everything was in place. Both arms of Hooker's plan had worked almost to perfection. Why then, did General Hooker order his men to wait for his arrival which delayed the advance of his army at Chancellorsville? Jackson and Lee were still at Marye's Heights with no sign they understood the danger they were in. All that was needed was to follow through with the final stage of the plan.

Robert Lee's Response to General Hooker

Stonewall Jackson learned of Hooker's crossing the Rappahannock in force at Kelly's Ford on the morning of April 29, while Robert Lee observed from Marye's Heights the crossing below Fredericksburg on the same day. Lee was not one to panic in the face of superior numbers. He recalled General Longstreet from his provisioning mission from the south, near Suffolk, and waited to see where Hooker's main strike would fall.

Jackson was less patient than Lee and eager to be at these ill-mannered invaders of his native land. He had played defense for too long; it was time the North felt the wrath of the South for the uncounted indignities heaped upon Southerners during this war.

On April 30, Lee and Jackson together rode along the heights above Fredericksburg. Lee carefully observed the strong entrenchments that General Sedgwick had erected to protect his beachhead on the south side of the river. Jackson wanted to attack this position but after careful examination decided it would be too costly. The cover the Yankees had from artillery on Stafford Heights was too much to overcome. Lee, as usual deferred to Jackson's judgment. But Lee was examining the Union position for a different purpose. Lee observed that the Federal troops were dug in too well; it did not look like a preparation for attack. He reasoned the Yankees did not plan their main blow from this direction and sensed that Hooker's main assault would come from up-river of Fredericksburg; Hooker would attack from the direction of Chancellorsville. It is there that Lee would see what Mr. J.F. Hooker, as Lee called him, was made of.

Once again Lee divided his Army in the face of a superior force. He left ten thousand men on the heights above Fredericksburg to hold Sedgwick's 1st and 6th Corps, numbering 42,000. Lee sent the rest of his Army, about 45,000 strong under command of General Jackson, to join General Anderson, now two miles east of Chancellorsville, at the eastern fringe of the Wilderness. Having been given the task of preventing the Federal Army from flanking Lee at Fredericksburg, Anderson was digging in, preparing to meet Hooker's Army; he knew he could not hold them for long without help. Jackson arrived at Tabernacle Church after sunrise of May 1. His orders were also to prevent General Hooker from advancing to Fredericksburg. To Jackson, holding the enemy meant only one thing: attack. In spite of the odds, around 11a.m., Jackson ordered his force to advance to Chancellorsville about four miles west. At 11:20 a.m., Jackson's men ran headlong into the Union Army.

Chancellorsville, April 30, 1862

When Union General Couch (2nd Corps) reached Chancellorsville on the evening of April 30, he noted

> *" the exuberant spirits at the success of their general in getting "on the other side" without fighting for a position" Couch writes, "As I rode into Chancellorsville that night the general hilarity pervading the camps was particularly noticeable; the soldiers, while chopping wood and lighting fires, were singing merry songs and indulging in peppery camp jokes." General Couch reported to Hooker's headquarters at the Chancellor House and found General Hooker was full of the usual bravado."*

To alleviate concern caused by his order to wait in Chancellorsville, General Hooker explained to his generals that General Sedgwick had crossed the Rappahannock just south of Fredericksburg with little opposition, U.S. Ford had been cleared of rebels, General Gibbon had been called from Falmouth with his 3rd Division, and General Sickles, and the 3rd Corps, were on the way from Fredericksburg to join them. At Chancellorsville, there would now be more than 77,000 infantry ready for a May Day destruction of the rebel army.

That evening General Hooker wrote a memo he ordered read to the troops while they rested around their campfires:

> *"It is with heartfelt satisfaction that the commanding general announces to the army that the operations of the last three days have determined that our enemy must either ingloriously fly, or come out from behind his defenses and give us battle on our own ground, where certain destruction awaits him. The operations of the 5th, 11th, and 12th corps have been a succession of splendid achievements."*

Chancellorsville May 1, 1862

Oddly, General Hooker did not issue orders for the "certain destruction" of Lee's Army until the next morning, and much of the morning hours were lost getting the columns ready to march. General Meade was ordered to advance with two of his divisions, the 1st and 3rd Divisions of his Corps, and form the left wing of the army. Charles Kelly marched with the 1st Division of Meade's 5th Corps. Their objective was to follow the River Road about six miles to Banks Ford, and secure a crossing there, which would greatly shorten their line of supply from Falmouth. The rest of Meade's 5th Corps, the 2nd Division, commanded by George Sykes, would advance on the Turnpike Road. Sykes would be closely supported by General Couch's 2nd Corps. General Sickles 3rd Corps would be held in reserve.

The right hand of General Hooker's "certain destruction", the 12th Corps, commanded by Henry Slocum, would advance on the Plank Road and join with Meade and Couch who were marching along the Turnpike Road. They would meet at the point the two roads intersected. General Hooker proclaimed, ***"after the movement commences, headquarters will be at the Tabernacle Church, about four miles to the southeast of Chancellorsville."***

To complete his master plan, General Hooker sent word to General Sedgwick, back at Fredericksburg to threaten a major attack against Lee's forces on Marye's Heights at 1 p.m. on May 1. Sedgwick was instructed not to follow through with the attack unless an opportunity presented itself to inflict major damage on the rebel forces.

To the east of Chancellorsville, on the morning of May 1, Jackson ordered General Anderson and General McLaws to stop the work of digging trenches and advance along the Turnpike and Plank roads toward Chancellorsville. When Union General Sykes first encountered Stonewall Jackson's skirmishers along the Turnpike Road, a couple of miles from their starting point, Sykes smoothly formed his Division into attack formation and met Jackson's main force. Outnumbered and under heavy pressure General Sykes halted and called for reinforcement. Jackson's troops were pushing him back when support arrived from General Couch's 1st Division, commanded by Winfield Hancock and accompanied by General Couch. The line was stabilized, and the Union forces prepared to move forward. Then something very strange happened.

A courier arrived with orders from Commanding General Hooker to ***"withdraw both divisions to Chancellorsville."*** General Couch, General Hancock, General Sykes, and a number of others could not believe what the courier was telling them. After being in the claustrophobic thickets of the Wilderness, it did not make sense to abandon the open ground to their front. The Union Army commanded some of the finest artillery in the world, but it became essentially useless when bogged down in the vines and brambles.

An aide was sent back to General Hooker explaining that the Union line was stable and all commanders wanted to move forward. Half an hour later they again received orders to withdraw to Chancellorsville, and were told that the Union right wing under General Slocum had been ordered to withdraw also. General Warren rode back to headquarters to find out what was going on while General Couch obeyed orders and began to withdraw. It was around 2 p.m. With the withdrawal well underway, General Couch received new orders, to hold until five o' clock. Struggling to contain his anger and frustration, Couch told the courier, ***"Tell General Hooker he is too late, the enemy are already on my right and rear. I am in full retreat."***

General Meade's 1st and 3rd Divisions, forming the left of the Union advance were also recalled. Charles Kelly's regiment, part of the 1st Division, had nearly reached their objective of Bank's Ford around dark when word came to withdraw. After an exhausting march in the mud, they circled back almost to their starting point, halted, countermarched, and re-countermarched, until around 10 p.m. when they established a position and sent out skirmishers. At 1:30 a.m. the next morning they were ordered back to Chancellorsville and arrived around daylight. Charles Kelly writes how sore his feet were from the long march.

> *"May 1 1863*
>
> ***Hookers Army has crossed the Rapidan River all right the 44th is incamped at Chancellorsville we started on a skirmish to feel of the Enemy which are in front have Been on the march all day came up to the front about dark was under fire about 2 hours had 3 men wounded one from company E mortally the others slightly this has been the hardest day I ever saw my feet are sore the day has Been very warm Sykes division has Been ingaged all day we have Been marching and feeling of their flanks."***

General Meade was furious. His confidence in General Hooker collapsed. He joined with the other Corps Commanders in believing General Hooker would lead them to defeat. He noted, referring to the ridge just outside of the Wilderness they had held earlier in the day, ***"My God, if we can't hold the top of a hill, we certainly cannot hold the bottom of it!"***

May 1 ended with Hooker's Army well entrenched. On Hooker's left, General Meade's Corps was stationed along the west side of Mineral Springs Run all the way to the Rappahannock River, protecting U.S. Ford. In the center, Generals Slocum and Couch covered the Orange Turnpike Road and the Plank Road where they intersected at Chancellorsville. To the west General Howard covered the right flank of the Army along the Orange Turnpike. General Sickles' Corps was held in reserve.

The bravado from General Hooker continued that evening. He announced to General Couch that he had Lee ***"just where I want him; he must fight me on my own ground."*** Couch was expecting something like this and he later wrote ***"but to hear from his own lips that the advantages gained by the successful marches of his lieutenants were to culminate in fighting a defensive battle in that nest of thickets was too much."*** Couch left General Hooker's headquarters ***"with the belief that my commanding general was a whipped man."***

Just what happened to General Hooker during the three hours his Army was marching toward Tabernacle Church? Why did he stop when victory over Lee was so close? Over the years what was going on in the mind of Joseph Hooker at this time has been the subject of much speculation. Perhaps it was information gotten from a rebel deserter, that General Longstreet's entire Corps was coming up from Suffolk and was only a day's march away from the rear of the Union Army. This turned out not to be true. General Lee would sometimes have one of his soldiers pretend to be a deserter and surrender to the enemy so he could plant false information. Perhaps it was the latest intelligence from observation balloons at Falmouth that reported columns of rebel troops ***"moving on the road toward Chancellorsville."*** Perhaps Lincoln's words to him ***"Beware of rashness"*** haunted Hooker's decisions. Or, as many believed, Joseph Hooker, in his mind's eye, had looked into the cold hard eyes of Robert Lee and found himself wanting.

Lee also was puzzled by General Hooker's actions, but hesitation in the face of an enemy was not who Lee was. He met with General Jackson at sundown that night and discussed how their much smaller army might do the most damage to the Federal juggernaut. Jackson believed General Hooker was in retreat and before sunup would head back beyond the Rappahannock; Lee thought not.

That night, as reports came in of strong Union entrenchments on Lee's right and center, Lee's focus shifted to the flank of the Union Army on his left. After a few hours' sleep, just as the night sky in the east began to turn orange, Jackson's cartographer, Major Jedediah Hotchkiss returned from scouting out trails leading west around the Union Army. He was full of excitement. He laid out his map before Lee and Jackson and showed them exactly what they were looking for. They could march west to Catharine Furnace, turn south until they reached Brock Road, march northwest to the Orange Plank Road and then turn northeast. Once on the Plank Road they would be just two miles from the rear of the Union army. The entire route was about ten miles long, and the roads were firm enough to support wagons and artillery. The heavy brush and thickets would screen their movements most of the way.

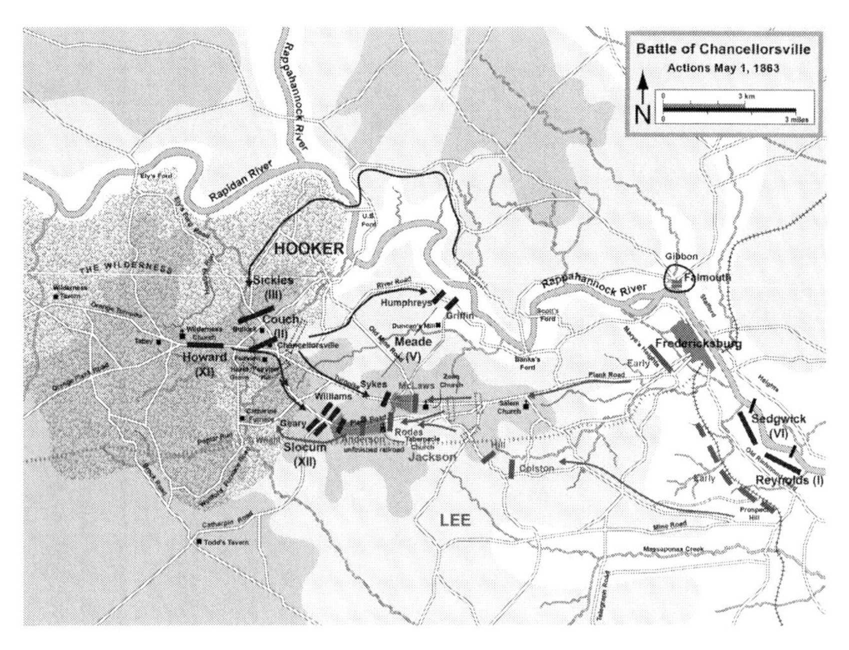

May 1 of the battle. Hooker's plan to fight through the Wilderness from Chancellorsville and establish his HQ at the Tabernacle Church seems to have evaporated. Charles Kelly is with Griffin, along the River Road. Sedgwick and Reynolds have crossed the river just south of Fredericksburg. Lee and Jackson have developed a plan to flank Hooker from the west near Howard's HQ at Wilderness Church. "Map by Hal Jespersen, www.cwmaps.com".

Chancellorsville May 2nd

"Saturday May 2nd 1863

the morning is fine we Expect to have a Tough day to day But we have got the best of the position and expect to clean the Rebs out"

Once again Lee divided his Army while positioned in front of an enemy with superior force. Lee was taking the biggest risk of his career. Jackson began the march around Hooker's flank with his entire corps of 27,000, plus artillery and cavalry, shortly before 8 a.m. of May 2. It was a fine sunny day. Jackson left Lee with two divisions commanded by General Anderson and General McLaws with just over 15,000 troops to hold General Hooker's force of what would soon be, upon arrival of the 1st Corps of General Reynolds, 90,000 strong.

At 2 a.m. that morning General Hooker issued orders for General Reynolds to leave General Sedgwick's force at Fredericksburg and march with the 1st Corps via U.S. Ford to join him at Chancellorsville. An odd decision considering how many troops Hooker already had at Chancellorsville and what he was expecting of General Sedgwick back at Fredericksburg.

As the day wore on, General Hooker began receiving a growing number of reports, some frantic, some more than frantic, concerning a large body of rebel troops with wagons and artillery moving to the west. Hooker got it in his mind these reports confirmed his fondest belief that the rebel army was in retreat. He told General Couch ***"Lee is in full retreat toward Gordonsville, and I have sent out Sickles to capture his artillery."*** As with many beliefs, nothing would change his mind until it was too late. Expecting Lee to be in full retreat by the next morning General Hooker, in the early afternoon of May 2, issued orders to his Corps Commanders to be ready at first light for a pursuit of Lee's Army.

To complete his plan, at 4:30 p.m., May 2, General Hooker ordered General Sedgwick, back at Fredericksburg to cross the river with his entire force, ***"capture Fredericksburg and everything in it, and vigorously pursue the enemy."*** General Sedgwick was confused. Did not the commanding general know he had crossed the river a couple of days ago? And if he now was to mount a major assault on the rebel army that was in the same very strong position from which it had so ingloriously defeated General Burnside, why was General Hooker constantly depleting his force, the latest example being sending the entire 1st Corps under

General Reynolds, to Chancellorsville? Why was General Hooker's massive army digging trenches at Chancellorsville while his much smaller force was ordered to vigorously attack the enemy?

Jackson Flanks the Union Army

Once Jackson's force started, it would take about four hours for his last man to get underway on the path to flank Hooker's Army. They started around 8 a.m. on May 2, 1863. That afternoon before the head of the column got to the turnoff point on Plank Road, General Fitzhugh Lee, a nephew of Robert Lee, approached General Jackson. Jackson followed Lee through some woods that led to a small hill. At the summit, they had a spectacular view of the entire right wing of the Union Army. Jackson immediately saw why Lee had brought him there; the intended turnoff on the Plank Road would lead his Army straight into the entrenched center of Hooker's right wing. If they proceeded two miles further up Brock Road, they could turn right on the Orange Turnpike and get closer than a thousand yards to the lightly-guarded extreme right of the Union Army, before becoming visible to the Yankees. Racing against the coming darkness, Jackson's men marched the additional two miles to the Orange Turnpike intersection, turned right, and began to form their line of attack. The Turnpike would form the center of their formation with a line stretching for a mile north and another line a mile south of the road, a two-mile long wave of death and destruction aimed at the flank of the Federal Army.

At 5:15 p.m., the last of Jackson's Brigades were still coming up when he gave the order to attack. Union General Howard, Commander of the XI Corps later reported that the first effect of the attack was ***"like a cloud of dust driven before a coming shower, appeared in the startled rabbits, squirrels, quail, and other game flying wildly hither and thither in evident terror, and escaping, where possible, into adjacent clearings."*** Within minutes, two dozen Confederate regiments emerged from what the Yankees believed to be impassable thickets, and smashed into the two regiments who held the Federal Army's right flank. The Federal regiments immediately collapsed and those that could ran for their lives. Panic spread even faster than the Union troops could run. Officers desperately tried to rally the fleeing men to form a line, with little effect. Jackson pressed on. He wanted nothing less than to cut all the way through the Union Army until he met up with Lee, and then to cut off the Yankees from retreat across U.S. Ford.

It took Joseph Hooker almost an hour to realize what was happening. He thought that the racket he heard from the west was General Sickles wreaking havoc on the rear of the column he believed to be Lee in retreat. Hooker had pulled Sickles from his reserve position earlier that day and weakened the XI Corps protecting the Army's right flank, to pursue the rebel retreat. Just before sundown, General Hooker's Headquarters at Chancellorsville was engulfed by a mob of stampeding and panicked Union soldiers fleeing from the wrath of Stonewall Jackson. Belief that General Lee was in retreat dissolved before General Hooker's eyes. General Couch later wrote that, Hooker ***"quickly mounted and flew across the open space to meet the onset, passing on his way stampeded pack-mules, officers' horses, caissons, with men and horses running for their lives."***

General Sickles' Third Division, being readily available, was immediately ordered to stem the rout. Throughout the Union Army, officers desperately tried to regain control of their troops. As the evening grew darker, the chaos increased. Blue and gray, fighting by the full moon, blundered into each other and many men died from friendly fire. In numerous places the thick underbrush of the Wilderness was on fire, consuming wounded who were too weak to flee. In the confusion, Stonewall Jackson was personally scouting out the front with his staff at about 9:30 p.m. Illuminated by the full moon, Jackson's group of officers was fired upon by his own men. The officers yelled in the direction of the fire ***"Cease firing! Cease firing! You are firing into your own men!"*** Believing the command to be a ruse another volley was let loose. A number of officers were killed, and Jackson was severely wounded. The next day, fourteen dead horses were counted where this incident occurred.

General Jackson was carried to an ambulance and brought to a makeshift hospital where his left arm was removed. At first he appeared to be recovering but a week later Thomas "Stonewall" Jackson died. He was 39 years old.

General Lee, on the night of May 2, still not aware just how serious Jackson's wounds were, had no intention of squandering all that had been gained by Jackson. Lee's orders that night were sent out to his commanders: ***"It is necessary that the glorious victory thus far achieved be prosecuted with the utmost vigor, and the enemy given no time to rally...Endeavor therefore, to dispossess them of Chancellorsville, which will permit the union of the army."***

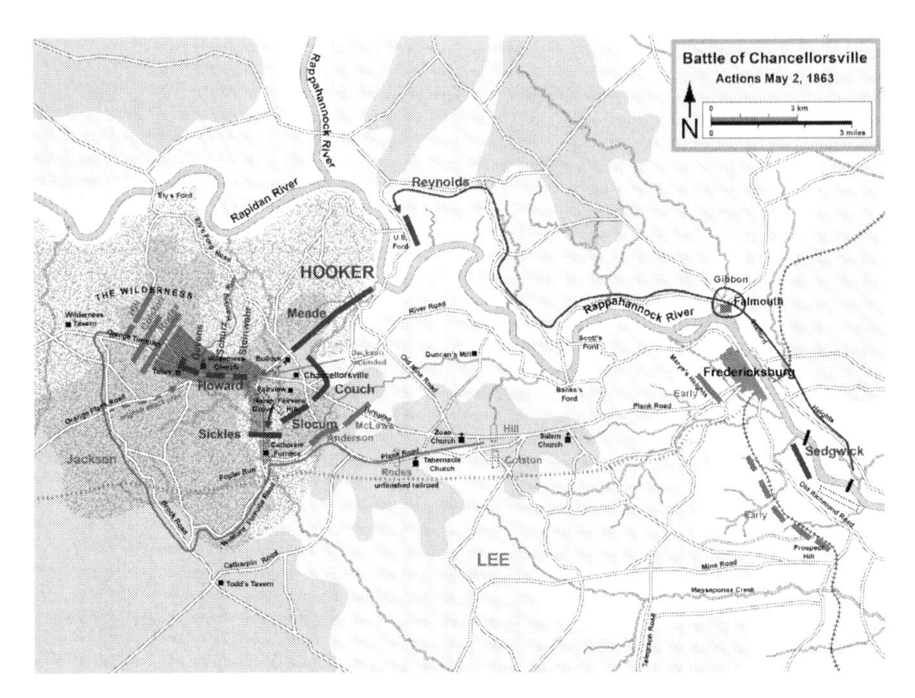

This map shows the route that Jackson took to flank Hooker's army. The evening of May 2 Stonewall Jackson emerged from the thickets along the Orange Turnpike with 27,000 men and smashed into Howard's XI Corps. Later that evening Jackson would be mortally wounded by friendly fire. General Reynolds has been ordered from Fredericksburg to aid General Hooker. Charles Kelley is with Meade's 5th Corps holding the approaches to U.S. Ford. "Map by Hal Jespersen, www.cwmaps.com".

Chancellorsville, May 3, 1863

Few would aid Robert Lee more in dispossessing the Federal Army of the crossroads at Chancellorsville than Joseph Hooker. During the moonlit night of May 2, and the morning of May 3, thousands of Union and Confederate soldiers died from enemy and friendly fire as Jeb Stuart, now filling in for Stonewall Jackson, attempted to join his approximately 20,000 men with Robert Lee's 16,000 men, and destroy the Yankees before they could flee back across the Rappahannock. By 1 a.m. of May 3, the only force between Stuart and Lee was General Sickles, who by then had grouped his men on a knoll called Hazel Grove, less than a mile southwest of Chancellorsville. Sickles knew his position was vital but also realized that Hazel Grove was jutting out from the Federal lines and vulnerable to attack from three sides. Sickles tried to convince General Hooker to reform the Union lines to include Hazel Grove. General Hooker was apparently focused on preparing a flanking maneuver on his right, and thought Hazel Grove too far ahead of his lines, and too vulnerable.

At daylight on Sunday morning General Hooker ordered General Sickles to withdraw from Hazel Grove and march the short distance to Fairview Hill, just outside of Chancellorsville. The result was that Lee could now join with Stuart; the gate to Chancellorsville was open. Even so, the heaviest and most costly fighting of the battle would occur in the next few hours as the Confederate army approached General Hooker's headquarters at the old mansion. As Sickles' men left Hazel Grove the position was immediately overrun, first by rebel infantry, then by thirty guns of rebel artillery. Now in a commanding position atop Hazel Grove, the rebels immediately began firing on Union troops commanded by Generals Couch and Slocum positioned near Fairview Hill just outside of Chancellorsville. These guns joined with an additional thirty guns from what, less than eighteen hours ago, was General Howard's XI Corps Headquarters along the Turnpike Road. And to the south along Plank Road, twenty four rebel guns were hammering Union positions at Fairview Hill and Chancellorsville.

"May 3rd 1863

started from the position we held yesterday we came around to the left of our lines Early this morning Expected to gain(going) to the front and we did But we was ordered to Build Breastworks we have Been under a heavy fire all day the first day we had 3 men wounded the first day of the fight to day we had 2 men out of company B 16th Michigan the fight has Been very severe all day Last Night the Rebs drove the 11 corps in But they Regained their position Before we Relieved them one Little I must note here this forenoon one man in the 16th Michigan was out at the front and was fired at By one of the Rebs the fellow started out the front after him found him up in a Tree shot at wounded him and Brought him in with him General Berry was Kiled this after noon his Division suffered heavy the Report say the Loss 1200 men in his Division this has Been a very hot day as far as fighting goes the impression is that we are going to Be atackted during the Night and sure enough the attemp was made at 3 different times But they were Repulsed at every point the pickets Report that the Rebs are going off at Doublequick time Retreating toward Gardinvile."

Most of the Federal generals did not see the setback caused by Jackson's flanking movement on the evening of May 2, to mean the battle was lost. Union forces still vastly outnumbered Robert Lee's forces. General Couch later wrote, ***"It only required that Hooker should brace himself up to take a reasonable, common sense view of the state of things, when the success gained by Jackson would have been turned into an overwhelming defeat... If he had remembered Mr. Lincoln's injunction (gentlemen, in your next fight put in all of your men), the face of the day would have been changed and the field won for the Union arms."***

It was not to be; Joseph Hooker was soon to learn the value of the position he had abandoned at Hazel Grove. A little after 9 a.m., after returning to his Chancellorsville headquarters from a morning scouting ride, he was leaning against a large wooden pillar on the southwest veranda. An artillery round (solid shot) smashed into the pillar, and split the pillar lengthwise. General Hooker was forcefully thrown to the deck of the porch, stunned. He was unconscious for a time. He was taken to the lawn on the north side of the building and upon regaining at least partial consciousness, he called for his horse. Later, General Hooker wrote that ***"his right side had turned livid."*** With help, General Hooker managed to mount his horse and ride in the direction of U.S. Ford, with his staff trailing after. A short distance later the pain caused him to stop and he ask for help to dismount. His staff laid him on a blanket and, not knowing what else to do, poured some brandy down his throat. It had been some weeks since General Hooker had allowed himself the pleasure of brandy and it may have given him a jolt. General Hooker got up, once again called for his horse, and was helped to the saddle. Still numb on his right side and far from being clear headed, rode off in the direction of U.S. Ford. As he was leaving, a solid shot fired from Hazel Grove hit the blanket he had been laying on and ***"tore up the earth in a savage way."***

Receiving no support in troops or ammunition from General Hooker, Generals Slocum and Couch were nearly out of ammunition and forced to join Sickles in withdrawing from Fairview Hill back to Chancellorsville. The Union rear guard division commanded by General Hancock fought desperately to keep from being overrun as artillery fire rained down on them from Fairview Hill. Soon, after a desperate struggle, they had to abandon Chancellorsville. They all retreated toward U.S. Ford. Robert Lee had achieved his objective, his army was reunited a little before 10:30 a.m. in the one hundred acre clearing surrounding the

Chancellorsville mansion. The majestic old structure, the victim of rebel artillery, was burning.

In the pre-dawn hours of that day, General Hooker had been able to consolidate his shaken troops into a strong defensive position centered on U.S. Ford, with the Rapidan River on his right and the Rappahannock River on his left. With the fall of Chancellorsville, General Hooker's entire force, including the newly arrived Corps of General Reynolds was now behind that line. In one of the many ironies of Chancellorsville, General Hooker's force of 90,000 was now surrounded and under threat by Lee's force of 43,000.

General Hooker had repeatedly telegraphed orders to General Sedgwick back at Fredericksburg on the night of May 2, and the morning of May 3, to come to his aid. As the morning of May 3 progressed, the messages became more frantic. Taking little account of the rebel force defending Fredericksburg that General Sedgwick was dealing with, General Hooker wrote just prior to his encounter with the porch pillar, ***"You will hurry up your column. The enemy's right flank now rests near the Plank road at Chancellorsville, all exposed. You will attack at once."*** The same message was resent around 10 a.m. General Sedgwick, fervently attempting to comply with his orders to take Fredericksburg, launched a three-pronged attack on the rebel positions at Marye's Heights. Once again Union soldiers were asked to assault the stone wall just west of Fredericksburg, but this time the number of rebel defenders was greatly diminished. Ten regiments of Union soldiers faced off against two regiments of Confederate defenders positioned behind that bloody wall. Two assaults failed, but on the third assault, the stone wall and all of Marye's Heights was taken. It was about 10:50 in the morning of May 3.

The latest demand from General Hooker for Sedgwick to come to what was essentially the rescue of Hooker's 90,000 man army with Sedgwick's 22,000 troops, reached Sedgwick about 11:30 a.m. Still recovering from the horrific battle of that morning, Sedgwick sent his troops marching to the west on the Plank Road toward Chancellorsville. Union General Gibbon remained in Fredericksburg to hold the town. It was about two in the afternoon when General Sedgwick got underway. A mile from Marye's Heights the Union troops met skirmishers under command of General McLaws, and behind them, 7,000 Confederate troops. As they neared Salem Church, the resistance became heavy. The "exposed" flank that General Hooker had referred to just a few hours earlier was nowhere to be found.

Flush with victory, Lee was far from finished with General Hooker. He intended to drive the Yankees into the Rappahannock; they would be forced to surrender or be slaughtered. While his men celebrated in the clearing at Chancellorsville that morning, Lee began the process of reforming his Army after a long night of brutal fighting. Men were fed, regiments were reformed, wounded were cared for. About the time Lee's forward units were ready to march toward Hooker's lines near U.S. Ford, a frantic messenger arrived from Fredericksburg. General Sedgwick, commanding the Union 6th Corps, had taken Fredericksburg, and was marching toward Lee's rear on the Plank Road. Lee's plan, in case this occurred, was for Jubal Early to withdraw south toward Guiney Station, the place where the wounded Stonewall Jackson would, in a few days, breathe his last breath. Lee hoped that General Sedgwick would follow General Early, but instead Sedgwick kept on the Plank Road, straight toward the flank of Lee's Army. General Hooker would have to wait.

As evening approached, after heavy fighting, General Sedgwick rested his exhausted troops for the night. His troops had been constantly attacking a very determined enemy since early that morning. The 6th Corps established a heavily guarded perimeter and tried to get some sleep.

Lee now saw an opportunity. Jubal Early had withdrawn from Sedgwick's attack for only a couple of miles down Telegraph Road, and when he determined that General Sedgwick was not in pursuit, he stopped. General Lee withdrew General Anderson from in front of the strongly defended Federal position along Mineral Spring Run, which was the left flank of Hookers position at U.S. Ford, and sent him to strengthen McLaws force in front of General Sedgwick, near Salem Church. Lee now had Sedgwick's 6th Corps held between General McLaws and General Early. Lee left Jeb Stuart with only 25,000 men to prevent General Hooker's army of 90,000 men from aiding Sedgwick. It turned out to be enough.

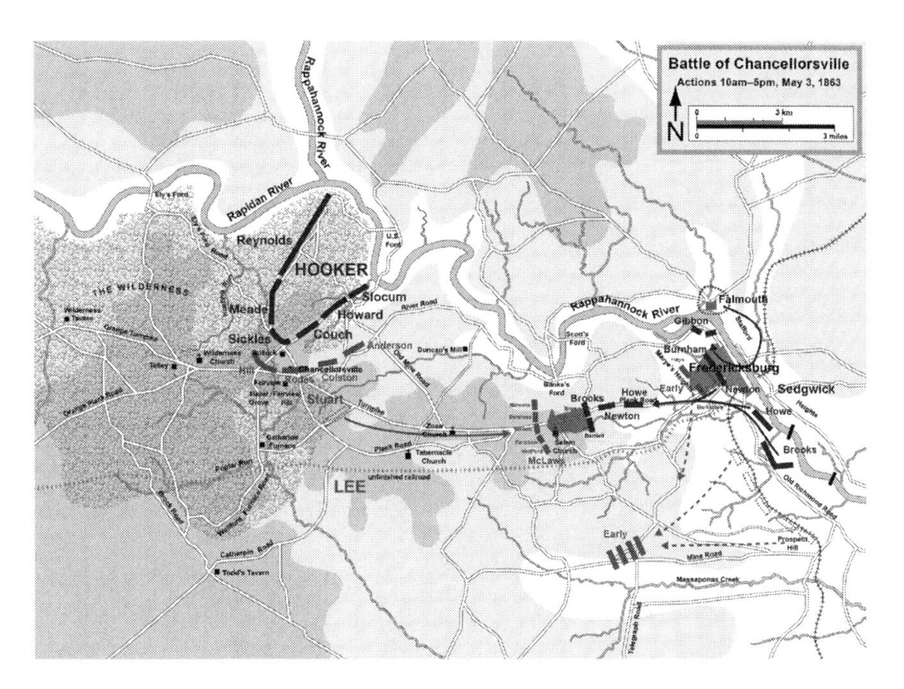

By the evening of May 3 General Hooker had withdrawn from Chancellorsville and built strong defensive fortifications around U.S. Ford. General Sedgwick had taken Fredericksburg and Marye's Heights and was marching toward Chancellorsville to relieve Hooker. Lee stopped Sedgwick's advance at Salem Church. "Map by Hal Jespersen, www.cwmaps.com".

Chancellorsville, May 4, 1863

"May 4th 1863

this day has the appearance of Being fine the impression seems to Be among the Pickets that the Rebs have skedadled But they have not withdrawn as yet what will Be done to day I dont know But the Enemy are up to some thing one of the prisoners Report that Jackson is Bound to Break through our lines at all hasards if he does come through it will be at the loss of his army for the union Boys are Bound to whip them in this fight the feeling in our army is good and they have confidence in Joe Hooker the commander the old fellow seems to Be everywhere on his fine white horse the Remainder of the day has Been Rather stil with the Exception of one or two slight Brushes I was on

> ***duty all Night Being called out 3 different times at 3 this morning the Reg't was ordered to get Ready to advance on the Enemy But we did not advance as ordered"***

General Lee arrived at Salem Church around noon on May 4. He planned to personally direct the destruction of the Union 6th Corps. By that time Jubal Early had retaken Marye's Heights and once again occupied the sunken road at the base of Marye's Heights. Union General Gibbon still occupied what was left of the town of Fredericksburg.

To perfect his plan Lee sent General Anderson's division around the south flank of General Sedgwick to join up with Jubal Early at Marye's Heights; several hours were spent getting Lee's army in position for the killing blow. The attack would come from the west commanded by McLaws, from the south commanded by Anderson, and from the east commanded by Early. The signal guns were fired at 6 p.m., and the battle began. There were pockets of savage fighting, but much of McLaws force was bogged down in heavy thickets common to the terrain and there was confusion among General Anderson's troops who, at one point, were firing into their own ranks. A heavy fog ended the attack after about an hour.

Full of frustration, Lee ordered his first night attack of the war. He would not give General Sedgwick an opportunity to dig strong entrenchments or to escape across the Rappahannock River. Lee's artillery shelled what in the darkness they hoped was Banks Ford, while his infantry groped in the fog and the dark looking for Sedgwick's Corps with little effect.

Chancellorsville, May 5, 1863

At sunrise on May 5, Lee's scouts learned that General Sedgwick had gotten all three of his divisions across the Rappahannock on a pontoon bridge erected at Scott's Ford, about a mile downstream of Banks Ford. Sedgwick was now out of reach of Lee's Army.

Back at Fredericksburg, Union General Gibbon had abandoned the town, crossed the Rappahannock, cut loose his pontoon bridges, and returned to Falmouth. Now, all that remained of Union forces south of the Rappahannock were the heavily entrenched troops with General Hooker at U.S. Ford. Deeply disappointed that he had missed an opportunity to destroy a significant portion of the Federal Army, General Lee ordered his weary men to march back toward Chancellorsville and deal with Joseph Hooker.

> ***"May 5th 1863***
>
> ***this is my Birthday to day and By the Looks of things I am going to have quite a Celebration the Enemy Began their work about 1/2 past 7 oclock A.M. But we Repulsed them in about 15 minutes our forces are strenght in their position as fast as they can our company are all safe as yet one of our men had a narrow eskape from a Bullett I am 29 years of age this day"***

As the 44th NY manned their fortified positions at U.S. Ford alongside the rest of the 5th Corps and the bulk of the Army of the Potomac, Charles Kelly observed his 29th birthday. Jeb Stuart continued to put pressure on the Union lines with his much smaller force while Charles wrote in his diary about the human carnage the battle had produced:

> ***"Yesterday our forces made an advance on the Enemy to feel of their position the Reg't that advance was the 4 Michigan they take 40 prisoners their Loss was 1 man Kiled and 8 wounded the Reg't that advanced Reported the woods were filed with Rebs which had been killed the day before our shells setting the woods on fire the consequence was that the wounded Rebs were Burned to death I mean those that could not get away our men Report the forest filled with dead Bodys"***

Charles Kelly did not know it, but General Hooker had crossed over the Rappahannock with his staff before dawn that morning, and ordered the Army to follow. His plan to destroy Robert Lee's Army had gone the way of General Burnside's plan at Fredericksburg last December. By noon, the Army of the Potomac had safely withdrawn to an inner line of defense just a little over a mile from the pontoon bridges at U.S. Ford, but then it started to rain. By midnight, the river had risen six feet and the pontoon bridges were being battered.

Chancellorsville May 6, 1863

Most of the army was still on the south side of the river and General Couch saw the rain as an opportunity. ***"We will stay where we are and fight it out,"*** he proclaimed. However, around 2 a.m., orders from General Hooker arrived directing the withdrawal to continue. One pontoon bridge was cannibalized to strengthen the other, and by 5 a.m., crossing of the infantry was well underway. The 1st Division of General Meade's 5th Corps, Charles Kelly's division, served as the army's rear guard. They were among the last to cross the bridge.

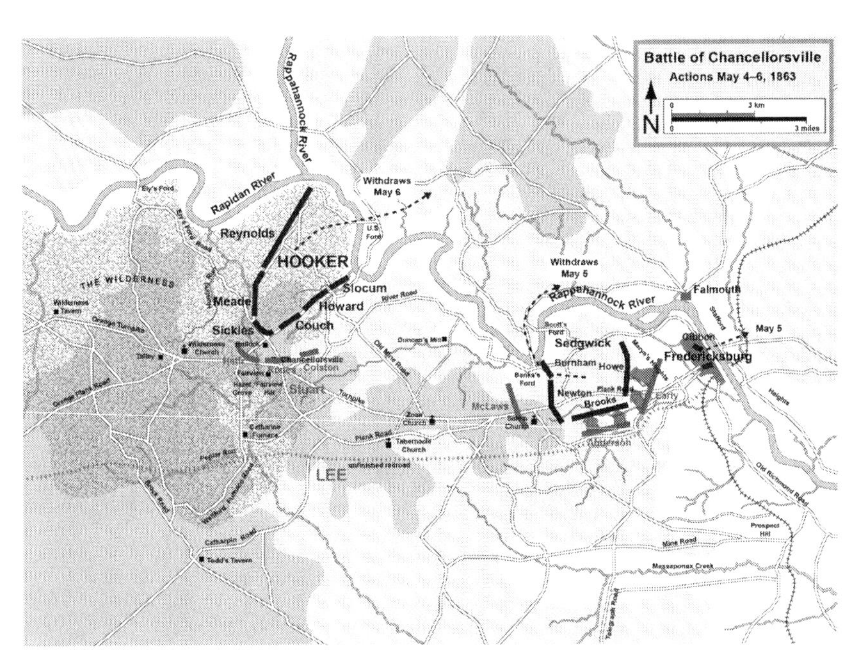

Sedgwick's advance on May 4 forced Lee to leave Stuart at U.S. Ford while he dealt with Sedgwick. Lee attempted to destroy Sedgwick's Corps with a three pronged attack the evening of May 4. Before dawn of May 5, Sedgwick had gotten his Corps across the Rappahannock, and beyond Lee's reach. On May 5, Gibbon withdrew from Fredericksburg leaving the town to the rebels. Lee marched back to Chancellorsville, intent on destroying Hooker's army but was too late. The Army of the Potomac crossed back over the Rappahannock the morning of May 6. Charles Kelly was in the rear guard of the retreat. "Map by Hal Jespersen, www.cwmaps.com".

Back to Stoneman's Switch

Charles Kelly writes about his experience serving as rear guard for the Army of the Potomac after he had returned to Falmouth:

> ***"Camp Near Kalmouth Va May 6, 1863***
>
> ***this had Been a fine morning no ingagement so far the picket Exchanged shots Regular some men of our Division were Killed to day in the Trenches and some on picket the order to Fall Back is understood By the commanders of companys it commenced Raining at sundown and Rained all Night very hard the order to fall in I have Just Rec'd that is to be Ready at 3 oclock in the morning of the 7th 1863 we have falling Back this morning and are the Rear guard of the army our division arrived at the River all Right and have crossed the River in good order it has Been the Hardest time I ever saw and I am about used up arrived in our old camp at 5 oclock in the afternoon slept in the tent with John McLaughlin Rested fine the Boys are Tired out"***

Charles' diary entry of May 7 was written after the 44th NY had crossed the Rappahannock on the morning of May 6 and marched back to their old camp at Stoneman's Switch. There had been no opportunity for sleep the night before. They arrived about 5 o'clock on the evening of May 6. In his diary, Charles wrote ***"it has been the hardest time I ever saw"*** and he was ***"about used up"***. His men were exhausted. The battle for Chancellorsville was over.

Lee had been delayed from reaching General Hooker's lines by the terrific storm that raised the banks of the Rappahannock to flood levels, and battered the pontoon bridges used by the Union army to escape across the river. When Lee arrived at U.S. Ford on May 6, it was too late. General Hooker and his Army were beyond his reach. General Lee returned with his army to Fredericksburg.

The entire battle had exacted a tremendous toll. The count for the Union was 1,606 killed, 9,672 wounded, and 5,919 missing or captured; for the South, it was 1,665 killed, 9,081 wounded, and 2,018 missing. Five generals, three Union and two Confederate, had been killed or mortally wounded. General Jackson's death stood out as being the most grievous blow to the South. Some believed that Lee would never be as effective as he had been with Stonewall Jackson at his side. As for Joseph Hooker, his days as Commander of the Army of the Potomac were numbered.

The Aftermath of Chancellorsville

Amidst the raging political storm in the North ignited by the defeat at Chancellorsville, General Halleck and Abraham Lincoln visited Joseph Hooker at his headquarters at Falmouth on May 7, 1863. Everyone knew the results at Chancellorsville were a disaster. General Hooker blamed his subordinates for the debacle, General Sedgwick for not coming to his aid, General Howard for the collapse of his right wing under Jacksons flanking attack, and General Stoneman for his ineffectual raid on Lee's supply lines. The northern newspapers blamed everyone involved including, and perhaps most of all, Abraham Lincoln. A number of General Hooker's subordinates, including his second in command, General Couch, refused to continue to serve under General Hooker.

"May 9th 1863

had a Restless Night of it did not sleep much I have a small Turn of the disentery which Bothers me very much the capt has gone to Acquia Creek this morning after something to Eat for the Mess I have Been quite sick for the Last 48 hours the President visited this place yesterday and the Rumor is that he told Hooker not to Risk a Battle with the Enemy unlys he was sure of winning it so as to keep Washington safe from an attack this is a Beautiful day the first of the kind we have had since we started on the march the Last time I think we are going to stay here for a while until we get clothing for the men capt Root of Co 33rd NYSV has Been mortally wounded at the storming of Fredericksburgh this Reg't has Been very Lucky in the Last fight"

Abraham Lincoln took a measured approach with General Hooker. On his visit he noted the ***"troops are none the worse for the campaign,"*** meaning that morale in the Army was still good and there were few desertions. The massive Army of the Potomac was still intact. He now knew that General Hooker was not the man he was looking for to destroy Lee's Army, but he had no obvious replacement in mind. The political atmosphere, which he understood far better than the military side of things, dictated that he wait. He urged General Hooker to regroup his forces and pursue Robert Lee. With that, he returned to Washington.

CHAPTER THIRTEEN

The Road to Gettysburg

Longstreet's Arithmetic

In Richmond, the Confederate States of America were celebrating another stunning victory by Lee. However, the death of General Jackson dampened everyone's spirits. On May 14, 1863, a high-level conference was held with generals and cabinet members headed up by Jefferson Davis, the President of the Confederate States of America. They all knew that despite Lee's victories the massive Union Army, just 50 miles to the north, was still intact. They also knew that to the west, General Ulysses Grant was threatening Vicksburg, and thus control of the entire Mississippi River. If Vicksburg fell, it would cut off the western Confederacy; Texas, Arkansas, and western Louisiana were a major source of men and material for the embattled South. What could now be done to improve their situation?

General Beauregard proposed a grand strategy which involved an all-out offensive against Union General Rosecrans, and the center of the Union Army. This would force Grant to abandon his plans for Vicksburg. Lee was very protective of his Army of Northern Virginia, and would have none of this plan which sent much of his army westward to be commanded by Beauregard. He argued that possible salvation of the Mississippi River for a season would mean the loss of Virginia forever. Instead, Lee proposed a second invasion of the North. He would take his army deep into Pennsylvania, north of Washington. This would allow the much-needed harvest in Virginia to go unimpeded; what's more, a major victory for the South, perhaps the fall of Washington, might at last collapse the will of the North to continue the fight, and invite foreign intervention on the side of the South. He presented his plan as one of two alternatives: he could withdraw to Richmond and prepare for a siege that the South would eventually lose, or he could invade Pennsylvania and perhaps tip the balance of the war toward the South, and maybe even end the war.

It was not a difficult choice. Only one of five cabinet members were willing to vote against the miracle worker Robert Lee.

Not everyone bought in to Robert Lee's choices however. For one, General James Longstreet, did not have confidence in Lee's plan; he wanted to employ offensive strategies but defensive tactics. At Fredericksburg, for his portion of the battle, he had inflicted 9,000 Union casualties while suffering less than 2,000 of his own, by carefully preparing a defensive position at the stone wall, backed by artillery on Marye's Heights. Longstreet understood that despite Jackson's flamboyant flanking maneuver at Chancellorsville the victory, which throughout both the North and South was being hailed as Lee's greatest victory and a work of military genius, was as much the work of Joseph Hooker as it was Robert Lee. Longstreet reasoned that if the Army of Northern Virginia fought four more such battles, with similar results, they would be reduced to a handful of men while the Army of the Potomac would still be over 60,000 strong with almost unlimited resources to replenish lost men and equipment. Arithmetic or no arithmetic, Longstreet was a soldier and he would follow orders. He began to prepare his men for a march north.

Lee returned to his army at Fredericksburg and began planning the invasion. Without General Jackson he needed to reorganize his army. The Army of Northern Virginia would now consist of three corps with three divisions each. The 1st Corps was of course under command of General Longstreet. The 2nd Corps went to Richard Ewell, who had lost a leg the previous summer, and the 3rd Corps, to A.P. Hill. Each corps would have five battalions of artillery. General Jeb Stuart would remain in command of the cavalry. For the invasion, the Army of Northern Virginia would have about 60,000 infantry, 5,000 artillery troops, plus 10,000 cavalry, for a total of 75,000 to 80,000 effectives.

Back near Falmouth, Charles writes,

"May 20th, 1863

I awoke this morning about 1/2 6 o'clock the day has every appearance of being fine it may Be somewhat hot in the middle of the day we Expect to move in the morning from the indications of things this army is not going to move very soon that is against the Enemy the order has just come that we move camp to day and away we go on the march for our New camping Ground the camp is a fine one the whole

Brigade incamp together in line of Battle this Regt is on the Extreme Left of the Brigade our New camping ground is 3 miles from the old one towards the picket Line"

Brandy Station

General Lee started out from Fredericksburg on June 3, 1863. By June 5, Longstreet's 1st Corps and Ewell's 2nd Corps made camp near Culpeper Court House. Six miles northeast from Culpeper, at Brandy Station, Jeb Stuart was using his 10,000 cavalry troopers to screen the movement of Lee's Army of Northern Virginia from General Hooker.

Full of "spit and vinegar" the thirty-year-old Jeb Stuart was not content to sit by and merely guard Lee's army. On June 5, he staged a grand review of his force complete with 9,000 cavalry and 4 batteries of artillery engaged in a mock battle, all for the entertainment of nearby residents, which included a number of the local ladies. Lee was unable to attend, so of course, on June 8, the grand review was repeated, this time without the mock battle. All of this commotion came to the attention of General Hooker.

Once again misreading Lee's intentions, Hooker believed that Jeb Stuart was preparing for another raid around his right flank to attack his supply lines. Hooker ordered General Alfred Pleasonton, commander of the Union Cavalry Corps, to cross the Rappahannock and disperse and destroy Stuart's corps. General Pleasonton decided to attack Stuart from two directions. General Buford would cross the Rappahannock two miles northeast of Brandy Station at Beverly Ford, while six miles downstream General Gregg would cross Kelly's Ford and attack from Stuart's rear.

It started on June 9, the day after Stuart's second grand review. At 4:30 a.m., General Buford crossed the Rappahannock in darkness and heavy fog and surprised Stuart's pickets. He quickly drove them back but Stuart's main body of men, shocked out of their sleep, were able to group on a low ridge above Brandy Station called Fleetwood Hill. Stuart's horse troopers, unaccustomed to being on the defense, were beginning to drive back Buford's cavalry when they got another unpleasant surprise. At 11:30 a.m., Gregg's artillery arrived from Kelly's Ford and opened fire on Stuart's rear flank. Gregg's cavalry followed. Five more hours of savage fighting ensued. Most cavalry battles of the war involved troopers riding to the front line of a conflict and dismounting, before engaging the enemy. This battle was different; it was mostly fought from horseback. Counting both sides, there were over 18,400 mounted horsemen and 3,000 Union infantry involved. After fighting all day, Pleasonton was unable to break through Stuart's forces. Upon hearing that Stuart had reinforcements on the way, Pleasonton abandoned the field and returned back across the Rappahannock. Union casualties were about 900, and Confederate casualties about 500. It was the largest cavalry battle in American history.

It was a close call for both Stuart and Lee, but Lee's main army remained undetected, and the march to the Shenandoah Valley continued. The large cavalry battle at Brandy Station should have given both Robert Lee and Jeb Stuart ample notice. Joseph Hooker had reorganized the Federal Cavalry into what was now a powerful and effective fighting unit; Jeb Stuart's cavalry would no longer go unchallenged. The Federal cavalry was now just as lethal as Stuart's 1st Virginia Cavalry. The lesson was driven home again on July 3, near Gettysburg.

Goose Creek Bridge and the Battle of Upperville

"June 17th 1863

made some coffie Eat Breakfast the Brigade Bugle Blared for to march so off we started the day is going to be very warm got in sight of Centreville Rec'd permission to Visit my Brother and sister found them without much Trouble made a short But pleasant Visit saw many old faces that was familiar to me when at home also saw Doctor Hammond and capt coleman and a great many of the Old boys had something good to Eat and changed my shirt that Regt is having a good soft thing of it But they don't see it as much as we did that are on the march all the while Unity wanted to know if I wanted any money and of course I never Refused that thing in my life"

For a brief period on June 17, Charles Kelly got a break from the long days of marching along the increasingly hot and dusty roads. When the 44th NY got within sight of Centreville, he received permission to visit his brother and sister along with some old friends. His brother Neil was a private in the 126th NY Volunteer Infantry, part of the 2nd Corps. His sister Eunice was serving as a nurse in the army. While in Centerville, he had a good meal, put on a clean shirt, and then rejoined his company. They marched 23 miles that day and camped in woods near Gum Springs, also known as Arcola. They were about five miles southeast of Aldie.

> ***"June 17th (continued)***
>
> ***we marched all day the weather is very warm the hotest I ever Experienced in my Life in the Roads the dust was about 6 inches in depth and the Road was filled by artillery, cavalry and infantry when night came I was about Beatout as much so as I was ever in my life before we camped in a piece of woods close By Derick so that the Brigade could wash off good for once and I never enjoyed anything so well in my Life I Laid down last night without any covering over me slept first rate"***

Nothing could have felt as good as washing off in a cool stream after marching 23 miles on dusty roads. Such was the life of an infantry soldier. The 44th NY arrived in Aldie on June 19, two days after a large cavalry battle between Stuart's 1st Virginia Cavalry and General David Gregg's Union cavalry. Still stinging from the embarrassment of being twice surprised at Brandy Station, Stuart's cavalry had been riding along the eastern edge of the Blue Ridge Mountains. They were protecting the numerous passes into the Shenandoah Valley where Lee's infantry was marching north. Stuart's cavalry troopers ran into stiff resistance at Aldie on June 17, and 1,500 of Stuart's troopers fought a four-hour battle, mostly mounted, against two thousand Union cavalry before withdrawing. The battle continued the next day at Middleburg.

On Sunday, June 21, General Pleasonton sent the Third Brigade of the 1st Division, 5th Corps, to reinforce General Gregg's cavalry pushing toward Upperville. Commanded by Colonel Strong Vincent, the Third Infantry Brigade included the 44th NY. That morning Charles and the rest of the Third Brigade had started from Aldie around 3 a.m., got to Middleburg around daylight, and around 7 a.m., near Upperville, encountered dismounted rebel cavalry. The rebels were in position behind a series of stone walls that ran at right angles to the road on the south side. Behind them, more Confederate cavalry waited. Two hundred yards beyond was a battery of six rebel guns. Colonel Vincent yelled, ***"stop that damned battery howling."*** The 16th Michigan Infantry Regiment went forward to dislodge the dismounted cavalry. The rebel force began firing and the 44th NY along with the 20th Maine were sent forward with instructions to ***"press the enemy hard and to pick off the gunners"*** who were manning the rebel battery. The 83rd Pennsylvania went through the woods on the Union left flank, emerged behind the stone walls, and attacked the rebels. The rebels withdrew in confusion and the 16th Michigan advanced on the double-quick. Colonel Strong Vincent reports that the enemy abandoned a fine Blakely gun[3].

The Third Brigade together with Gregg's Cavalry continued to drive the enemy troopers from one position to the next until the rebels made a stand on the west side of a small stream called Crummer's Run. Rebel artillery immediately began inflicting casualties on Union troops. While responding with Union artillery, Union infantry and cavalry flanked the rebel position and once again had Stuart's troopers on the run. Step by step Stuart's men were driven back nearly four miles until they entrenched behind a stone wall overlooking a narrow gorge where a four-arched stone bridge crossed Goose Creek. From there, Stuart's troopers fired a volley into the Union cavalry unit as they prepared to cross the bridge. An hour-long artillery duel ensued. The 83rd Pennsylvania was ordered to ***"carry the bridge on the run"*** while skirmishers from the rest of the Brigade were ordered to ford the stream and turn the enemy's flank. Under heavy fire, the bridge was taken, the enemy flanked and driven back with Union cavalry hot in pursuit. Stuart's troopers were driven beyond Upperville to Ashby's Gap. The exhausted Union infantry, not able to keep up with either Union or Confederate cavalry, took positions near Upperville. The Third Brigade was relieved by the First Brigade around 6 p.m. allowing the 3rd Brigade to withdraw one mile toward Middleburg where they camped for the night.

---

[3] Blakely guns were muzzle-loading rifled cannon sold to the Confederate States of America by British Captain Alexander Blakely. Captain Blakely designed the gun and had them made under contract by private foundries in England. The gun captured by Colonel Vincent was probably a 2.75 inch mountain Blakely, the smaller brother of a series of much larger Blakely guns. The mountain Blakely was light enough to be used by cavalry units and was a deadly weapon with good range.

Charles Kelly wrote briefly about that long day in his diary.

> ***"June 21st 1863***
>
> ***started this at 3 o'clock this morning got to Middelburg at Daylight went to the front and left Traveled about 2 miles from the Vilage before we commenced skirmishing turned out our flankers ahead one battery of the Enemy are playing on our Regt we advanced perhaps a 1/2 mile when D.E. Mapes was wounded by a shell from the Enemy guns Mapes from Co. 6 also Mosher of company 5 a fine fellow was killed at the same time our forces drove the Rebs from Middlebourg to thurafair gap and some say through the gap we have had a hard Day of it was Relieved at Night by the 1st Brigade and Loss in the engagement 1 man in the 44th Regt was 1 Killed 2 wounded"***

It is interesting to note that Charles writes they drove the enemy to Thoroughfare Gap, when actually it was Ashby's Gap. Thoroughfare Gap is south of Aldie, cutting through the Bull Run Mountains.

Even though Stuart had been constantly pulling back his troopers from superior Union forces since June 17, his mission was successful. His skilled delaying tactics prevented the discovery of Lee's main force, and gave Lee's infantry time to traverse the Shenandoah Valley and reach Maryland.

That night, after pursuing Confederate cavalry on foot since early that morning, and being constantly under enemy fire, Charles was exhausted. Even so, he still had time to appreciate the beauty around him, and of course, his hungry men took full advantage of the abundance of local farms.

> ***"this is the finest part of Va. I have Been in yet the crops Look fine the Buildings are good and the homes in good condition part of the day was very warm the Boys are foraging at a great rate they having a good part of the country to work in I never was so Tired in my Life as I was Last night we encamped for the night … with nothing But my overcoat and Blanket over me"***

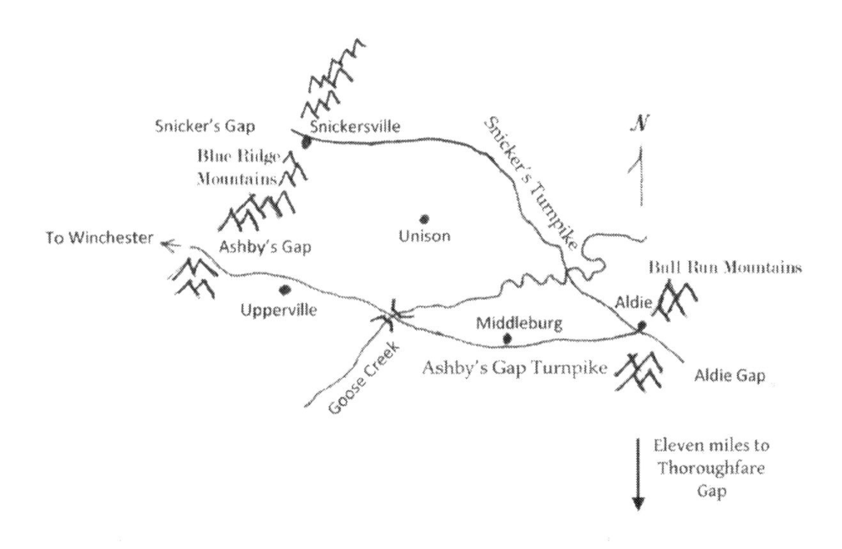

Aldie, Middleburg, Upperville; June 17 to June 21, 1863. Unison is the place where Jeb Stuart began his two day battle with advanced units of General Hookers army in November of 1862, which delayed the Army of the Potomac's attempt to get between Lee and Richmond. Now Stuart protected Lee's army as they marched north, in the Shenandoah Valley, toward Pennsylvania. Most roads are not shown.

On June 25, the 44th NY left Aldie via Carter's Mills and Leesburg, crossed the Potomac River at Edwards Ferry, and spent the night about four miles from the river. They marched 20 miles that day. The march continued for two more days, and on the evening of June 27, made camp about three miles from the city of Frederick. There they joined the bulk of the Army of the Potomac who were bivouacked in the area.

The morning of the 27th, General Hooker ordered General French to evacuate Harpers Ferry and, with his 10,000 men, join in the pursuit of Robert Lee's Army. Back in Washington, General Halleck got wind of the order and sent word for French to ***"pay no attention to General Hooker's orders."*** For Joseph Hooker, this was the last straw. Since Chancellorsville, Hooker had been constantly bickering with Halleck, mostly over what Hooker considered to be contradictory orders and orders that undermined his authority. At one p.m., he sent the following telegram to General Halleck:

....

Maj. Genl. H. W. Halleck, Sandy Hook, June 27, 1863, 1 P.M.
Commander in Chief,

> My original instructions require me to cover Harpers Ferry and Washington. I have now imposed on me in addition an enemy in my front of more than my number. I beg to be understood, respectfully, but firmly, that I am unable to comply with this condition with the means at my disposal, and earnestly request that I may at once be relieved from the position I occupy.

Joseph Hooker, Major General.

....

After Chancellorsville, there was little support for General Hooker in Washington. Lincoln, Halleck, and Secretary of War Edwin M. Stanton had all agreed that if Hooker were to tender his resignation it would be accepted. Colonel James Hardee left Washington around 7:30 that evening with orders for General Hooker and General George Meade, commander of the 5th Corps. He arrived at Frederick at 3 a.m. on June 28, woke Meade up, and informed him that he was now in command of the Army of the Potomac. General Meade and Colonel Hardee then went to General Hooker's headquarters and notified him that he was relieved of command. The largest battle of the war would begin not far from Frederick in three days. The new army commander had little time to prepare.

General Meade spent the remainder of June 28, developing a plan to deal with Lee. He appointed General George Sykes to take his place as commander of the 5th Corps, which included the 44th NY.

On the morning of June 29, the 44th NY left Frederick with the rest of the 5th Corps, and marched 18 miles. That night they camped between the small villages of Liberty and Jonesville. A hard rain during the night soaked everyone. Before it got light on the morning of June 30, the bugles were sounding, and the march resumed at 4:30 a.m. The 44th NY was leading the Third Brigade, which was leading the 5th Corps. After marching 23 miles they arrived at Union Mills and spent the night. By 9:30 a.m., July 1, they were back on the road. They crossed the Maryland State line into Pennsylvania about noon.

The 5th Corps received a heartfelt welcome as they crossed into Pennsylvania. Just the day before, the locals had endured Confederate General Stuart's cavalry passing through and taking all the horses, cattle, and provisions that could be found. The rebels paid for the goods with useless Confederate currency.

The 5th Corps reached Hanover late in the afternoon of July 1, and began to set up camp and have something to eat. While cooking supper rumors began running through the camp of a desperate battle that was occurring at Gettysburg. The 1st and 11th Corps had been attacked by overwhelming numbers of rebel troops and had been driven back at great loss. General Reynolds, a greatly admired general who commanded the 1st Corps, was dead.

Charles writes;

> ***"July 1, 1863***
>
> ***started this morning at half past 9 o'clock in the day The march was some what slow we are encamped at Hanover, a village in Penn The Rebs were here last night and had quite a Brush the Rebs have taken all that the people had in the shape of horses and cattle Left Hanover at 6 o'clock p.m. on the way to Gettesbourgh encamped 6 miles this side of the Town we have had a hard march to day got into camp about 11 o'clock at night we are to start in the morning at five o'clock"***

Lee's 2nd Corps under General Ewell Marches North

Three weeks earlier, back on June 8, Confederate General Richard Ewell's 2nd Corps, together with Longstreet's 1st Corps had reached Culpeper on their march north from Fredericksburg. They continued the march north from Culpeper on June 10, with Ewell's Corps in the lead, headed to Pennsylvania. A.P. Hill's 3rd Corps remained in Fredericksburg. Joseph Hooker, still at Falmouth, immediately knew when Lee withdrew most of his troops from Fredericksburg and wanted once again to flank the forces holding the city and destroy at least part of Lee's Army.

Both Lincoln and Halleck prevented him from interjecting his army between Lee's forces. Hooker's frustration with both Lincoln and Halleck grew. On June 12, Ewell entered the Shenandoah Valley near Front Royal with 20,000 men. He had two objectives: first, to travel north with the Blue Ridge Mountains on his right, acting as a screen to keep the Union Army ignorant of his location and second, to destroy the 8,000 man garrison of Union troops at Winchester, commanded by General Robert Milroy.

Winchester

Milroy believed he could hold the earthen forts he had been improving on the approaches to Winchester, and ignored advice to evacuate the town. On June 11 and June 14, General Halleck ordered Milroy's commanding officer, General Schenck, to have Milroy withdraw his force to Harpers Ferry. Milroy responded by telegraph the he was well prepared to hold Winchester and could hold it against any force ***"the rebels could afford to bring against it"***. Milroy did begin to comply with his orders to evacuate and that day sent 114 wagons full of supplies north to Harpers Ferry. However, on June 12, Milroy received orders from General Schenck to hold his position and await further orders. At that point, rebel forces cut off all communication between Milroy and his commanding officer stationed in Baltimore. The order to hold his position was the last order Milroy received from General Schenck.

At the time, Milroy and Schenck had no idea of the location of Lee's main forces, or what was bearing down on the town of Winchester. On the evening of June 13, General Milroy learned that Ewell's entire 2nd Corps was at his doorstep. Ewell had marched 70 miles in three days. General Schenck sent telegrams to Milroy telling him to withdraw, but all of the telegraph lines to Winchester were cut. After a number of engagements with Ewell's Corps, by the evening of June 14, Milroy's situation was hopeless. By failing to withdraw when possible, Milroy gave Ewell's troops time to surround his command.

Abandoning 200 wagons, an enormous amount of supplies and 23 guns, which he spiked, Milroy set out with his division around 1 a.m. on June 15, headed toward Harpers Ferry. Spiking a gun consisted of driving an iron nail into the touch-hole of a cannon, the passage at the breach of a gun (back of the barrel) that ignited the main charge inside the barrel. Spiking a gun made it useless until a skilled blacksmith could repair the damage.

They were about 4 miles north of Winchester when at 3:30 a.m. Milroy's column was ambushed from two sides. After two hours of fighting, mostly in darkness, Milroy's division fell apart. Milroy's only orders were, ***"Every man fight your way through to Harpers Ferry."*** About 4,000 Union prisoners were taken, and the division suffered 400 killed and wounded. Milroy made it to Harpers Ferry that night with 1,200 troops after a 30-mile forced march. Milroy was relieved of command; it was the last command he would hold.

Longstreet Moves North

Longstreet's 1st Corps marched north from Culpeper on June13, following the east side of the Blue Ridge Mountains, crossed into the Shenandoah Valley at Ashby's Gap and Snicker's Gap, and then marched on to Winchester. They arrived a couple of days after Union troops under Milroy had been defeated and routed. While crossing into the valley, Longstreet's men were protected by Jeb Stuart's cavalry, which, as we have seen, delayed a Union advance at Aldie, Middleburg, and Upperville. Hooker, not knowing where Lee's main body was, had chosen not to press beyond Ashby's Gap. On June 22, after Longstreet reached Winchester, Ewell's 2nd Corps continued north and crossed the Potomac at Shepherdstown and Williamsport. From there they moved on to Hagerstown and the next day, Chambersburg. By June 28, Ewell was nearing Cashtown, and General Longstreet, having crossed the Potomac on June 24, and June 25, was at Chambersburg.

Ewell had sent cavalry units ahead into southern Pennsylvania about a week before his main body of infantry, and "procured" many horses, cattle, and large quantities of supplies, all paid for with Confederate paper currency. Ewell's troopers returned on June 22. The cavalry raid and word of the coming Confederate infantry sent waves of panic and hysteria throughout the farms and small towns of southern Pennsylvania.

CHAPTER FOURTEEN

Lee Invades Pennsylvania

Land of Milk and Honey

When the Confederate infantry reached Pennsylvania they were shocked at how prosperous the farmers seemed, and how lush the countryside was in comparison to the war-ravaged farms of Virginia. To use a Biblical expression, it was a land of milk and honey. The local inhabitants however, were not inclined to share their abundance with Lee's Army and everyone who could fled north with what cattle, horses, and household goods they could manage. Those who remained were obliged to trade whatever the rebel army felt it needed for Confederate dollars, which everyone knew were worthless. The farmers of southern Pennsylvania saw the invaders as ragged, shoeless, and filthy, but noted all were well armed and under strict discipline.

General Jubal Early takes York

General Ewell sent General Robert Rode's Division to Carlisle and General Jubal Early's division through Gettysburg to York and on to Wrightsville on the Susquehanna River. The plan was to capture the bridge that crossed the Susquehanna River at Wrightsville and make a two-pronged attack from Carlisle and Wrightsville on a great prize, Harrisburg, the capital of Pennsylvania. Passing through the small town of Gettysburg on June 26, 1863, General Early's troops encountered some resistance from local militia who were easily driven away. General Early met with the town leaders of Gettysburg and demanded a requisition of supplies to be furnished to his men by the town. The town leaders claimed they could furnish no supplies as the people there were poor and supplies were not to be had. A search of Gettysburg revealed 2,000 rations in railcars intended for the local militia, but little else.

The Confederate troops moved on and arrived at York on the morning of June 28. The mayor and other town officials met them on the outskirts of the town and surrendered York to General Early. Early sent troopers on to Wrightsville to secure the bridge across the Susquehanna River. It was the world's longest covered bridge, more than a mile long and 40 feet wide, with a track for railroad traffic and another for wagon traffic. Defended by 1,200 green local militia, the Union volunteers were easily driven back across the bridge and as they fled, they set fire to the wooden structure. Early's troops fought the fire but were unable to stop destruction of the bridge. They did stop the fire from spreading on the Wrightsville side of the river and saved most of the town of Wrightsville from burning.

At York, General Early announced a levy on the city of $100,000 in cash, 2,000 pairs of shoes, 1,000 hats, 1,000 pair of socks, and three days rations for his troops. The next evening, after the destruction of the bridge over the Susquehanna River, and saving Wrightsville from the fires started by Union troops, General Early had a somewhat heated discussion with the city leaders of York over an appropriate amount for the levy. He was interrupted by word from Lee that General Meade was now in command of the Army of the Potomac, had crossed the Potomac River, and was now at Frederick. General Early was ordered to rejoin his Corps and unite with General Lee.

On June 30, at 5 a.m. General Early's division left York. Early had managed to get about 1,200 pair of shoes, all the hats, socks, and rations levied, and $28,600 in cash from the town of York. The Mayor claimed that was all the cash there was; all the bankers had fled with their money to Philadelphia. Early believed the mayor had made an honest effort and let the matter go. As he departed from York he left a message for the town on a subject he felt very deeply about;

"To the Citizens of York:

I have abstained from burning the railroad building and car shops in your town, because, after examination, I am satisfied the safety of the town would be endangered; and acting in the spirit of humanity which has ever characterized my government and its military authorities, I do not desire to involve the innocent in the same punishment with the guilty. Had I applied the torch without regard to consequences, I would have pursued a course that would have been fully vindicated as an act of just retaliation for the many authorized acts of barbarity perpetrated by your own army upon our soil. But we do not war upon women and children, and I trust the treatment you have met with at the hands of my soldiers will open your eyes to the monstrous iniquity of the war waged by your government upon the people of the Confederate States, and that you will make an effort to shake off the revolting tyranny under which it is apparent to all you are yourselves groaning.

J.A. Early, Major General, C.S.A."

In future campaigns the Federal Army would not be as careful of the lives and property of civilians as Jubal Early was, while in Pennsylvania.

As Jubal Early moved his troops through the Pennsylvania countryside to rejoin General Ewell's Corps, they encountered a number of people who were making mysterious signs to his troops. Upon investigating, he learned that some enterprising Yankees had passed through a short time before claiming, for a fee, to reveal secret signs to the people that would prevent the rebels from molesting them or their property. The signs were claimed to have their origin with the Knights of the Golden Circle, a secret society founded in 1854. The aim of the society was to establish a new country known as the Golden Circle where slavery was legal. This new country would have its capital in Havana, and once the southern United States had joined the Golden Circle, it would annex Mexico, Central America, parts of South America, and most of the Caribbean, if necessary by force. Secret knowledge, mysterious symbols, and strange rituals all played a big part in the order. Several members of President James Buchanan's administration were members of the order, as were many high officials in the Confederate States. To this day, the Knights of the Golden Circle are mentioned in whispered conversations about secret symbols, mysterious brotherhoods, and the search for lost Confederate gold.

General Early reported that his troops knew nothing of these matters and that *"the purchasers of the mysteries had been badly sold."*

Jeb Stuart Rides Around the Union Army (Again)

It was not until June 28 that Robert Lee learned of the change in command of the Union Army, and that Federal infantry has crossed the Potomac and were now near Frederick. It had been almost a week since Lee had heard from Jeb Stuart who was supposed to be acting as his eyes and ears. Lee, who by then was at Chambersburg, felt blind and frustrated. Stuart commanded six cavalry brigades; two were guarding the Blue Ridge passes, one was with Ewell approaching the Susquehanna, and the remaining three were with Stuart on another one of his rides around the Union army. Lee did not know it but Stuart was 70 miles away, with 6,000 troopers, just a short distance from Washington. Stuart had no idea where Lee was.

Stuart left Salem just after midnight on June 25. His orders were to collect all the supplies he could for the Army but at the same time to screen the movements of Elwell's Corps. He was to break off any encounters with large Union forces. Stuart headed east, passed through the Bull Run Mountains, and ran smack into the Union Army. He turned south. Feeling as frustrated as Lee, his orders were to cross the Potomac as soon as practicable, he then turned north and finally rested his exhausted men and horses at Fairfax Courthouse. Pushing on, desperate to reach Lee's army, he continued north. At Rockville, Maryland, his troopers captured 125 newly built Federal wagons filled with supplies headed toward Frederick. It was a worthy prize, but it slowed him down and delayed his re-joining Lee. Lee remained "blind" to the whereabouts of much of the Federal Army.

While passing through Hanover, just one day before the arrival of Charles Kelly and the 5th Corps, Stuart encountered Union cavalry and had a desperate struggle with the Federals. He was nearly captured. He suffered over a hundred men killed, wounded, or missing. The way west was blocked by Union troops so Stuart again pushed north, and passed through York on July 1. Finding that Jubal Early had left there the day before, he pressed on to Dover with his 17 mile-long column. His horses and men were nearing the point of collapse. Still not knowing where Lee was, Stuart headed to Carlisle, 25 miles away. Stuart's cavalry arrived in Carlisle late on July 1. It was then that two of his scouts arrived and reported they had found Lee at Gettysburg where there was a terrific battle in progress; his orders were to join Lee at once. After burning about half of the Federal army barracks buildings in Carlisle, at 1 a.m. on July 2, one week after setting out, Stuart put his exhausted troopers on the march to Gettysburg, 30 miles away. Stuart reached Lee late in the afternoon of the July 2, and arrived to an icy reception. Those who witnessed the reception, knowing how much Jeb Stuart revered Lee, described it as ***"painful beyond words"***.

Some reports of the time believed that Lee unjustly treated Jeb Stuart and that Lee had, if used properly, plenty of cavalry to act as his ***"eyes and ears"***. They point out much of Stuart's path had been forced by Union troop locations and Stuart was acting within his orders as far as possible.

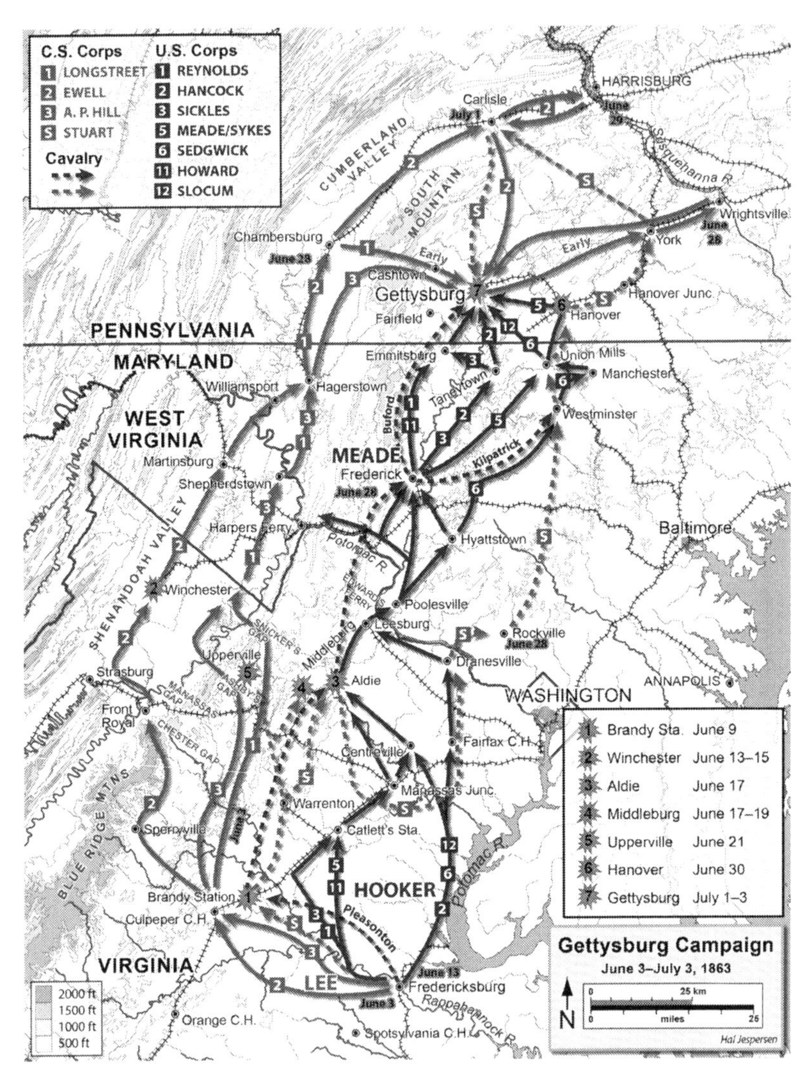

There is a wealth of information in this map by Hal Jespersen. The route north from Fredericksburg, for each of Lee's Corps commanders, is shown. Stuart's long ride around the Union army is also shown. Jubal Early's march through Gettysburg, to York and the bridge over the Susquehanna River at Wrightsville are indicated, and Ewell's near capture of Harrisburg before he was called to Gettysburg is illustrated. Charles Kelly is with the 5th Corps, traveling from Fredericksburg, through Aldie, Frederick, and Hanover, and from there to Gettysburg. "Map by Hal Jespersen, www.cwmaps.com"

Meade Orders Gettysburg Occupied

Meade had now been in command of the Army of the Potomac for three days. Both he and Lee were hurtling toward what would be the largest battle of the war in a place that neither wanted to fight. They both had lost control of events in the field.

Lee's staff made light of General Meade as being slow and overly cautious, but Lee had known Meade from his West Point days and commented, ***"General Meade will commit no blunder on my front and if I make one he will make haste to take advantage of it."***

On June 29, A.P. Hill, one of Lee's most aggressive generals, sent General Heth ahead to Cashtown where his Division made camp. There is a story that when Jubal Early passed through Gettysburg on June 26, his men had overlooked a large cache of shoes hidden in the town. Having got wind of this cache General Heth became determined to find those shoes. Although unlikely to be true, it makes a good story. What is more likely is that no less than ten roads converged on the small town, which made it important to both sides who were maneuvering for position in southern Pennsylvania.

On June 30, Confederate General Heth sent a brigade under command of Johnston Pettigrew to scout out Gettysburg. Pettigrew encountered Federal cavalry entering the town from the south on the Emmitsburg Road and withdrew to Cashtown. Lee had issued orders to avoid a general engagement, and Pettigrew had no idea what force was behind the troopers he encountered. The Union troopers passed through Gettysburg just before noon and camped west of Seminary Ridge, along the Chambersburg Pike.

Pettigrew had run into Union General John Buford in command of two brigades of cavalry, a force of about 2,800. The troopers were pickets for the 1st Corps, commanded by John Reynolds, who was less than six miles away; General Howard, commander of the 11th Corps and General Sickles of the 3rd Corps were not far behind. General Meade was digging in at Taneytown, 12 miles to the south. Beginning to have doubts about his plan to attack Lee, Meade had determined to make a defense near Taneytown along Pipe Creek, stretching from Middleburg to Manchester. Meade ordered the 1st Corps and the 11th Corps to occupy Gettysburg to secure approaches to the Potomac.

CHAPTER FIFTEEN

Gettysburg the Battle

July 1, 1863

On the morning of July 1, 1863, Union cavalry General Buford spread his troopers west of Gettysburg on both the north and south side of the Chambersburg Pike along Willoughby Run. Whether it was for shoes or not, General Heth, now under orders from Lee to occupy Gettysburg, came at the Union troopers with infantry lines three deep, under command of General James Archer. An excellent officer, it was Archer who had led the attack on Hazel Grove and broke the Union defense at Chancellorsville. Union and Confederate soldiers, both ordered to occupy Gettysburg, clashed south of the Chambersburg Pike at Willoughby Run. General Heth, believing he had the battle won, sent in another brigade, north of the road under command of General Joseph Davis, nephew of the President of the Confederacy, Jefferson Davis, to cinch the deal.

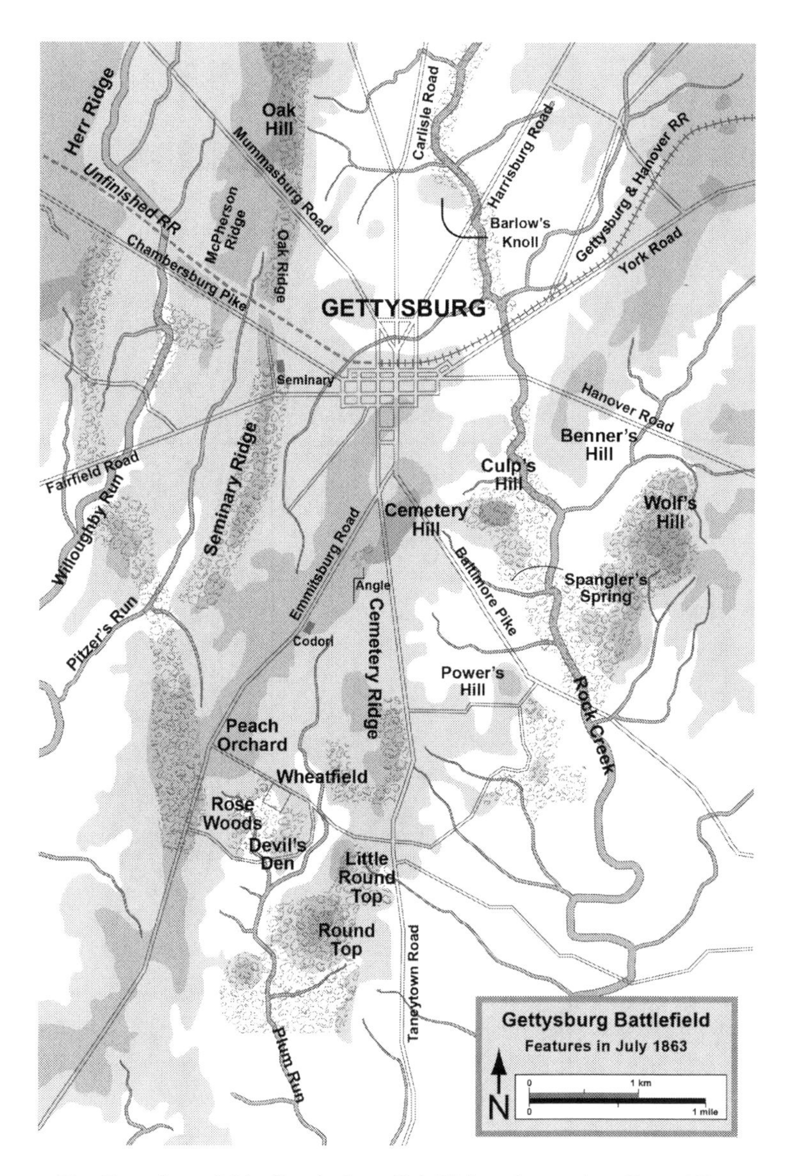

The Gettysburg field of battle from Oak Hill in the north to Round Top in the south. "Map by Hal Jespersen, www.cwmaps.com".

General Reynolds Arrives

General Buford's men, greatly outnumbered, were driven back from Willoughby Run and formed a line at the crest of McPherson's Ridge. General Buford had been watching the progress of the battle from the cupola of a local Lutheran Theological Seminary and did not like what he saw. Badly outnumbered, he was getting ready to pull out when John Reynolds, commander of the Union 1st Corps, arrived. It was about 8:30 in the morning. Reynolds told him the 1st Corps would be there in less than an hour and asked him to hold out. Buford said he would try. After sending word to Generals Howard and Sickles to get to Gettysburg immediately, Reynolds rode back to his lead division, under command of General James Wadsworth and led them cross-country from the Emmitsburg Road, over Seminary Ridge, and up the Chambersburg Pike toward McPherson's Ridge.

Reynolds sent one of Wadsworth's brigades to the north of Chambersburg Pike and one to the south, the latter being the shorter march for the troops. Around 10 a.m., while positioning his troops on the south side of the road, General Reynolds was shot and killed by a rebel marksman firing a minie ball from the woods ahead. John Reynolds, considered by many to be the best general in the Union Army, was the highest-ranking soldier killed at Gettysburg.

Meanwhile, Confederate General Archer, also on the south side of the road, led his men splashing across Willoughby Run. They rushed uphill toward the crest of McPherson's Ridge and there met a massive volley from the first of Wadsworth's brigades, famously known as the Iron Brigade. They had expected light fire from the carbines of Buford's cavalry but this was heavy infantry fire. Outnumbered and overwhelmed, they pulled back across the stream with heavy losses. Seventy-five rebels were captured, including General Archer.

On the north side of the road, the Confederate attack commanded by General Davis, was faring better. General Reynold's reinforcements rushing to the north side of the road had further to go and there was less cover than enjoyed by the brigade south of the road. Upon arrival, with no time to prepare a defense, the fresh Union troops were driven back to Seminary Ridge by a vigorous charge. The gray coats rushed over the crest of McPherson's Ridge and into the quarter mile wide valley beyond. The rebels funneled into a deep unfinished railroad cut and started up the slope of Seminary Ridge when two additional Union regiments, sent by the new commander of the 1st Corps, appeared on the slope above and ordered them to throw down their guns. Two hundred-fifty rebels surrendered; the rest ran westward. General Davis lost half of his command.

General Rodes Arrives

Around 1:30 p.m., General Robert Rodes, commander of one of Ewell's divisions, still seething because he had been called back from the north just when Harrisburg was within his grasp, came marching south on the Carlisle Road looking for a fight. What he saw was two armies facing off on two parallel ridges extending south from Oak Hill. The Union army's right flank was only a half mile away but now, aware of his presence, was beginning to fold back to face him. He deployed three brigades, held another in reserve, and attacked the Union's northern flank around 2 p.m. Not having taken the time to do adequate reconnaissance, the middle brigade of the three stumbled into a Union ambush. The Federal troops fired at near point-blank range into the surprised rebels. Half the brigade was killed or wounded. Aggressive assaults with little reconnaissance had worked for the Confederate Army before, but not now. Rodes' other two brigades finally reached their assigned objectives, aided by the reserve brigade, and came down hard on the Union flank. The bluecoats were driven back.

That afternoon Lee arrived from Chambersburg, and around 2:30 p.m. surveyed the battlefield from Herr Ridge. General Heth wanted to press the attack but Lee was hesitant. Longstreet had not yet arrived and Lee did not know what was before him. The Federal troops could be a corps or he could be facing the entire Union Army. Lee was sorely missing his cavalry, his eyes and ears, and was constantly asking, ***"Where is General Stuart?"***

General Early Arrives

However, as Lee watched the battle, he saw Rodes' Brigades recover from their clumsy attack and push forward. Then Jubal Early's division arrived from York along the Harrisburg Road. General Early immediately formed a line, three brigades wide, and positioned artillery to fire on Howard's flank. The artillery fire was very effective. At the same time, Early sent a brigade forward, commanded by General John Gordon, to support the left of Rodes' line. They engaged with Union infantry on a wooded hill west of Rock Creek near the northeast edge of

Gettysburg. As soon as Gordon's infantry brigade was engaged, Early sent in two more brigades, with artillery following. After a brief but savage fight, the Union troops, consisting of the 1st Division of Howard's XI Corps, collapsed and attempted to reform behind a low ridge in the direction of the town. General Early's troops took numerous prisoners, including the Union commander of the 1st Division, General Francis Barlow, who was severely wounded in the fight and left for dead by his men.

General Early's two additional brigades, which were on the east side of Rock Creek, advanced toward Gettysburg on General Gordon's left, and as described by General Early, ***"[drove]back into the town in great confusion the second line of the enemy."***

Watching Ewell's troop's drive the enemy back into the north side of Gettysburg caused Lee's hesitation to evaporate. He sent in Generals Heth and Pender, part of Lee's 3rd Corps, attacking from Seminary Ridge, into the town. By 4:30 p.m., Union troops were being driven out of Gettysburg.

Cemetery Hill and Cemetery Ridge

The panicked Federals, now commanded by General Howard, formed a line on Cemetery Hill, just a half mile south of the center of Gettysburg, and a hundred feet higher in elevation than the town. Howard immediately saw the importance of Cemetery Hill and was determined to hold it at all cost. About a half mile to the east was another small, rocky, and wooded hill which was 50 feet higher in elevation than Cemetery Hill, known as Culp's Hill. The two knolls were connected by a saddle of rocky ground and overlooked a ridge, called Cemetery Ridge, that extended two miles to the south from Cemetery Hill, running parallel with Seminary Ridge, which was about a mile to the west. The southern end of Cemetery Ridge dropped down into a low, timbered, and marshy area at which point a pair of conical heights emerged. The smaller one, reaching fifty feet higher than Cemetery Hill, was called Little Round Top, and the knoll just beyond was called Round Top. Round Top was a hundred feet higher in elevation than Little Round Top. From Culp's Hill to Round Top was a little less than four miles.

It was not until early afternoon of July 1 that General Meade learned General Reynolds was dead, a fierce battle was underway at Gettysburg, and the outcome was in doubt. Meade was shocked. Meade, who was overseeing construction of fortifications near Taneytown along Big Pipe Creek, his chosen location to meet the rebel Army, sent General Winfield Scott Hancock to take charge of the situation twelve miles to the north at Gettysburg. Hancock, with a small staff, arrived around 4 p.m. An officer who rode with him wrote, ***"Wreck, disaster, disorder, almost panic that precedes disorganization, defeat and retreat were everywhere."*** Hancock found General Howard desperately trying to stave off a general retreat, a position that General Howard had also found himself in two months earlier at Chancellorsville. After examining the terrain, General Hancock decided to hold Culp's Hill, Cemetery Hill and Cemetery Ridge. He sent reinforcements to Culp's Hill and Cemetery Hill, and extended the Union line along Cemetery Ridge. He saw this as a good defensive position, ***"although somewhat exposed to be turned by the left."*** Hancock sent word to Meade that he would hold until more Federal troops arrived.

General Longstreet Arrives

About that time, James Longstreet arrived, riding several hours ahead of his troops, and joined Robert Lee. He too saw that the Federal line was exposed on the Union left. He very badly wanted to swing around the Union flank at Little Round Top and position his troops between the Federals and the city of Washington, forcing Meade to attack what would by then be fortified positions. Lee would have none of it. The enemy was on Cemetery Hill and that was where he would attack them. Lee had sent somewhat vague orders to General Ewell to take Cemetery Hill but before Ewell even received those orders, Lee received a message from Ewell saying he thought he could take Cemetery Hill if General A.P. Hill would attack at the same time from the west. Lee responded that the only support he could give was artillery but repeated his earlier orders to ***"carry the hill occupied by the enemy, if he found it practicable, but to avoid a general engagement until the arrival of the other divisions of the army."*** As Union troops poured in from the east and took positions on Culp's Hill, Cemetery Hill, and along Cemetery Ridge, Longstreet sensed that it was not the time to argue with General Lee. Longstreet mounted his horse and road back toward Cashtown to hurry the arrival of his troops, who were six miles away.

The Powerful Drug of Victory

General Lee was flush with the powerful drug of victory. Once again, he had met the Union Army and driven it from the field. Lee remembered The Peninsula, 2nd Manassas, Fredericksburg, and Chancellorsville; and indeed they were all remarkable achievements. But it is difficult not to recall the words of James Longstreet, after Lee's stunning victory at Chancellorsville, that four more such "victories" would leave the Army of Northern Virginia with a handful of men, while the Army of the Potomac would remain strong. The Yankees could easily replace their losses. The south could not. Lee was using up his Army.

Confederate casualties for the day were about six thousand, Union casualties not quite nine thousand. In places, the fighting had been some of the bloodiest of the war. When General Lee ordered Heth's Division to sweep Seminary Ridge around 2:30 p.m., the 26th North Carolina Regiment ran headlong into the 24th Michigan. When they started, the 26th North Carolina was 843 men strong. In less than an hour, they were 212 men strong. The 24th Michigan, who they attacked, suffered 73% casualties. General Heth was knocked unconscious in the fight and remained so for over 24 hours. Still, Lee was pacing back and forth anxious to hear guns from Cemetery Hill that would herald Ewell's attack on the rocky fortress. There was four hours of daylight remaining to complete the destruction of the Yankee Army and Lee wanted to make good use of those hours.

To Lee's regret, General Ewell was not Stonewall Jackson. Using the discretion in his orders, Ewell decided that without help from General Hill he could not, with any chance of success, attack the constantly increasing Union forces on Cemetery Hill. Ewell's troops were sorely battered from the days fighting, Cemetery Hill was bristling with Union artillery, and there were rumors of a Federal column soon arriving along the York Pike. By 6:30 p.m., Union troops had been driven from Gettysburg, and the valley became quiet, the first day of the battle was over.

General Lee was not unaware of Longstreet's arithmetic, but he knew that he could not position his Army in one place and let the larger Union Army come to him. He did not have that luxury. He was receiving no help from Richmond in keeping his supply routes open or in replenishing his losses. He could not advance on Baltimore, Harrisburg, or Washington, with Meade's Army to his rear, and he could not sustain his own army if he stayed in one place. His only option was to crush Meade's Army of the Potomac, now in his front.

When General Longstreet rode to the west to hurry his troops, he was still determined to change Lee's mind, from wanting to attack the Yankees to finding a good position and letting the Yankees do the attacking. As Longstreet left Lee's headquarters, Charles Kelly, a dozen miles away to the east, had his coffee, pork, and hardtack interrupted by rumors of a large battle at Gettysburg. It had been a long tiring day of marching to reach Hanover, and now the 44th NY learned their day was not over. By 6 p.m., they were again on the march. As they marched, a rumor spread up and down the long column of the 5th Corps that McClellan had just replaced General Halleck as Commander of the Union Army. Cheers and hurrahs travelled in great waves along the entire column. Of course, there was no truth to the rumor. They kept going until around 11 p.m. and stopped for the night six miles short of Gettysburg. The entire 5th Corps was exhausted.

Gettysburg, July 2, 1863

General Meade arrived at the top of Cemetery Ridge after midnight on the morning of July 2, and did a moonlight inspection of his lines. From the ridge, he saw thousands of rebel campfires arrayed around Gettysburg and knew that this is where he would have to make his stand. His plan to form his army along Pipe Creek was gone. He would fight Lee at Gettysburg.

Union troops continued to arrive for the rest of the night and spread south along Cemetery Ridge. Around 5 a.m., as part of Meade's actions to strengthen Culp's Hill, Meade ordered General Geary to have two divisions from the 12th Corps leave their isolated position far to the left, where they formed a line from Cemetery Ridge to the base of Little Round Top. They were ordered to withdraw and take up position on the Union's far right at Culp's Hill. General Sickles was ordered to take up Geary's position with part of the 3rd Corps. When he received the order General Geary was reluctant to leave because relief troops had not yet arrived to take up his position at the base of Little Round Top. General Geary sent a Staff officer to Sickles' headquarters, explaining the importance of the position, and requested that one of General Sickles' officers be sent to acquaint himself with the position so Sickles would be ready to post his troops when they arrived. For an answer all he got was, ***"General Sickles will attend to it in due time."*** Having no option, General Geary sent his men from the base of Little Round Top to Culp's Hill.

General David Birney, commander of Sickles' 1st Division, arrived at Little Round Top around 7 a.m. and formed a line extending from near the base of Little Round Top to the position held by the rest of Sickles' 3rd Corps. He formed his picket line 300 yards to his front along the Emmitsburg Road.

Longstreet Prepares to Attack the Union Left

On July 2, despite Longstreet's protests, General Lee directed him to prepare to attack the far southern flank of the Union Army on Lee's right, which made up the Union left. Oddly, his orders were not issued until 11 a.m. that day. Longstreet commanded three divisions, two of which were present: one commanded by John Bell Hood and the other by Lafayette McLaws. Longstreet's 3rd Division, commanded by George Pickett, was still in-route to the battlefield.

Lee's plan was to flank the Union forces on his right with Longstreet's two divisions, which had about 15,000 men. Richard Anderson's division, and then William Pender's division would attack in echelon, folding up the Yankee forces as the attack went from south to north, along the Emmitsburg Road. At the same time, Hill's three divisions, commanded by General Rodes, General Early, and General Johnson, would attack Cemetery Hill and Culp's Hill from the north, mostly to hold the Union troops on the hill, but also to advance if the opportunity presented itself. General Hill's signal to attack would be the moment he heard Longstreet's guns begin the attack from the south.

As the afternoon unfolded, a number of problems for both sides became apparent. For Longstreet, a poorly scouted route resulted in a confused and tiring trek that added miles of marching for his men who were try to get into position, while at the same time attempting to avoid detection by Union flagmen on Little Round Top. This only added to Longstreet's reservations about Lee's plan. In addition the Union line was not on the Emmitsburg Road near Gettysburg as Robert Lee believed and had planned for. The Union line was above the Emmitsburg Road to the east, on Cemetery Ridge. The biggest surprise of all was when General Hood finally reached his position at the far right of the Confederate line. From directly west of Devil's Den, and Little Round Top, General Hood saw an entire corps of Union troops clustered on a small knoll covered with peach trees, a half mile to his north, and nearly a mile ahead of the Union line on Cemetery Ridge. They were farther south and west than Lee had planned for. This force could flank his position if he followed orders. This was not part of the plan!

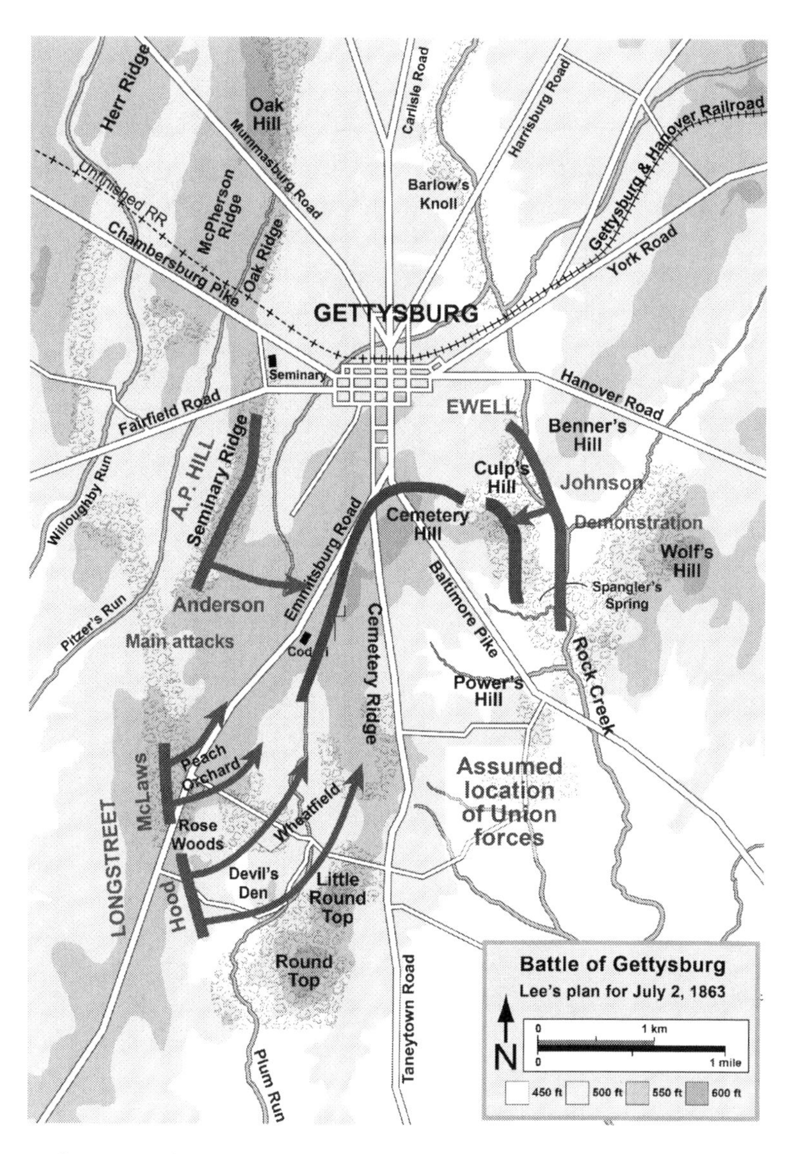

General Lee's plan for the 2nd day at Gettysburg. When General Hood arrived at his starting position on the far right of Lee's army, he saw an entire Union corps stretching from Devil's Den to the Peach Orchard and then north along the Emmitsburg Road. This was not part of Lee's plan and, if Hood followed orders, there would be large numbers of Union troops on his right flank and to his rear. Lee would not change his orders. "Map by Hal Jespersen, www.cwmaps.com".

It was not part of General Meade's plan either. Meade thought the 3rd Corps, commanded by General Dan Sickles, was up on top of Cemetery Ridge protecting the Union left flank, which is where he had put Sickles six hours earlier. Instead, the 10,700 men of the 3rd Corps were almost a mile to the west, strung out from Devils Den to a peach orchard and then north along Emmitsburg Road. To the right of the 3rd Corps was now a large gap between the 3rd Corps and the 2nd Corps. The 3rd Corps was supposed to be on the left of the 2nd Corps up on Cemetery Ridge. But now the gap created by General Sickles being forward of the Union line by almost a mile created a perfect path for Confederate General Anderson to march to the top of Cemetery Ridge and attack the Union forces on Cemetery Hill and Culp's Hill from the rear.

In addition, Little Round Top was empty, except for a handful of signalmen. Unlike its bigger cousin to the south, Little Round Top had been logged off less than a year before. It formed an unobstructed platform to station artillery and rain death down on the Union line. Although General Sickles' 3rd Corps had been given the task of defending this knoll when General Geary was sent to Culp's Hill that morning, Sickles men were a quarter of a mile west of the base of Little Round Top with their far left flank at Devil's Den.

Dan Sickles, a consummate politician, spent the rest of his life defending his decision to move his Corps forward without orders and without notifying the commander of the 2nd Corps, General Hancock, whose left flank he left twisting in the wind. Sickles' reason centered on four acres of high ground, which rose 20 to 30 feet in elevation above the surrounding terrain and made up the only high ground between Seminary Ridge and Cemetery Ridge. The high ground was covered with one of local farmer Joseph Sherfy's peach orchards and would forever after be known as "the Peach Orchard". General Sickles believed that if the rebels had possession of the peach orchard knoll, they would deliver an assault on his position ***"with advantage and force that would have given Lee the victory."*** General Sickles' decision cost the Union Army dearly, and cost Sickles his right leg, which, after 34 years of politicking, he leveraged into being awarded the Congressional Medal of Honor for conspicuous gallantry in the field. He always believed that by delaying General Longstreet, he had saved the Union Army from defeat at Gettysburg.

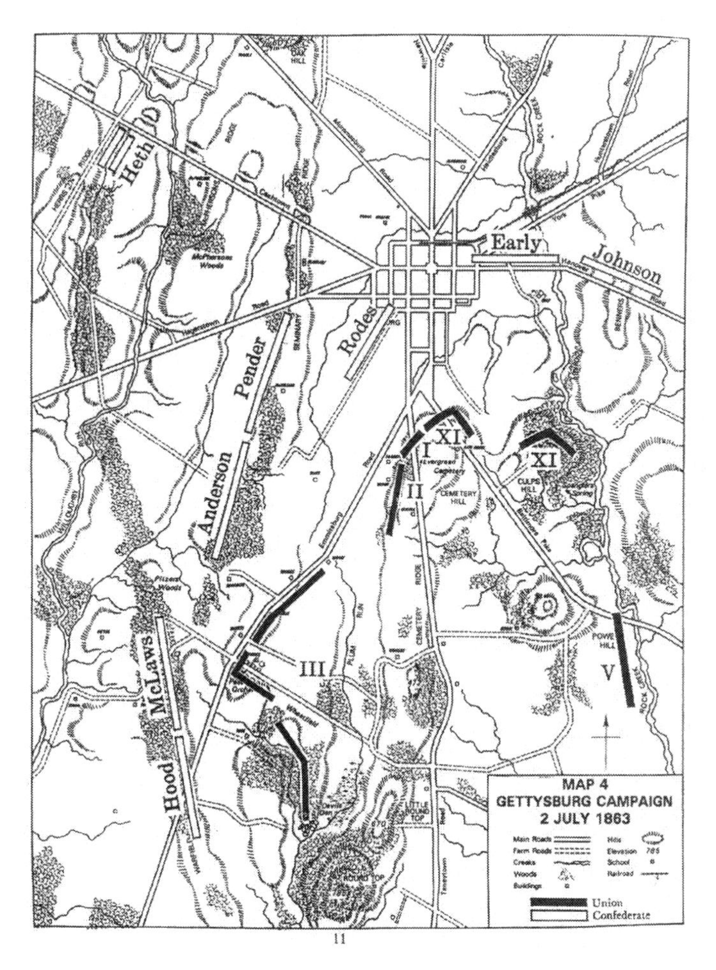

This map shows the positions of the Union and Confederate Armies around Gettysburg at approximately 3 pm, July 2nd. Little Round Top is at the lower center of the map, and at this time was not occupied by Federal troops with the exception of a signalman squad. Charles Kelly is with the 5th Corps, near the point that the Baltimore Pike crosses Rock Creek. The Peach Orchard and Wheatfield are shown occupied by Sickles' 3rd Corps at this time. Devil's Den is directly west of Little Round Top. The large gap in the Federal line between Sickles' 3rd Corps and Hancock's 2nd Corps is evident. The Trostle Farm house (referred to below) is a little north of the Wheatfield road on the west side of Plum Creek, also called Plum Run. Note that elevations are shown at Round Top, Little Round Top, and other places. For example, the elevation of Little Round top is shown as "670 feet". (This map is courtesy of the Army University Press, Gettysburg Staff Ride Briefing Book, U.S. Army Center of Military History)

Lee had also taken note of the small knoll covered with peach trees, and believed when Longstreet reached the peach orchard he would be south of the Union line and therefore able to establish his artillery on the knoll without resistance. When Lee learned the peach orchard was occupied by Union troops his conviction of its importance grew; he later wrote, ***"it appeared that if the position held by it could be carried, its possession would give facilities for assailing and carrying the more elevated ground and crest beyond."***

Charles Arrives at Gettysburg

Charles Kelly was woken around 3:30 a.m. on July 2, by the blare of bugles. After a hasty breakfast, his men, along with the rest of the 5th Corps, were on the march. They reached the Union position at Cemetery Ridge around 7 a.m. The 5th Corps waited there in reserve, behind the right of the Union line. Around 2 p.m., the Union 6th Corps arrived, and took up the position of the 5th Corps, which was moved to south of the Baltimore Pike on the west side of Rock Creek.

It was about an hour after noon on July 2 that General Sickles began to move his 3rd Corps down from Cemetery Ridge to take possession of the peach orchard. Around three o'clock, Longstreet began an artillery barrage while his troops formed into a line of attack. Hearing the rebel guns on his left, General Meade ordered the 5th Corps forward and rode with members of his staff to see what Sickles was doing. Meade had placed Sickles' 3rd Corps on his left flank that morning. He was shocked at what he saw. Riding up to Sickles, showing remarkable constraint, he told Sickles, ***"General I am afraid you are too far out."*** Claiming he could hold his position if supported, Sickles offered to withdraw his corps. General Meade could see that Sickles' 3rd Corps was stretched along a front longer than could be defended with the troops Sickles had, and saw it was too late to withdraw without triggering a disaster. Meade said he would send the 5th Corps and a division of the 2nd Corps to support Sickles' position. General Meade, artillery shells exploding in the air around him, rode off to get more help with thoughts of Chancellorsville and other Union disasters running through his head.

Little Round Top

Before General Meade rode out to meet with General Sickles, he ordered his Chief Engineer, General Warren, to investigate the firing of guns on his left flank. ***"Warren! I hear a little peppering going on in the direction of the little hill off yonder. I wish that you would ride over and if anything serious is going on... attend to it."***

Little Round Top; July 1863. (Library of Congress)

General Warren headed out toward "the little hill yonder" with his staff. Aided by Lieutenants Washington Roebling, Ranald Mackenzie, and others, Warren had chosen his staff well. For example, Lieutenant Roebling, a consummate engineer, would attain worldwide fame after the war for supervising the construction of the Brooklyn Bridge, at the time the longest suspension bridge in the world. Roebling's father, John Roebling, designed the bridge with his son's participation in every phase of the design.

Lieutenant Mackenzie would achieve the rank of Brigadier General before the end of the war. Ulysses Grant regarded Mackenzie as the most promising young officer in the Union army.

Years later, Roebling wrote of Warren's arrival at the base of Little Round Top. ***"Arriving at the foot of the rugged little Knob [Little Round Top] I ran up to the top while Warren stopped to speak to General Weed. One glance sufficed to note the head of [General John Bell] Hood's Texans coming up the rocky ravine which separates Little and Big Round Top. I ran down, told General Warren, he came up with me and saw the necessity of immediate action."***

Before going to the summit, Warren convinced General Weed, on his way with the 5th Corps to support Sickles, to send some guns up Little Round Top. Warren continued with Roebling to the summit and as Lieutenant Roebling reports, Warren immediately saw what others had seen, including the handful of flag signalmen on Little Round Top. For some time they had been trying to get someone's attention to the impending danger. Warren saw that if immediate action was not taken, Little Round Top would shortly be a Confederate stronghold that he believed could imperil the Union Army position along Cemetery Ridge.

Warren sent Lieutenant Mackenzie to General Sickles, with an urgent request to send troops to the knoll. Sickles refused, saying that his whole command was necessary to defend his front. There are numerous accounts of exactly what happened next and exactly when it happened. The accounts vary, but apparently Lieutenant Mackenzie continued on to General Sykes (5th Corp) with a note from Warren requesting at least a Division be immediately sent to him. General Sykes promptly sent a Captain from his staff to General Barnes, commander of the 1st Division of the 5th Corps, ordering a brigade to Little Round Top.

The Extreme Left Flank of the Federal Army

The courier rode hard toward the head of the 5th Corps column, which was momentarily halted while on its way to reinforce General Sickles. General Sykes and General Barnes were up ahead scouting a position for their troops to aid Sickles' left. The courier was searching for General Barns when Colonel Strong Vincent, commander of the Third Brigade of the 1st Division, interrupted him and asked what his orders were. Upon learning that a brigade had been ordered to Little Round Top, Vincent, whose brigade was just then near the north east corner of the base of the knoll, immediately detached from the rest of the 5th Corps. His brigade of four regiments, the 20th Maine, the 16th Michigan, the 83rd Pennsylvania, and the 44th New York, went at double-time, up the slope, and over the knoll. It was shortly before 4:30 p.m. on July 2.

The Third Brigade passed near the summit of Little Round Top on the east side. Colonel Vincent rode ahead and scouted the positions he wanted each of his regiments to occupy. When his men arrived Vincent immediately deployed his troops about two thirds of the way down the south and the west slope of Little Round Top with the 20th Maine facing roughly to the south. The 83rd Pennsylvania was immediately to the right of the 20th Maine, and Charles Kelly, with the 44th New York, was on the right of the 83rd Pennsylvania. They were facing southwest. The 16th Michigan, on the right of the 44th NY, was facing west.

The 44th New York and the 83rd Pennsylvania

Skirmishers were immediately ordered out in front of each regiment of the Third Brigade. The 44th NY sent Company B commanded by Captain Larabee. After advancing down the hill about two hundred yards, Company B ran headlong into the Confederate line of battle; the rebels were three deep, coming fast up the hill. Captain Larabee was killed; those who could made it back to the line of the 44th NY, and the rest were killed or captured. The first of three rebel regiments to hit the Union line was the 4th Texas. They charged directly into the 44th NY. When the rebels reached within forty yards of the 44th NY's line, a massive volley stopped them, and heavy firing continued for some time as the 5th Texas and the 4th Alabama joined the 4th Texas in the attack on the 44th NY and 83rd Pennsylvania. Finally, the Confederate forces fell back and then made another assault, this time extending their attack from the 44th NY to the 20th Maine on Vincent's left flank. It was about a quarter after five on that hot sunny afternoon when the Texan and Alabamian regiments were driven back. The 44th NY then turned their fire to their right front to help protect the left flank of the 16th Michigan. During the attack, two more Confederate regiments arrived from the summit of Round Top, Colonel Oates' 15th Alabama, along with the 47th Alabama. They joined in the assault on the Third Brigade, charging straight into the 83rd Pennsylvania and 20th Maine. They too were driven back. Colonel Vincent's Third Brigade now held the extreme left flank of the Union Army.

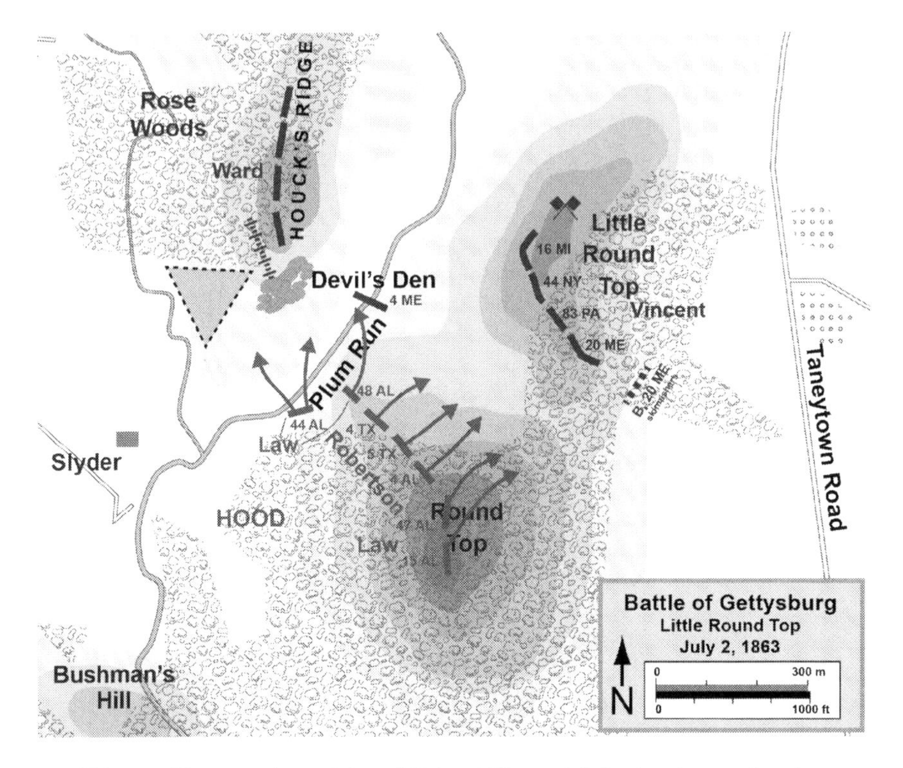

This map illustrates the position of Colonel Vincent's brigade minutes after they arrived on Little Round Top. Charles Kelly is with the 44th NY. "Map by Hal Jespersen, www.cwmaps.com".

Colonel James Rice, commander of the 44th N.Y., and later commander of the Third Brigade, described the first hour after arrival at Little Round Top:

> ***"The brigade had scarcely formed in line of battle and pushed forward its skirmishers, when a division of the enemy's forces, under General Hood, made a desperate attack along the entire line of the brigade. He approached in three columns with no skirmishers in advance... Massing two or three brigades of his force, he tried for an hour in vain to break the line of the Forty-Fourth N.Y. and the 83d Penn., charging again and again within a few yards of these unflinching troops. At every charge he was repulsed with terrible slaughter."***

Colonel Oates and the 15th Alabama

A half hour earlier, around 4:30 p.m., the 15th Alabama, commanded by Confederate Colonel William Oates, was at the extreme right of General Hood's division. They had already marched 25 miles that hot dry day. As part of General Hood's attack, they advanced up the west side of Round Top driving a few Union skirmishers before them. The 47th Alabama joined them on their left. They reached the summit of Round Top around 5 p.m., exhausted. Colonel Oates believed that Round Top was the perfect place to position artillery to rain down on Little Round Top and Cemetery Ridge; He saw the position as key to winning the entire battle.

A few minutes after reaching the summit of Round Top, a member of General Law's staff, arrived and asked Colonel Oates why he had halted. The captain informed Oates that General Hood had been severely wounded and that General Law was in command of the division; his orders were to press forward. Protesting that General Law could not know the importance of holding this position, and that Round Top should be occupied with artillery, Oates reluctantly ordered his tired troops down the north slope of Round Top toward Little Round Top. Joining in the attack around half past five, not aware that twenty minutes earlier Vincent's Third Brigade had occupied the ground immediately to their the front, the 15th Alabama and 47th Alabama got within 40 or 50 paces of a rocky ledge running parallel with the Alabaman's line when according to Colonel Oates, the Yankees ***"poured into us the most destructive fire I ever saw."***

After a brief pause, around 5:30 p.m., Charles Kelly's entire Third Brigade was hit again, this time by six regiments from Texas and Alabama, three of which came crashing into the 83rd Pennsylvania and 44th NY. The 15th Alabama charged into the 20th Maine, the 47th Alabama into the 83rd Pennsylvania and 20th Maine, while the 48th Alabama flanked the 16th Michigan.

The 16th Michigan

The 44th NY tried to protect the left flank of the 16th Michigan with oblique fire, but the right of the 16th was flanked by the 48th Alabama and fell apart. While trying to rally his brigade's right flank, Colonel Vincent was mortally wounded. Colonel James Rice, commander of the 44th NY, assumed command of the Third Brigade. Command of the 44th NY went to Lieutenant Colonel Freeman Conner.

General Warren, at the signalman's station on the north side of Little Round Top was unaware of the arrival of the third Brigade on the south side of the knoll. Accounts vary as to the exact details, but General Warren, accompanied by Lieutenant Roebling rode down the north slope of Little Round Top and intercepted Warren's old brigade, commanded by General Stephen Weed, a friend of General Warren. Warren took responsibility and detached the 140th New York, commanded by another friend, Colonel Patrick O'Rourke, and headed them up the knoll at double time, guided by Lieutenant Roebling, to the western crest of Little Round Top. It was about 5:30 p.m. Warren then returned to General Meade's headquarters; Roebling, with the 140th New York, arrived at the western crest of the hill shortly after Vincent had fallen.

The 140th NY, five hundred men strong, plowed into the rebel assault against the 16th Michigan and prevented the 16th Michigan's complete collapse. Three more Union regiments soon followed, and the gray coats were driven back. The fighting had been horrific. Colonel O'Rourke was hit in the neck by a minie ball and killed. General Weed fell victim to a sharpshooter from Devils Den and was mortally wounded. 1st Lieutenant Charles Hazlett, who commanded two 10-pound Parrott rifles that had been manhandled up the hill with Lieutenant Roebling and a number of others straining at the wheels, rushed to attend to the fallen General Weed. He too was killed. The assault on the 16th Michigan had been a near thing. For the time, the right flank of the Third Brigade was secure.

The 20th Maine

The fourth regiment in Vincent's Brigade, the 20th Maine Infantry Regiment, commanded by Colonel Joshua Chamberlain, was on the extreme left of the Third Brigade which was on the extreme left of the entire Union Army. Chamberlain states in his report of the battle that Colonel Vincent expected a desperate attack would occur here that would attempt to turn his position, and ordered him to "hold that ground at all hazards". It was the last order Chamberlain would receive from Vincent. After establishing his line to take advantage of, as Chamberlain described it, ***"the rough, rocky, and stragglingly wooded ground,"*** he detached his Company B, commanded by Captain Morrill, together with some sharpshooters to cover his left flank. From his left, they moved downhill to the smooth and thinly wooded hollow at the southern base of Little Round Top, and across toward the base of Round Top.

After failing to collapse the center of the Third Brigade, the gray coats, as expected, did attempt to flank the 20th Maine by attacking from Chamberlain's left. When Colonel Oates'15th Alabama, believing they would find an unguarded flank, got within a dozen yards of Chamberlain's line the Union troops opened up on them and drove them back. The assault continued for some time. Chamberlain reports that at times squads of the enemy broke through his line and the fighting was hand-to-hand; ***"the edge of the fight rolled backward and forward like a wave."*** The 83rd Pennsylvania and 44th NY, after what was now three assaults, continued to protect Chamberlain's right, and prevented the 20th Maine from being flanked. Chamberlain, around 6 p.m., then saw the 15th Alabama massing at the base of the hill in two lines directly to his front, preparing for another assault.

A few minutes later, as his men prepared for yet another assault, Colonel Oates, learned that the 47th Alabama on his left, was outflanked by the 83rd Pennsylvania, and parts of the 44th NY. The Yankees poured fire into the 47th Alabama, cutting down the rebels and severely wounding their commander, while driving the regiment from the shelter of the large rocks and trees near the base of the hill. After heavy losses, the 47th Alabama left their wounded commander on the field and retreated in confusion up the north face of Round Top. Oates also learned that there were Union troops to his right and on his flank: they turned out to be Captain Morrill's Company B, with the 14 sharpshooters that Chamberlain had placed there earlier. Colonel Oates had lost over 130 men out of the 500 he had started the day with, and his men were out of water, low on ammunition, and exhausted. Colonel Oates' brother, Lieutenant John Oates, had just been struck by eight minie balls and killed. The Colonel figured it was time to go. He sent out word to prepare to retreat and regroup near the summit of Round Top. Minutes later, Colonel Joshua Chamberlain attacked.

Chamberlain knew a third of his regiment had been killed or wounded, and those still fighting were down to their last one or two rounds of ammunition. Some had no ammunition. They could not withstand another assault. Running out of options, he ordered his men to fix bayonets and charge. Fortune smiled on Joshua Chamberlain that day; his desperate attack turned out to be perfectly timed with the normal confusion of Colonel Oates getting his regiment's withdrawal underway. Colonel Chamberlain describes what happened next,

> *"At that crisis, I ordered the bayonet. The word was enough. It ran like a fire along the line, from man to man, and rose into a shout, with which they sprang forward upon the enemy, now not 30 yards away. The effect was surprising; many of the enemy's first line threw down their arms and surrendered. An officer fired his pistol at my head with one hand, while he handed me his sword with the other. Holding fast by our right, and swinging forward our left, we made an extended "right wheel" before which the enemy's second line broke, and fell back, fighting from tree to tree, many being captured, until we had swept the valley and cleared the front of nearly our entire brigade."*

Peach Orchards and Wheat Fields

The struggle on the slopes of Little Round Top was a small part of the battle that day.

Confederate General John Bell Hood started his attack on the Emmitsburg Road at four p.m. as ordered. Three times he had requested he be allowed to send troops south around Round Top and attack the enemy flank. He saw that advancing up the Emmitsburg Road with part of the Union 3rd Corps now on his right flank, rather than to the north near Gettysburg as Lee believed, made no sense. His Commander, General Longstreet, agreed but could not get Lee to change his orders. A few minutes after the attack began, General Hood was hit with shrapnel from a bursting cannon shell and severely wounded. General Evander Law took command of his division.

By 5 o'clock Hood's Division, now Law's Division, had driven the Yankees from Devil's Den and Sickles' left was retreating toward Plum Run. By six o'clock Confederate General McLaws' division had hit Sickles hard at the peach orchard and along Emmitsburg Road. General Law's and General McLaws' troops hit Union General David Birney's Division, part of General Sickles 3rd Corps, from three sides and nearly destroy it as a fighting unit. The casualties were severe. The peach orchard was abandoned by Sickles' troops around 6:15 p.m. During the fight, General Sickles was severely wounded; he would lose his right leg. Later, General Birney, now in command of Sickles' 3rd Corps, watching the survivors of his division gather around him on Cemetery Ridge, whispered to one of his officers, ***"I wish I were already dead."***

Confederate General Anderson's division assaulted Cemetery Ridge through the gap created by Sickles but was driven back by General Hancock's 2nd Corps with heavy casualties on both sides. It was a frantic struggle all along Hancock's position, one that Lee's troops almost won. At one point just before 7:30 p.m., the Confederate forces were driving Hancock's men before them. Some Confederate units made it to the top of Cemetery Ridge and were in sight of Meade's headquarters, but without support were unable to hold the position. In danger of losing his artillery at the base of Cemetery Ridge, and perhaps his entire line, General Hancock declared that he needed five more minutes to allow help to arrive. He ordered eight companies of the 1st Minnesota, totaling 262 men, to charge into the Confederate assault. They were outnumbered six to one but managed to stall the rebels at Plum Run. In fifteen minutes, the 1st Minnesota lost 82% of its men. General Hancock got his five minutes.

Savage fighting continued across a 19 acre wheat field located about half way between the peach orchard and Cemetery Ridge. Driven back through the wheat field to Plum Run, the Yankees left 4,000 dead and dying soldiers, both Union and Confederate, behind. Meade poured in reinforcements and by 7 p.m., his line began to stabilize just east of Plum Run. By eight o'clock, some ground west of Plum Run had been re-gained by Federal forces, with the bulk of the Union Army positioned along Cemetery Ridge. There was now a solid line of Federal troops from Little Round Top, all along Cemetery Ridge, to Cemetery Hill, and on to Culp's Hill, just as General Meade had intended that morning.

Cemetery Hill and Culp's Hill

On the north end of the battle, General Richard Ewell started his artillery barrage onto Culp's Hill and Cemetery Hill as soon as he heard Longstreet's cannon from the south. He had placed a twenty-gun battery atop Benner's Hill that stretched across the Hanover Road about a mile east of Gettysburg. Benner's Hill was 1,000 yards from Culp's Hill and about 1500 yards from Cemetery Hill. Major Joseph Latimer, a rising star in Lee's Army, commanded the Confederate battery, he was 19 years old. One of General Ewell's staff officers wrote of Latimer that he was ***"idolized by his own men and the infantry of his division as well. The latter called him the 'Boy Major' and sometimes cheered him as he passed-a distinction they conferred on very few."*** The Federal artillery on Cemetery Hill and Culp's Hill outgunned Latimer, both in quantity and in quality. Thirty-seven well-protected

Federal guns bore down on the Confederate guns positioned on the bare unprotected Benner's Hill, and after an hour-long artillery duel, Latimer began withdrawing his guns. Only four of Latimer's guns remained in action on the hill when, around dusk, a bursting shell hit both Latimer and his horse; the horse fell and pinned Latimer to the ground. His left arm had to be amputated. Joseph Latimer died from gangrene on August 1, 1863, less than a month before his twentieth birthday.

It wasn't until after 8 p.m. that Confederate General Edward Johnson attacked Culp's Hill with 4,700 troops. General Meade, who had pulled troops from his right and sent them to face Longstreet's attack on the Federal left, had depleted Culp's Hill of defenders. General George Green and his 1,400 troops were tasked with holding the Federal right, which was the far right of the entire Federal line. Green also provided protection for the Baltimore Pike, a primary line of supply for General Meade. Colonel Lewis Stegman, commander of the 102nd New York, which was part of General Green's brigade, later wrote that depleting the Federal right ***"nearly proved a calamity to the whole army, it was a suicidal move."***

General Johnson's attack flanked the outnumbered Federal defenders and drove them from the base of Culp's Hill back toward the summit. Fortunately for the Federal army, General Green, age 62, was at heart an engineer. He had ordered the construction of strong fortifications that allowed his brigade to hold off multiple attacks from Johnson's much larger force. It was General Green's finest hour. Late that night, troops from the 1st Corps and the 11th Corps were sent to shore up General Green's brigade and the assault stalled. Sporadic gunfire continued throughout the night while both sides reinforced their numbers.

At the same time that General Johnson began his attack on Culp's Hill, Jubal Early attacked Cemetery Hill with two brigades. Early's men came from the south edge of Gettysburg, turned west, and charged the Federal troops at the base of Cemetery Hill. Remnants of the Federal 11th Corps at the bottom of the hill were overrun. As General Early advanced up Cemetery Hill, there was vicious hand-to-hand fighting, especially around Federal gun emplacements, which were savagely defended. Confederate Major Samuel Tate of the 6th North Carolina wrote afterward,

> *"75 North Carolinians of the Sixth Regiment and 12 Louisianans of Hays's brigade scaled the walls and planted the colors of the Sixth North Carolina and Ninth Louisiana on the guns. It was now fully dark. The enemy stood with tenacity never before displayed by them, but with bayonet, clubbed musket, sword, pistol, and rocks from the wall, we cleared the heights and silenced the guns."*

The Federal accounts of the battle for Cemetery Hill are not quite as generous to the Confederates as Major Tate's account, but Major Tate gives a credible first hand description of the struggle. At any rate, the Confederate attack, finally driven back with the help of reinforcements from the Hancock's 2nd Corps, caused heavy losses on both sides.

Nightfall on Little Round Top

That night, as it grew dark over the battlefield, Charles Kelly wrote a few words in his diary about the long day he and his Company had endured. He was still on the southern slope of the rocky knoll called Little Round Top.

> *"July 2, 1863*
>
> *struck tents started to march the front The country is Rough The first corp was in the fight yesterday also the 11 corp Our men took 5000 prisoners and 11 pieces of artillery Genl Reynolds was Killed. Genl Doubleday was wounded slightly Our forces took Genl Hill prisoner the Rebs are on one side of the Town and we are on the other We have a Large force here at the present time The day is warm and showery it is the opinion around that we have got a good position Henderson has fell to the Rear a alot stronger went into the fight at 4 o'clock this afternoon Take our position on the left had a hot time of it had 2 men of the company Killed and 10 wounded the Regt Lost 27 men Killed and 78 men wounded the 2 men in our company names were R. McElbright and Frank Griswold the capt was hit in the Bowels slightly Capt Larabee of Company B was Killed Capt W.M. Bourne of co K and Lieut Thomas of the same co were wounded Lieut Dunham of co D was Killed Lieut Gilman of co F was wounded in the Breast"*

In Company C of the 44th NY, by now considered by Charles to be like family, Corporal Richard McElligott, age 22, was killed, as was Frank Griswold, age 18. They died during the two hours the Third Brigade held off the assault at Little Round Top. Both Richard and Frank had joined Company C at the same time as Charles. Company C counted 10 wounded including Captain Bennet Munger, Charles' commanding officer. He would recover. They had marched 200 miles with little food or rest to arrive at the southern slope of this small hill. During the fighting one third of the 44th NY were killed or wounded.

Around 9 p.m., the 20th Maine received orders to march across the small valley to their front and occupy Round Top. Requesting support, parts of the 83rd Pennsylvania and the 44th New York advanced into the darkness and joined the 20th Maine. They remained there until relieved by the First Brigade on the morning of July 3. It is not clear if Charles Kelly spent the night on Round Top or Little Round Top. The Third Brigade then moved to the rear of the left center of the Federal line along Cemetery Ridge.

In his diary, Corporal Erastus Goodrich, Company A, 44th NY, age 24, writes about the evening of July 2nd.

> ***"At night of July 2nd, our company was on picket in our front at the foot of the hill. The ground was literally covered with dead and wounded. It was the worst picket duty I ever performed. Will never forget it. The Rebs were principally Texan troops. They said it was the first time their brigade had ever been repulsed. I spent all my time, while on picket, attending to the wounded, giving them water, fixing them in easy positions, cutting off shoes and helping them in every way I could. It was terrible, some crying, some praying, some swearing and all wanting help."***

Many questions could be raised about what was achieved at Little Round Top. Certainly, the men of Vincent's Third Brigade, and the Alabama and Texas regiments who attacked them, pushed the limits of what men could endure. The same could be said for many other brigades and regiments at other points of the battle. General Longstreet, General Law, Colonel Oates, General Warren, Colonel Vincent, and many others saw Little Round Top as being the position that would determine the winner or loser of the entire Gettysburg campaign. However, Confederate General Hood, before he was severely wounded, did not agree. He believed that Longstreet should go entirely around the larger hill, Round Top, and attack from there. Before the struggle for Little Round Top, General Longstreet wanted to do the same only, after going around the larger hill, to dig in and let the Federal's attack them. He asked General Lee again to do so on the following morning.

Neither General Lee nor General Meade placed much importance in Little Round Top beyond use as an observation point, both seeing Cemetry Hill and Cemetery Ridge as being the key to the battle. General Lee had not ordered an assault on Little Round Top, and General Meade only became interested in the hill because of General Warren. The reality was that the only part of Little Round Top that could be used to endanger the Federal line was its north slope. As Federal troops discovered, the rocky stump-covered north slope was notoriously difficult to maneuver artillery on and almost impossible to maneuver troops on. If the South had gained control of the hill, and somehow got enough artillery up the hill to threaten the Federal line, they would have made as easy a target for the Federals as the Federals were to them. In addition, it would have been very difficult for Lee to supply the north side of the slope; it was too vulnerable to being cut off and destroyed by the Federals. Lee did not have enough troops for such a venture.

Such questions have no answers, but in no way diminish what men did there.

Gettysburg July 3, 1863

"July 3, 1863

slept But little Last night the muscats Began about 5 o'clock pretty sharp was Relieved about 7 o'clock this morning By the first Brigade the Regt was gathered together some of them cooked coffie and the order was given to fall in the men Expected to go to the Rear But we only changed positions going from the Left of our Lines to the center things are very quiet at this point all day one man was wounded on our Line that is one company line heard from the capt this morning they say he is feeling comfortable his wound Being slight the names of the wounded men in our company are as follows Sargent Habert wounded in Leg sargent Kinner slightly in face fit for Duty Corp McElligott shot in the Bowels and Killed R.C. Phillips in the wrist Dansenburgh in arm Graham in Bowels Warren in the Leg Harrington Houghton in the head Wm Smith in the shoulder nothing of importance happened this after noon on our camp But they had some hard fighting on our Right Wing"

In Charles diary entry of July 3, 1863, the ***"hard fighting on our Right Wing"*** that he refers to is one of the most well-known events of the war.

The bloodshed of the previous day did not diminish Robert Lee's determination to break the Federal Army arrayed before him. The image of federal leaders, surrounded by the ruin of the Army of the Potomac, coming to him, seeking an end to the war, and offering recognition of the Confederate States of America, still burned inside of him. The morning of July 3, Lee rode south and met Longstreet to discuss what was to happen this day. Longstreet had lost perhaps 6,000 men the day before while attacking the Federal lines, many of them friends. Once again, he strongly recommended going around Round Top and digging in for a Federal attack. ***"The enemy is there,"*** responded Lee, pointing to the northeast, ***"and I am going to strike him."*** The two Generals, over a period of three hours, twice rode the full length of the proposed line of attack. ***"General,"*** Longstreet entreated, ***"I have been a soldier engaged in fights by couples, by squads, companies, regiments, divisions, and armies, and should know well as anyone what soldiers can do. It is my opinion that no 15,000 men ever arrayed for battle can take that position."***

In response, General Lee pointed to a clump of trees about a mile away, up on Cemetery Ridge, not far from Meade's command post; that would be the object of the attack Lee proclaimed. He firmly believed that once penetrated, the Federal line would fall apart. Years later James Longstreet wrote, ***"Never was I so depressed as upon that day."***

While on the ride with Longstreet, General Lee was surprised to hear guns from the north. It was General Johnson, renewing the attack on Culp's Hill as ordered the previous night. That morning, Lee had sent orders for the attack to be delayed in order to coordinate with the coming assault on Cemetery Ridge, but the orders arrived too late. General Green's trenches, heavily reinforced during the night, stopped the attack, and by 11 a.m., Johnson was driven back to his starting point suffering heavy casualties. He did not take part in the attack against Cemetery Ridge later that day. Poorly coordinated attacks were a problem for Lee's army throughout the Gettysburg campaign.

A little after 1 p.m., 159 Confederate guns opened up on Cemetery Ridge. They formed a line two miles long starting at the peach orchard and continuing north along the Emmitsburg Road. The Federal guns answered back for about two hours then gradually stopped firing to conserve ammunition, and confuse the enemy as to the effectiveness of the Confederate fire. The valley between the two armies filled with smoke. Hoping but not convinced that much of the Federal artillery was destroyed, his guns almost out of ammunition, Colonel Edward Alexander, Longstreet's artillery chief who had so effectively commanded Longstreet's guns at Fredericksburg, urged the infantry attack to begin while he had some ammunition left to support them. Resupply for his guns was an hour away. It was now or never.

Alexander's artillery did have some effect on the Federal Line. General Meade, while having lunch with his staff officers was nearly killed by a rebel shell. One of his orderlies was cut in two. Sixteen horses belonging to Meade's staff died a horrible death while tethered to a fence outside of Meade's headquarters. For a time, shrapnel rained down behind the Federal line but defense of the Ridge was not impaired.

About 3 p.m., 12,500 men emerged from the trees growing along the base of Seminary Ridge and headed for the clump of trees, three quarters of a mile away on Cemetery Ridge that Lee had chosen as their objective. This action would achieve fame as "Picket's Charge," although the commanding General was James Longstreet acting under orders of Robert Lee. General George Picket, on Lee's right, commanded three of the nine brigades that formed the initial attack. On the left, General James Pettigrew commanded a division. During the assault, Pettigrew's horse was shot out from under him; he pushed forward on foot. A short while later he suffered a painful arm wound. A third division commanded by Isaac Trimble attacked on Lee's left, behind Pettigrew's division. General Trimble, severely wounded in the leg and left on the battlefield, would serve out the rest of the war as a Federal prisoner. For those interested in such things, historians refer to the attack as the Pickett-Pettigrew-Trimble Charge.

They came in a well-disciplined line, over a mile wide, with parade ground precision, bayonets fixed. One Federal soldier said it was ***"the most beautiful thing I ever saw."*** Federal artillery opened up on them from three sides. Crossing the Emmitsburg Road, Lee's men ignored their dead and wounded and continued to within 400 yards of the Federal line. The Yankees were huddled behind a long stone wall. It was then that the Federal gunners switched to canister shot in their smooth bore guns (which made up only a portion of the Federal artillery). These guns, when loaded with canister shot, became oversized shotguns that could destroy whole platoons with a single load of iron or lead balls. The blue-clad troops behind the stone wall joined in with their rifled muskets or in some cases smooth bore muskets. Years later, in his history of the 8th Ohio Volunteer Infantry, Lieutenant Colonel Franklin Sawyer described the effect of the Union guns on the rebel charge; ***"They were at once enveloped in a dense cloud of smoke and dust. Arms, heads, blankets, guns and knapsacks were thrown and tossed into the clear air."*** In places along the Federal line, Yankee troops chanted: Fredericksburg! Fredericksburg!

At one point, Lee's attack did penetrate the stone wall, not far from the clump of trees, at a turn in the wall now known as The Angle. Rebel General Lewis Armistead, with his hat held high on the tip of his sword, led his men over the wall near The Angle, driving back the 71st Pennsylvania, which left a 200-foot wide gap in the Federal line. For a few minutes, near the Angle the screams, rebel yells, musket fire, and clash of bayonets, drowned out all other sounds. Receiving no help from his left or right Armistead and the three hundred men who followed him over the wall had to surrender or die. There were no officers left to order a retreat. Armistead, hit three times before he fell, died two days later in a Federal hospital.

In less than an hour, it was over. Even Lee's remarkable men could see it. Most of the officers leading the charge were dead or wounded; more than 6,000 of their comrades were killed, wounded, or captured. The futility of the attack, now obvious, left no choice but to turn around and walk back to the Confederate line or be killed. As they straggled back to Seminary Ridge, still hammered by Federal artillery, Robert Lee and James Longstreet were there to meet them. As Lee rode among them, he shouted repeatedly, ***"It's all my fault."***

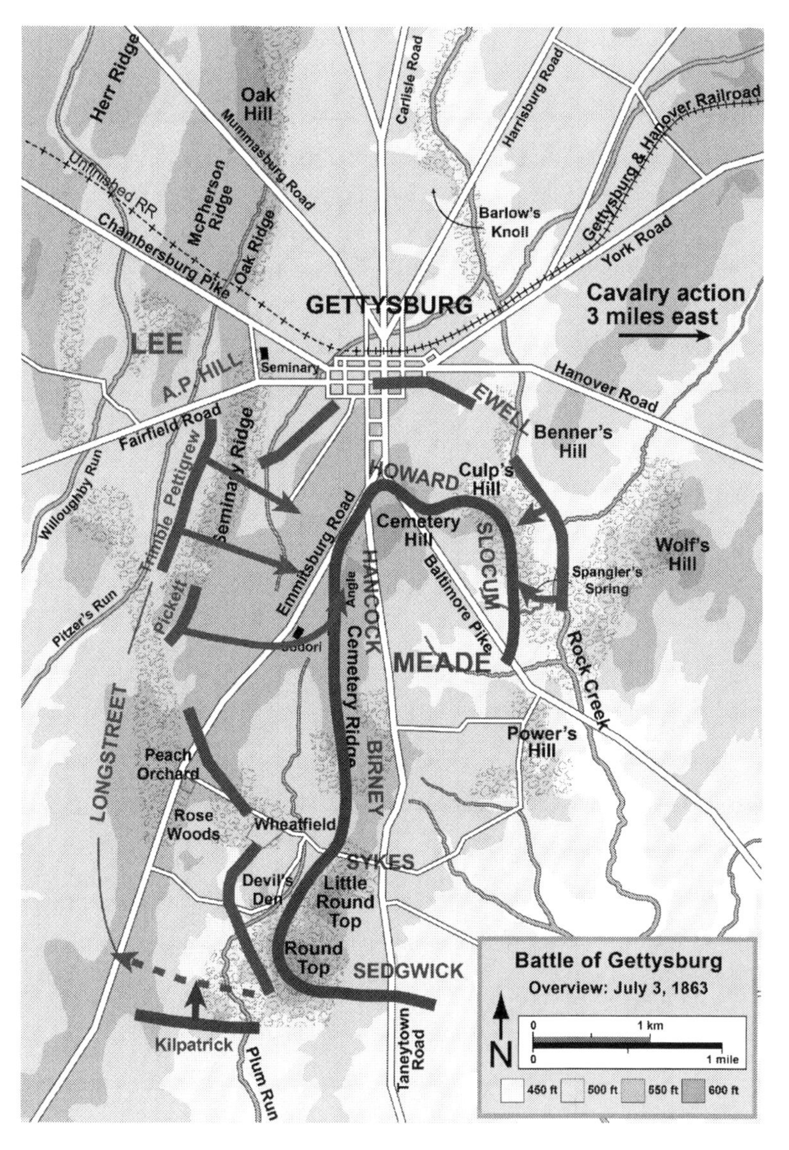

Day 3 at the Battle of Gettysburg ended Lee's invasion of the north. Together with Grant's victory at Vicksburg in the west the following day, Gettysburg ended southern hopes of forcing a military solution on the North that would end the war, and force the North to recognize the Confederacy as an independent nation. "Map by Hal Jespersen, www.cwmaps.com".

For Lee, nothing remained but to prepare for the counter-attack he believed was sure to come. When he rode up to General Pickett and urged him to ready his division for defense, Pickett responded with bitterness, ***"General Lee, I have no division."***

However, General Meade held fast to his plan to fight a defensive battle, and passed on the opportunity to counter-attack; to do so would have involved concentrating his reserve forces, which Meade had not done. Even though, on July 3, Meade became the first of Lincoln's generals to anticipate what Lee was going to do, he did not plan for a killing blow to the Army of Northern Virginia. To Robert Lee's great relief there was no counter-attack. As the sun set on that hot, muggy, bloody day, Lee entrenched his broken army on a line from Oak Hill to the Peach Orchard.

During the Gettysburg campaign, the Federal Army incurred a little over 23,000 killed, wounded and taken prisoner out of a total engaged of 104,000. The Confederate Army counted 28,000 killed, wounded, and taken prisoner. They had started out 73,000 strong. General Lee lost a third of his officers including six generals killed. General Trimble, left on the battlefield by his men, lost a leg. General Hood lost the use of his left arm. General Heth was knocked unconscious for 24 hours but recovered. Two of Lee's generals, including Isaac Trimble were wounded and captured. Robert Lee's army was no longer the same army that had invaded Pennsylvania a few weeks earlier.

Five Federal generals were killed; Sickles, who lost a leg, joined with three other severely wounded northern generals.

The suffering was not confined to just the men. At Gettysburg, three to five thousand horses and mules died while serving their masters.

On the afternoon of July 2nd, the 9th Massachusetts Battery was ordered to cover the retreat of Hancock's 2nd Corps. They made a stand at Trostle Farm located about one third mile east of Emmitsburg Road, just west of Plum Creek. Earlier that day the farm had been General Sickles' headquarters. They held the position until 6:30 p.m. In three hours the 9th Massachusetts Battery expended over three tons of shot and shell, including ninety-two rounds of canister. The 9th Massachusetts Battery bought enough time for Hancock's troops to reform east of the Trostle House. The battery lost 27 men, killed and wounded. There was one surviving officer and one surviving sergeant. Catherine Trostle filed a claim for damages sustained on the farm during the battle. In her claim, she noted, "16 dead horses were left by the door of the house, and probably 100 lay around the farm."
(Library of Congress)

When word reached Washington of the battle, the elation was soon tempered by the fact that Lee's Army was still intact. Abraham Lincoln's emotions ranged from being angry to being distraught. Why had there been no counter-attack?

When news of Gettysburg reached England, lingering hope of recognition for the South died its final death.

Even though Robert Lee was still capable of winning stunning victories, there were no more Confederate offensive campaigns during the war; the assault on Cemetery Ridge ended all of that. When Lee gave the order for the assault, it seemed like he had somehow forgotten his thousands of dead comrades who died so easily when they charged Malvern Hill on the Peninsula, or the piles of blue-clad soldiers, shot down in front of the stone wall at Fredericksburg.

CHAPTER SIXTEEN

Lee Heads for Home

July 4th, 1863

As the sun rose over Gettysburg the next day, both Armies braced for an attack that did not come. Charles Kelly again makes a few brief comments in his diary:

> ***"July 4, 1863***
>
> ***all still along the Lines it Looks as if the Rebs were falling Back this is a Tough 4th of July it Began to Rain this morning and Kept it up al day and all night the News are that we have the Rebs flanked I learned this afternoon that the 2nd corps was engaged on the 3rd I have heard nothing of Neil or Dave since the fight commenced"***

In this entry of July 4, Charles mentions that he did not learn of the engagement of the 2nd Corps on the previous day until the afternoon of the 4th. He is referring to Pickett's Charge.

It soon became clear to Meade that Lee was digging in all along his line with no intention of renewing the attack that day. Federal troops, in a soaking rain, began the grisly task of burying the dead. Wounded were cared for, ammunition and rations brought forward, and the Federal army waited for what was to come next.

Lee knew exactly what needed to come next. In contrast to his often open-ended orders given during the battle at Gettysburg, he now gave precise instructions to each of his Corps Commanders. Lee realized that the days when he could rely on Stonewall Jackson to do what needed to be done, without detailed orders, ended that moonlit night at Chancellorsville two months earlier. Lee, low on food and ammunition, told his commanders, ***"We must now return to Virginia."***

Under command of General John Imboden, Lee's wounded left Gettysburg that day in a train of wagons seventeen miles long. They would pass through Cashtown, Chambersburg, Greencastle, and Hagerstown, and then cross the Potomac into Virginia near Williamsport. Generals Longstreet, Ewell, and Hill would hold Seminary Ridge until after dark. They would then abandon Gettysburg. Leaving campfires burning on Seminary Ridge, Hill's Corps went first, and Longstreet followed. The driving rain muffled the sound. Ewell's turn came around 2 a.m. with Jeb Stuart's cavalry guarding the flank. By now, the roads were muddy, slowing the march. The infantry would pass through Fairfield to Hagerstown and cross the Potomac at Williamsport, the same crossing used by the train of wounded.

Even before Lee's Army had slipped away during the night of July 4th, while Federal troops glared at the rebels from Cemetery Ridge less than a mile away, General Meade sent a word of congratulations to his weary men ***"for the glorious result of the recent operations... Our task is not yet accomplished, and the commanding general looks to the army for greater efforts to drive from our soil every vestige of the presence of the invader."***

When Lincoln got wind of General Meade's message to the Army of the Potomac, he was furious. ***"Great God is that all? Will our generals get that idea out of their heads? The whole country is our soil."*** In these few words, Lincoln summed up the vast gap between his understanding of what this war was about as compared to that of his generals.

On July 4, over 900 miles to the southwest, Union General Ulysses Grant received the surrender of the entire Confederate garrison, over 30,000 soldiers, at Vicksburg. Under siege for 47 days, Confederate General John Pemberton, out of food and ammunition, and with no help in sight, gave in to the single-minded Ulysses Grant. The entire Mississippi was now under Federal control. It was another blow to the Confederacy, perhaps greater than the one they had just suffered at Gettysburg.

Leaving Gettysburg

After the battle of July 3, both sides were exhausted and in need of rest, supplies, and horses for the cavalry, artillery and supply trains. There was little rest to come. For the North, General Meade had been in command only a few days, yet during that time a great many of his officers had been killed or wounded, and there was bickering among the remaining high-ranking officers, maneuvering for position and arguing about the next move the army should make. Before he had even finished burying his dead, General Meade starting getting telegrams from Washington expressing the disappointment of General Halleck and Abraham Lincoln. Why had there had been no counterattack on Lee's forces after the assault on Cemetery Ridge? Why had Lee's Army been allowed to leave Gettysburg?

The criticism, and what must have seemed to Meade as micro management from those nowhere near the battlefield, did not sit well. After all, even before Meade was sure that Lee was leaving Gettysburg, Meade had ordered Cavalry General Hugh Kilpatrick, to attack the rear guard of Ewell's 2nd Corps train of wagons headed for Williamsport.

Kilpatrick, was one of the few cavalry commanders in the Federal army more reckless than George Custer. The most direct path to Williamsport from Gettysburg was through South Mountain via Monterey Pass, a few miles southwest of Fairfield. Kilpatrick left Emmitsburg around 3 p.m. on July 4, with 5,000 cavalry troopers. At Monterey Pass, starting around 9 p.m. and continuing until the next morning, during a terrific thunderstorm, there were continual engagements in complete darkness, with only lightning to guide the chaotic fighting. In the end, Ewell lost 280 wagons, about a third of his train, 1,500 men, mostly taken prisoner, and thousands of cattle. Major Charles Capehart of the 1st West Virginia Calvary was awarded the Congressional Medal of Honor to recognize his charge into the rebel train with sabers and revolvers before dawn on July 5.

"July 5, 1863

started for the front this morning sent out skirmishers at dawn But no Enemy to Be found staid until about 2 o'clock for our old lines the Rebs are on the Retreat for South mountains the 3 Brigade is on the Road for Frederick City had a hard march this Night the Roads are very muddy"

On July 5, after discovering that Lee had withdrawn his army from Gettysburg, General Meade sent General Sedgwick's 6th Corps, up to now held in reserve, to pursue the fleeing Confederate army. They followed Lee's path to Fairfield in the heavy rain. When Lee was passing through South Mountain, General Meade decided not to attack him in the easily defended passes of the mountain. He ordered the 6th Corps to leave Fairfield, march to Emmitsburg, and join his army in a race to Middletown, attempting to cut Lee's Army off on this side of the Potomac.

On July 5, Charles Kelly's 44 NY, rejoined the 5th Corps around 5 p.m., and began marching south along the Emmitsburg Road toward Frederick and Middletown. They marched along the muddy road until midnight and camped along Marsh Run. That day, Captain Bennet Munger, commander of Company C of the 44th NY, was given leave to return to his home in Yates County, New York, to recover from the wound he received on July 2, defending Little Round Top. He would return August 19. Charles Kelly was now ranking officer of Company C, of the 44th NY.

On the same day, General Elwell's 2nd Corps, the last of Lee's infantry to leave Gettysburg, reached Fairfield, nine miles southwest of Seminary Ridge. To the west, during the evening of July 5, the head of General Imboden's wagon train of wounded reached Williamsport, where they found their route to the Shenandoah Valley blocked. A Federal cavalry raid had destroyed the pontoon bridge across the Potomac, and the River was too swollen to ford. An immediate effort began, using what boats could be found, to move Confederate wounded across the river.

July 6, 1863

"July 6th, 1863

started this morning for the city* (Frederick) *traveled about 1 mile camped for the Night"

Lee's Army was ahead of Meade in the race to the Potomac. On the July 6, Longstreet with his 1st Corps reached Hagerstown around 5 p.m. It was still raining. The train of Lee's wounded had passed through earlier that day. The order for the train was to make no stops for any reason until they reached Williamsport, even though many of the wounded had not eaten for 36 hours. General Imboden, leading the train, later wrote of that long line of wagons:

"... The storm continued, and the darkness was appalling. There was no time even to fill a canteen with water for a dying man; for, except the drivers and guards, all were wounded and utterly helpless in that vast procession of misery. During this one night I realized more of the horrors of war than I had in all the two preceding years."

July 7, 1863

"July 7th, 1863

started this morning along the foot of the Mountain it has Rained all day did not go to Frederick passed through Midleton encamped there over night of the 9th started for the mountain once more encamped in them 9th Left the hills"

It was July 7 when Abraham Lincoln first learned of Ulysses Grant's victory on the banks of the Mississippi River far to the west at Vicksburg. The news renewed him and filled him with hope. He immediately sent word to his commander of Armies:

"Major Genl Halleck

We have certain information that Vicksburg surrendered to General Grant on the 4th of July. Now, if Gen. Meade can complete his work so gloriously prosecuted thus far, by the litteral(sic) or substantial destruction of Lee's army, the rebellion will be over.
Yours truly,
A. LINCOLN"

The Race to the Potomac

General Grant's victory at Vickburg intensified the push for Meade to finish off Lee's Army and end the war. At 2 p.m. on July 8, General Meade wrote a detailed letter to General Halleck trying to convey what he was dealing with in his attempts to do exactly what he was repeatedly being asked to do;

"Letter from George Gordon Meade to Henry Wager Halleck, July 8, 1863

July 8, 1863, 2 P. M. Gen'l Conch learns from scouts that the train is crossing at Williamsport very slowly. So long as the river is unfordable the enemy cannot cross. My cavalry report that they had a fight near Funkstown, through which they drove the enemy to Hagerstown where a large infantry force was... From all I can gather the enemy extends from Hagerstown to Williamsport... Their cavalry and infantry pickets are advanced to the Hagerstown and Sharpsburg pike, on the general line of the Antietam. We hold Boonsboro, and our pickets, four miles in front, toward Hagerstown, are in contact with the enemy's pickets. My Army is assembling slowly; the rains of yesterday and last have made all roads but pikes almost impassable. Artillery and wagons are stalled; it will take time to collect them together. A large portion of the men are barefooted. Shoes will arrive at Frederick today and will be issued as soon as possible. The spirit of the Army is high; the men are ready and willing to make any exertion to push forward. The very first moment I can get the different commands, the artillery and cavalry, properly supplied and in hand I will, move forward. Be assured I most earnestly desire to try the fortunes of war with the enemy on this side of the river, hoping, through Providence and the bravery of my men to settle the question, but I should be wrong not to frankly tell you of the difficulties encountered. I expect to find the enemy in a strong position, well covered with artillery, and I do not desire to imitate his example at Gettysburg and assault a position when the chances are so greatly against success. I wish in advance to moderate the expectation of those who; in ignorance of the difficulties to be encountered, may expect too much. All that I can do under the circumstances, I pledge this Army to do."

General Meade again wrote to General Halleck just one hour later responding to further dispatches from Halleck. His frustration with Washington is growing,

"Letter from George Gordon Meade to Henry Wager Halleck, July 8, 1863, 3 P. M.

My information as to the crossing of the enemy does not agree with that just received in your dispatch. His whole force is in position between Funkstown and Williamsport. I have just received information that he has driven in my cavalry force in front of Boonsboro. My Army is and has been making forced marches, short of rations and barefooted. Our Corps marched yesterday and last night over 30 miles. I take occasion to repeat that I will use my utmost efforts to push forward this Army."

By 5 p.m., General Halleck again wrote to General Meade hoping to diffuse some of the frustration evident in Meade's letters,

"Letter from Henry Wager Halleck to George Gordon Meade, July 8, 1863, … 5 P. M.

Do not understand me as expressing any dissatisfaction. On the contrary your Army has done most nobly. I only wish to give you opinions formed from information received here. It is telegraphed from near Harpers Ferry that the enemy have been crossing for the last two days. It is also reported that they have a bridge across. If Lee's Army is divided by the river, the importance of attacking the part on this side is incalculable -- such an opportunity may never occur again. If on the contrary he has massed his whole force on the Antietam, time must be taken to also concentrate your forces -- Your opportunities for information are better than mine. Brig. Gen. Kelly was ordered some days ago to concentrate at Hancock and attack the enemy's right. Maj. Gen. Brooks is also moving from Pittsburgh to reinforce Kelly. All troops arriving from New York and Fort Monroe are sent directly to Harpers Ferry unless you order differently. You will have forces sufficient to render your victory certain. My only fear now is that the enemy may escape by crossing the river."

That night Charles Kelly and the 44th NY camped near Middletown. The next morning, by 9 a.m., they were on the march. They crossed over South Mountain and camped near Boonsboro.

Reveille sounded early on the morning of July 10. The men of the 44th NY had a hasty breakfast, and shoes, along with other supplies were distributed. The march began at 6 a.m. They crossed Antietam Creek and sent out pickets, who soon ran into enemy pickets, in an affair now called Jones' Crossroads.

Charles Kelly writes:

> ***"July 10, 1863***
>
> ***the day was very warm crossed Antietam Creek encamped for the Night in front of the Enemy about 1/2 miles from the old Battle ground sent out skirmishers to the front Lieut Munger was Detailed as one of the officers to go with them the Regt has Been ordered out on picket company B went on post"***

It should be noted, to avoid confusion, that Lieutenant Munger, referred to often in Charles' diaries, was the nephew of Captain Bennet Munger, who was at the time absent from the regiment, recovering from wounds received at Little Round Top.

Charles was now close to his old campground near Antietam Creek, where his company first joined with the 44th NY, less than a year ago. He was also close to the site where General Hooker had fought a bloody battle with Lee, which the south called The Battle of Antietam. At Antietam, General Hooker failed to prevent Lee's Army from crossing the Potomac River and escape the grasp of the Federal army.

By July 12, most of the Army of the Potomac was again facing off against Lee's entire Army of Northern Virgina. Lee had formed his troops into a semi-circle around Williamsport with the swollen Potomac River on his right and rear, and Conococheague Creek on his left. His men had completed four miles of entrenchments along this line, fortified with the same artillery that had caused such harm to the Federal army at Gettysburg. Less than a mile to the east, stretching from the Potomac to Hagerstown, the Federal army stared down the muzzles of those rebel guns, waiting for Meade to decide what to do. Some of the troops remembered what artillery did to the gray-clad rebels who assaulted Cemetery Ridge just a few days before. Others, at night, still had visions of piles of blue-clad soldiers in front of that awful stone wall at Fredericksburg, just seven months ago.

That night Meade called a meeting with his corps commanders and took a vote. This is something Meade had done at Gettysburg, to the great frustration of those in Washington. Five of the six corps commanders who were present were opposed to attacking Lee's line. Meade telegraphed the results of the poll to Washington and got a quick reply from General Halleck:

> ***"You are stong enough to attack and defeat the enemy before he can effect a crossing. Act your own judgment and make your Generals execute your orders. Call no coucils of war. It is proverbial that councils of war never fight. Do not let the enemy escape."***

Meade hesitated, which was never a good idea when facing Robert Lee. Meade spent most of July 13, scouting Lee's lines, looking for weak spots. He prepared to attack the next morning. As the Federal army advanced on the morning of July 14, they discovered Lee's trenches were empty and the Army of Northern Virgina had crossed to the other side of the Potomac. During the previous three days the rebels managed to build enough pontoons by tearing down abandoned houses, and using what other lumber they could find, to reach across the river. One wonders what might have happened had General Burnside showed such initiative when he first arrived at Fredericksburg. By dawn of July 14, Ewell's 2nd Corps had crossed, soon followed by Longstreet's 1st Corps, artillery, wagons, and all. By then, the river had fallen just enough to allow Hill's 3rd Corps to wade, neck deep, across the ford at Williamsport, with soldiers of lesser stature being helped by taller men. General Heth's men covered Hill's retreat, and then followed, fighting as they went.

While serving as rear guard at the pontoon bridge, Johnston Pettigrew's brigade was suddenly attacked by about forty Federal horsemen, who made a suicidal assault on the retreating rebels. They may have been drunk. In the fighting that followed, all forty of the Yankees were killed. General Pettigrew, thrown from his horse and fighting on foot, pistol blazing, was shot in the stomach. He refused to be left behind and made it over the bridge, dying three days later. The last of Lee's army crossed the bridge, cut the anchor ropes, and sent it floating down the Potomac.

When the Federal army crossed into Lee's entrenchments on July 14, their hesitation seemed justified. Colonel Charles Wainwright wrote about what they found:

> ***"We pushed on to this place at a pretty good rate, passing directly through their line of works. These were by far the strongest I have seen yet; evidently laid out by engineers and built as if they meant to stand a month's siege. The parapet was a good six feet wide on top, and the guns, which were very thick, were all placed so as to get a perfect cross fire and to sweep their whole front. When shall we learn to put up such field works?"***
>
> ***—Col. Charles S. Wainwright, U.S. Army, July 14, 1863."***

Lee's Army marched for two days and stopped near Bunker Hill, twenty miles from the Potomac. As his exhausted army rested, he reported to Richmond, ***"The men are in good health and spirits but want shoes and clothing badly."*** In spite of massive losses, Lee was ready to replenish his army with men and supplies and *"resume operations"*. He was already planning counter attacks from higher up the Shenandoah Valley should the Yankees pursue.

Abraham Lincoln did not respond to the news from Williamsport with the resilience of Robert Lee. Hearing that Lee's army had crossed the Potomac into Virginia set loose within Lincoln old demons of depression and despair. Those demons were relentless. They would not stop whispering to him; all of the men who suffered so much at Gettysburg did so for nothing; the opportunity to end this war was gone; hundreds of thousands more will suffer and die. Heartsick, Lincoln spoke to Secretary of the Navy, Gideon Wells, ***"Our army held the war in the hollow of their hand and they would not close it."***

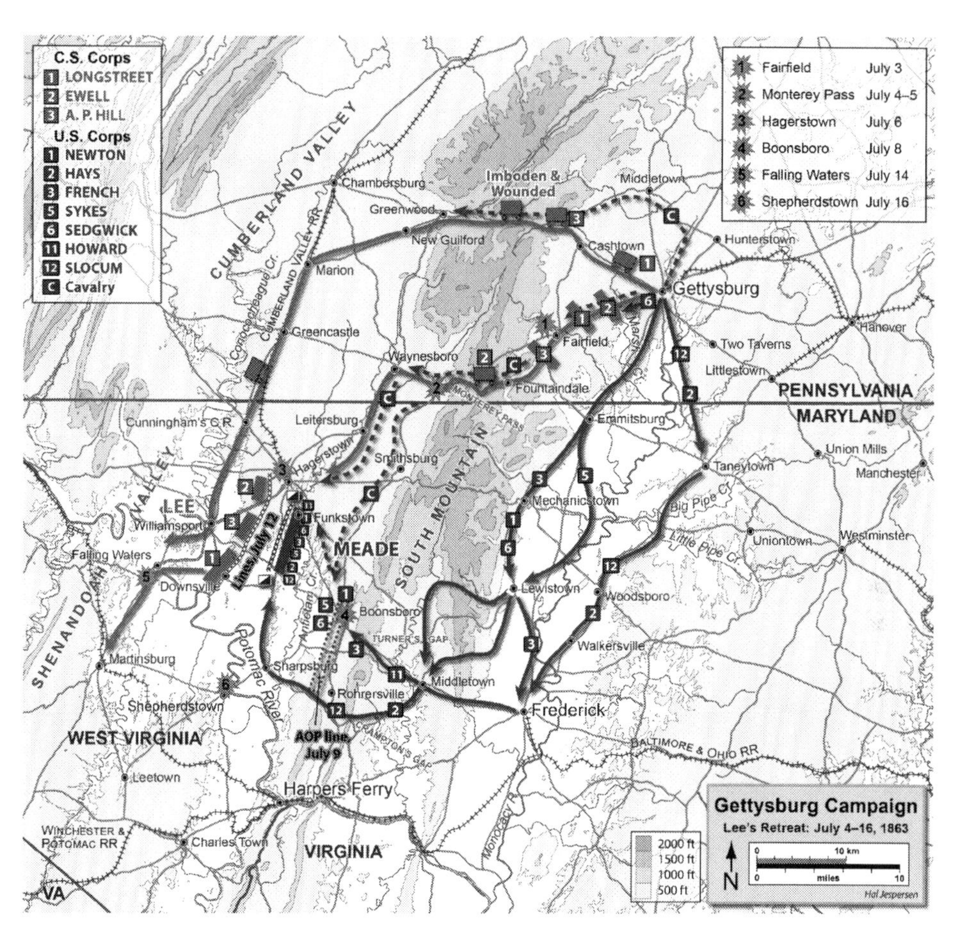

General Lee leaves Gettysburg. Lee's train of wounded go through Cashtown and Greencastle to Williamsport. Lee's three infantry corps travel through Fairfield, and through South Mountain at Monterey Pass. From there they travel through Hagerstown and reform their lines at Williamsport. Meade's army follows, mostly through Middletown. By July 12, Charles, with the 5th Corps, is not far from where he first joined the 44th NY along Antietam Creek, less than a year earlier. "Map by Hal Jespersen, www.cwmaps.com".

"The Gettysburg Story"

That afternoon, on July 14, Robert Todd Lincoln, President Lincoln's oldest son, visited the president. He had recently finished his spring semester at Harvard. Years later Robert recounts that he entered his Father's study shortly after the Battle of Gettysburg and found him in tears with his head bowed in his arms. He had seen his Father cry only once before. His Father told him he had just learned Meade and his generals had decided not to pursue Lee and now the opportunity of ending this bitter struggle was lost. According to Robert, the President told him that he had sent a dispatch to Meade telling him to attack Lee, cost what it might, before he could cross the river. Robert recalls being told that the message stated: ***If you fail, this dispatch will clear you from all responsibility and if you succeed you may destroy the dispatch and take all the glory and victory for yourself.***

This story did not come to light until years after the meeting between father and son, and Robert was the first to say it relied totally on his memory. Some have considered this story to be myth. Try as they might, historians have found no written evidence that such a dispatch was written, and no evidence has been found that Meade ever received such a message. An excellent article can be found about the *"Gettysburg Story,"* written by John Hoffmann, in the *Journal of Abraham Lincoln Association*, published by the University of Illinois Press, Volume 38, Issue 1, 2017. For the rest of his life, on the few occasions that Robert mentioned the story, he claimed it to be factual, always admitting the story relied on memory alone.

General Halleck wrote to Meade of the President's ***"great dissatisfaction"*** resulting from Lee's escape across the Potomac without the army giving him battle. He told Meade ***"it will require an active and energetic pursuit on your part to remove the impression that it has not been sufficiently active before."*** Meade, who had been doing a job that he did not want, for less than three weeks, responded by asking to be immediately relieved from command of the army. Lincoln and Halleck backed off. The northern papers were full of accolades for Meade's victory at Gettysburg. Now was not the time to find a new general for the Army of the Potomac.

Lee was back behind the Rapidan River by August 4. For his men, over sixty days of continuous marching and fighting had ended. The Gettysburg campaign was over. Both Meade's and Lee's armies were now at about the same locations as when the campaign started.

CHAPTER SEVENTEEN

After Gettysburg

Draft Riots

The escape of Lee's Army was not the only thing Abraham Lincoln was struggling with that summer. In March of 1863, the Federal Army was running low on volunteers, which prompted Congress to passed the Enrollment Act. For the first time, the use of a draft was authorized to fill depleted ranks of the Federal army. Draftees would be chosen by lottery as needed. The draft pool included single, able bodied men, between the ages of twenty and forty-five. After that group was depleted, married men between the ages of twenty and thirty-five entered the pool. Draftees were chosen by lot. Black Americans were not eligible. A man could avoid the draft by finding someone to act as his substitute or by paying $300, and many found substitutes among the multitude of newly arrived immigrants.

There was wide-spread resistance to the draft but nowhere as much as in the City of New York. New York's economy had close ties to the South, and since Lincoln's Emancipation Proclamation there was fear among the working class that freed slaves would come to New York and take their jobs. Violent protests began in lower Manhattan on July 13, and evolved into race riots. Mobs ransacked public buildings, Protestant Churches, homes of abolitionists, and many homes belonging to Black Americans. Mobs attacked the Colored Orphan Asylum on 44th Street and 5th Avenue, burning it to the ground. Many Black residents of New York City fled, never to return. One hundred and twenty people died. Lincoln sent in Federal Troops to stop the riots, and by July 17, an uneasy calm had returned to the city.

On the March

For Charles Kelly, more long marches lay ahead. At 4 a.m. on July 15, the 5th Corps left Williamsport, passed through South Mountain, and stopped for the night near the little village of Burkittsville. They had marched 20 hard miles. They left at daylight the next morning and marched till noon. The next day they started out around 4 p.m., in a heavy rain, crossed the Potomac, and halted for the night at Lovettsville, six miles southeast of Harpers Ferry. On July 20 they reached Upperville, on Goose Creek, where Charles had fought against Jeb Stuart's cavalry on June 21. Continuing south, the 3rd and 5th Corps had minor encounters with Confederate pickets, but Robert Lee did not want a general engagement. The 5th Corps marched beyond their supply trains and for a couple of days their rations came from the abundant supply of berries they found along the way. By July 27, they were about three miles south of Warrenton, and went into camp. On August 4, they continued the march and arrived the morning of August 7 at Beverly Ford on the Rappahannock River. They built fortifications along the river and for a while settled into camp life. Going out on picket, practicing drills, cooking, writing letters to home, camp duties, cards, checkers, and an occasional game of baseball filled their time. For the officers, reciting tactics to the their new commander, Luitenant Colonel Conner, and improving their leadership skills was a constant occupation. Fresh bread, plenty of rations, and a dry place to sleep all helped to rejuvenate the exhausted army who had been lacking all of these things for many weeks.

Always on Charles' mind was letters from home. Seldom does a day go by that letters are not mentioned in his diaries. He often writes that he received a letter from home reporting the folks back in Penn Yan were in good health. If more than two or three days went by without receiving a letter, Charles became anxious and frustrated, inquiring in his diary why no one back home had seen fit to write. He wrote many letters to his mother and siblings, and an occasional letter to Dick Mahar, who had rented his saloon when Charles entered the service. Mail coming to the regiment was a time the men looked forward to, and often when no mail arrived by noon, Charles would write that he expected a letter before the end of the day. The mail system for the Army of the Potomac was remarkably efficient, rivaling our modern postal system; letters written by Charles often arrived in Penn Yan after two or three days. Soon after, Charles was looking for a return letter. News from home did not always portray idyllic small town life. On Oct 9, Charles writes;

> ***"I sent a letter home stating that I did not want to hear from them again until Father stoped drinking whiskey."***

Charles also greatly valued the newspapers he received by mail. *The Penn Yan Gazette* and *The Yates County Chronicle* helped him to maintain his connection with home.

August 29, 1863, was a solemn day for the 5th Corps. On that day, five men were executed for desertion. Charles writes in his diary:

> ***"Aug. 29, 1863***
> ***this has Been an eventful day there were five men shot for Desertion here today it was a solemn spectical to Look upon they were all from the first Div of our corps they were Executed in presence of the troops it was a sader sight to see five men marching under guard with their coffins carried in front of them a splendid band playing the Death March the different Friends marching with the prisoners one of the men was a Jew and a Jewish Rabbi was with him also a Catholic priest and a Methodist were there to perform the Rites of their different faiths they were Executed in presence of 14,000 soldiers the mere preparation for the Execution had a Better Effect on the men than the Execution itself Jacob Stroub was brought back under arrest charge desertion it will go hard with him on trail he has on Citizens clothes we are making out pay rolls for the months of July & Aug this is saturday will finish our muster rolls tomorrow the nights are very cold here at this time."***

The 5th Corps remained in camp at Beverly Ford until September 16, when they crossed the Rappahannock River and marched to within two miles of Culpeper. On October 10, the 1st and 5th Corps advanced to the Rapidan River and encountered enemy cavalry. Having completed their reconnaissance, they started back toward the Rappahannock at dawn on October 11, with Confederate cavalry making frequent attacks on their rear guard. After crossing the Rappahannock River, they camped at the Beverly Ford campsite.

Early on October 12, the 2nd, 3rd, and 5th Corps were once again ordered to cross the Rappahannock, where they formed a line of battle. The enemy was plainly visible on a range of hills four miles in the distance. To the left, toward Bristoe Station, Federal cavalry were plainly seen in a hotly contested battle with Confederate cavalry. As the infantry advanced, expecting a major engagement, the Confederate infantry withdrew. The men spent an uncomfortable night not knowing if the rebels would attack their line. When they learned that Lee was attempting to flank the Federal line and get between the Federal army and Washington, the Army of the Potomac was once again in motion.

The 5th Corps was on the march shortly after 1 a.m., October 13, headed for Centreville, to stop Lee from getting at Washington. They again crossed the Rappahannock River a little after daylight, halted briefly for breakfast, and resumed the march. Charles Kelly's brigade acted as rear guard. After marching 22 miles the army stopped at Catlett's Station for the night. Reveille sounded at 2 a.m. on the morning of October 14, but the 44th NY did not get underway until after daylight. They halted that evening two or three miles from Manassas Junction, looking forward to some food and hot coffee, but were ordered to extinguish their fires to avoid becoming targets of the enemy.

Battle of Bristoe Station October 14, 1863

Lee's 3rd Corps, commanded by General Hill, attacked the rear guard of the Federal 5th Corps but failed to note the approach of the Federal 2nd Corps., commanded by General Warren. A bad mistake. The 2nd Corps was following the 5th Corps, and had just arrived from Auburn. Warren deployed his corps behind an embankment of the Orange and Alexandria Railroad near Bristoe Station and from there ambushed the Confederate troops who were advancing against the rear guard of the 5th Corps. Ordered on the double quick, the chance for a hot meal and rest now gone, the main body of the 5th Corps rushed back to support Warren. By the time they arrived, what is known as the Battle of Bristoe Station was over. General Warren captured 5 pieces of artillery, 450 prisoners, and drove the rebels back. The North suffered about 580 casualties, the South about 1,380 casualties. When Warren saw that Lee was coming to aid of the Confederate 3rd Corps, Warren withdrew and continued the march toward Centreville. After the Federal army was gone, Lee's army destroyed a large section of the Orange and Alexandria Railroad from Bristoe Station to Rappahannock Station by tearing up the ties and bending the rails.

Arriving too late to help General Warren, the 44th NY once again changed their direction and continued the march toward Washington. They kept going until 2 a.m. and finally camped two miles beyond Bull Run. They marched thirty miles that day. They made an early start on October15, and passed through Centreville, stopping for the night near Fairfax Courthouse, about ten miles from their starting point. After a cold, rainy, muddy, and miserable march in the dark through the evening of October 16, camp was again made a mile from Centreville. On October 17, the 44th stayed in place. Sunshine brought some relief from days of little sleep, little food, and exhausting marches.

Reveille sounded at 3 a.m. on Oct 18. By daylight the 44th NY was underway. What followed was a month of almost continual marching and counter-marching over ground that Charles Kelly had passed over many times. It was the life of a soldier during the War of the Rebellion.

The 5th Corps stopped on October 19, 1863, near the Battlefield of First and Second Manassas (1st and 2nd Bull Run) where so many men of the 44th NY died in late August of 1862. On that day Charles writes in his diary:

> ***"...it was a hard march in Looking over the Battle field one finds some of the Dead not Buried yet it is a hard sight the men Lie where they fell on that day one of our officers was Over the ground where the 44 fought that day the field Looks Dreadful now and animals unBuried some of their hands above ground others with their heads skuls with the hair on some of the men Recognise their comrades that were killed at that time one Lieut knew his Brother By his Teeth another soidier saw a crowed of soldiers Looking at some graves when he went there he found that one of his Brothers was Burried there a Number of such cases happened while we were on the ground the day was very pleasandt the men feeling fine and it is my opinion if the Rebs gives us Battle on this ground we will whip them good this time We are within 1 mile from Grovetown it is with sad feelings that I think how many men were killed Sure Last year But we have a fine man in comdg of the Army he understands his Bussiness."***

General Lee and General Meade jockeyed for position during this time, with little effect. On November 7, there was a clash near Rappahannock Station when General Sedgwick launched a brutal night-time bayonet attack on General Jubal Early's troops who were guarding a pontoon bridge from the north side of the Rappahannock. The Yankees overran Early's troops, took 1,600 prisoners, and eight guns, and occupied Brandy Station. Lee retreated to south of the Rapidan River.

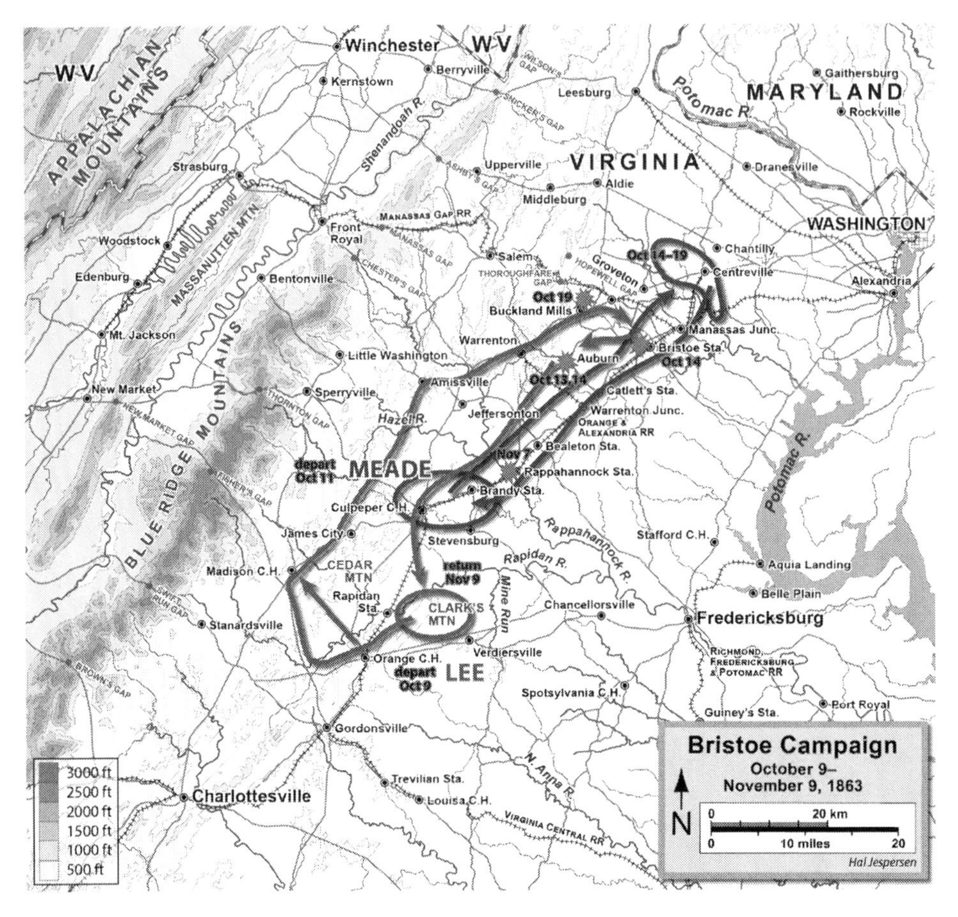

Charles Kelly's life in the fall of 1863, consisted of endless long marches, and fighting in a number of battles, meant to protect Washington from Lee's Army of Northern Virginia. "Map by Hal Jespersen, www.cwmaps.com"

Charles Travels to Washington

On November 5, 1863, Charles received leave to travel to Washington to be examined for a "colored Regt". Being given command of one of the Black American regiments then being formed was a path to promotion for lower ranking Federal officers. After walking three miles carrying his satchel, Charles got on board a train to Alexandria and stayed at the Marshal House Hotel. The next morning, he left

Alexandria around 8 o'clock and arrived in Washington an hour later. He found the location of the Examining Board, presented his papers, and was ordered to report every morning till he was examined by the Board. Alone in Washington that night, Charles attended Ford's Theater and saw a production of Shylock, or The Merchant of Venice. Charles felt the production was not firstrate and wrote that he was ***"lonesome in Washington."*** The next morning he was examined by two officers and afterward went to a store and bought some much needed clothing. That night Charles attended Grover's Theater to see Oliver Twist and commented that it was ***"well done".*** Charles managed to stretch out his visit and as was his way, encountered old friends and made new ones along the way. He arrived back at his regiment around dark on November 11.

Lincoln At Gettysburg

It was November 18, 1863, when Abrahan Lincoln traveled by train to the battlefield at Gettysburg to say a few words during the dedication of the Soldier's National Cemetery. The next afternoon, following a two hour speech by Edward Everett, Lincoln spoke for just minutes, delivering these powerful words:

> ***"Four score and seven years ago our fathers brought forth on this continent, a new nation, conceived in Liberty, and dedicated to the proposition that all men are created equal.***
>
> ***Now we are engaged in a great civil war, testing whether that nation, or any nation so conceived and so dedicated, can long endure. We are met on a great battle-field of that war. We have come to dedicate a portion of that field, as a final resting place for those who here gave their lives that that nation might live. It is altogether fitting and proper that we should do this.***
>
> ***But, in a larger sense, we can not dedicate—we can not consecrate—we can not hallow—this ground. The brave men, living and dead, who struggled here, have consecrated it, far above our poor power to add or detract. The world will little note, nor long remember what we say here, but it can never forget what they did here. It is for us the living, rather, to be dedicated here to the unfinished work which they who fought here have thus far so nobly advanced. It is rather for us to be here dedicated to the great task remaining before us—that from these honored dead we take increased devotion to that cause for which they gave the last full measure of devotion—that we here highly resolve that these dead shall***

> ***not have died in vain—that this nation, under God, shall have a new birth of freedom—and that government of the people, by the people, for the people, shall not perish from the earth."***

Lincoln's assistant secretary John Hay noted that during his address Lincoln looked mournful, almost haggard; Lincoln's face had a ***"ghastly color"***. Upon returning to Washington, Lincoln suffered a protracted illness and was later diagnosed with a form of smallpox.

The Mine Run Campaign

As Abraham Lincoln addressed the crowd and the nation at Gettysburg on November 19, General Meade started a new campaign against the Army of Northern Virginia. By November 28, the two armies faced off against each other with a small creek between them called Mine Run, a tributary of the Rapidan River. In the heavy rain of November 28, the 44th NY suffered three wounded while relieving pickets. Just across the creek, the rebels were heavily entrenched waiting for the Yankees. Corporal Adgate Gregg of Company H, 44th NY, was chosen to check how deep the creek was; dangerous duty for a young man. Setting out with a pole for measuring the depth of the water he found that Mine Run was shallow enough to ford, but the banks of the creek were four to ten feet high, with clear open ground on the other side, sloping up to the rebel entrenchments bristling with artillery. Difficult ground, to say the least.

General Meade ordered General Warren, then commanding the 2nd Corps, to attack at 8 a.m. the next day. As the sun came up and the fog lifted, General Warren examined the rebel position. He saw no chance of a successful assault. Sending word to Meade, he strongly advised against an attack. General Meade rode to the front and, after his own examination of the Confederate position, reluctantly agreed with General Warren. Charles wrote in his diary that the Enemy position was ***"as good as ours was at Gettysburg."*** Meade's army retired during the night of December 1, and 2, ending the Mine Run Campaign and the winter campaign of 1863.

When the Army of the Potomac withdrew from Mine Run Charles wrote on December 2 and 3:

> *"We have done the Largest marching that we Ever have done since I have been With the Regt from our front to the River is 13 miles we have came that Before Breakfast We then made some coffee as that was all we had to Eat our stay was short so off we started once more and traveled to Stevensburg and staid there All night But had Nothing to Eat the Night was Very cold started from Stevensburg this morning at Eight O'clock our men feel the worst for the Wear and being without rations...We arrived at Rappahannick Station at 10 o'clock This afternoon had orders to Bivouac For the Night and take up our Position in the morning"*

For the month of December, 1863, and much of Janurary of 1864, the 44th NY was camped north of the Rappahannock River guarding the Orange and Alexandria Railroad. The nights were bitterly cold and the ground frozen. The men were furnished no shelter beyond their canvas tents. The Colonel of the Regiment sent men out looking for boards so he could winterize his tent, a privilege not available to the enlisted men. Charles was lucky enough to find an abandoned "shanty" that he shared with a couple of other officers. Even this shelter was not available to him on the many nights he was with his men on picket duty.

Home for Christmas

The afternoon of December 18, Charles received permission to go home on furlough. That night he got on board a cattle car headed to Washington. Charles reports that he ***"had a very poor Time the Night was very cold"***. After waiting for trains in Washington and Baltimore, Charles arrived in Penn Yan around eight a.m. on December 21.

Charles was a man who genuinely liked people. He spent his Christmas break from the war visiting with family, especially his parents and siblings; seeing as many old friends as possible; and settling accounts with various business people like Richard Mahar, who owed him money for rent of his saloon. He attended the Catholic Church in Penn Yan and heard a sermon from Reverend English, after which he concluded the Reverend was not much of a speaker. He attended a wedding and went to a dance for the benefit of sick soldiers. Everywhere he went he ran into old friends. On New Year's Eve, he stayed up all night with friends and reports that he drank a great deal of whiskey. He also saw his old sweetheart, Martha Kane. She would not speak to him.

On New Year's Day, 1864, Charles left Penn Yan by freight train and headed back to his Regiment. His train left about noon. During the ride to Washington, Charles wrote that he had spent $140 while home, a considerable sum for an officer who made about $105 a month. He arrived in Baltimore at 8 o'clock in the morning after an extremely cold ride. By noon of January 2, he was in Washington, where he learned the train back to his Regiment was not leaving until 9:50 a.m. the next morning. That evening, Charles attended the theater and had drinks with Lieutenant Willard of the 18th Cavalry. He boarded a freight train to the front on the morning of January 3, and arrived at his regiment around 4 p.m.

On January 7, Charles was placed in command of Company I of the regiment. Rail guard duty continued, and Charles often mentioned the bitter cold they all experienced during the long nights riding on top of the railroad cars.

Around January 20, Charles' commanding officer, Captain Bennett Munger left the Company to become Inspector of the prisoner-of-war camp at Elmira, New York. Charles was now ranking officer in Company C of the 44th NY.

Camp at Alexandria

Later that month the 44th NY was ordered to the city of Alexandria; they would now be guarding supply trains from their starting point at Alexandria, just across the river from Washington. From there, each night, about 25 men of the 44th NY would travel on top of boxcars headed for the front. They would usually leave in the afternoon and return, if no delays were encountered, by noon of the next day.

On January 25, the 44th NY arrived in Alexandria by freight car about 2 a.m. to begin the duty. The day they arrived, they sent out eighty men guarding three trains.

This photo shows the camp of the 44th NY at Alexandria from behind the camp, with the city in the background. Each company had an arched entryway leading to a street dedicated to that company. The center archway was higher than the company archways, and led to the Regimental Headquarters. (Library of Congress)

This was a plum assignment that lasted a little over three months. After a few days, the Regiment established a model campsite just outside of Alexandria with wooden planks for floors in their tents and stoves to keep off the cold. On January 31, Charles writes,

> ***"This day has been well spent in fixing up my tent I have Made a fine Bunk and floor In my tent things are all quiet Here no Mail from Home to Day..."***

Another advantage of being in a camp for more than a few days was the opportunity for officers to hire a servant to do their cooking and other chores. Lower-ranking officers would usually join with two or three other officers of similar rank and share the cost of a cook that could be as high as $20 a month. Charles purchased a stove for his tent and a stove for his servant, who most likely lived elsewhere. Hired cooks and servants were often escaped slaves referred to as contraband.

In August of 1861, Congress passed the Confiscation Act permitting court proceedings for confiscation of any property being used to support the Confederate independence effort, including slaves. Most Black Americans were still considered property. The following March Congress passed legislation forbidding all officers or persons in the military or naval service to return escaped slaves to their owners. Thousands made their way to Federal Lines and more than a hundred contraband camps were established. The men would often work for the Army or Navy and later in the war many would join "colored regiments" to fight for the Union. Often, schools were established for the children in these camps. By the end of the war, ten percent of the Federal Army consisted of Black Americans.

In early February, Charles learned that his efforts to be promoted to Captain would probably, at least for the time being, go nowhere. With free time on his hands, Charles began to grow restless and started to think about life after the Army. Charles did not do well with idle time and notes in his diaries that he was drinking considerable amounts of ale and whiskey.

Charles quickly settled in to life at Alexandria. He spent his time guarding trains headed to the front, which, except for the miserably cold and often rainy nights, he enjoyed. He wrote home often and began going into Alexandria several nights a week to attend the theater or play billiards. He saw *Macbeth, Our American Cousin*, and a number of other plays popular at the time. On Friday, March 11, Charles crossed over the Potomac with a group of officers to see the city of Washington. That evening, they attended Grover's Theater for a production of *Richard the Third* starring Edwin Booth, the brother of John Wilkes Booth. During the play Charles saw President Abraham Lincoln and Secretary of State William Seward, who were also attending the play. Charles notes that the piece ***"was finely played"***.

It was not unusual for Lincoln to attend plays. On one occasion, when Lincoln was asked why he so often attended the theater he replied:

"I have not come for the play, but for the rest. I am hounded to death by office-seekers, who pursue me early and late, and it is simply to get two or three hours' relief that I am here. After a slight pause he added: I wonder if we shall be tormented in heaven with them, as well as with bores and fools?"

In early March of 1864, Ulysses Grant was promoted to the rank of lieutenant general, and made Commander of all Union Armies. Grant established his headquarters at Culpeper and developed his plan for the coming spring, which, at last, involved much of the Federal Army being coordinated in its actions to defeat the South. Lack of coordination was a constant problem for the Federal forces up to this point. The overall plan was simple: as General Tecumseh Sherman put it, ***"He was to go for Lee and I was to go for Joe Johnston."***

Grant would travel with General Meade and the Army of the Potomac. They would follow Robert Lee wherever he went until the Army of Northern Virginia was destroyed. There would be no halt to the campaign until the thing was done. Sherman would travel south from Chattanooga. His orders were to defeat Joe Johnston's Army of the Tennessee and take Atlanta, Georgia. Benjamin Butler would advance on Lee from the southwest up the James River, Nathaniel Banks would take Mobile, Alabama, and Franz Sigel would capture granaries and rail lines in the Shenandoah Valley. The smaller campaigns of Butler, Banks, and Sigel would prove to be unsuccessful; victory or defeat rested in the hands of Grant and Sherman. Charles Kelly's days guarding trains, and attending theater in Alexandria were numbered.

The South was also carefully considering what its course of action would be once the roads dried out enough to support artillery and wagons. By now, Confederate President Jefferson Davis knew there would be no recognition or aid coming from England or France. The South would stand or fall on its own. Also, the hope of Lee capturing large northern cities such as Baltimore or Washington had died on Cemetery Ridge, that awful day at Gettysburg.

Vastly outnumbered in men and everything else needed to secure the freedom of the South, there remained but one course of action that might compel the Yankees to quit their invasion of Davis' homeland and allow the South to live in peace. Abraham Lincoln would be up for re-election in November. If the South won enough battles and made pursuit of the war painful enough for the North, support for Lincoln might well erode. The Federal Presidency might end up in the hands of someone like George McClellan, whose party's platform called for an immediate cessation of hostilities and a negotiated settlement with the Confederacy. McClellan himself thought the war should continue until the Union was restored, but did not advocate the end of slavery. The conflicts within his party weakened McClellan's chance of success, but getting Lincoln out of office that November was the one realistic hope left for the Southern cause. It was a long shot, but in the spring of 1864, that was all Jefferson Davis had to work with.

This photo, taken March 20, 1864, shows the main archway into the camp of the 44th NY at Alexandria Virginia. At the top of the arch is the red Maltese Cross, emblem of the 1st Division of the 5th Corps of the Army of the Potomac. Below that hangs the number designation of the Regiment. On the sides of the archway are plaques commemorating battles fought by the 44th New York. Charles Kelly is in the front row, sitting, third from the left. (Library of Congress)

On Easter Sunday, March 27, 1864, Charles came in to Alexandria from train duty and attended church. He was well pleased with the service. When he returned to camp he noted that some of the officers were drunk and that it was having a bad effect on the regiment. Charles had not had any liquor for some time and he notes that he felt better for it.

The next day, the regiment had dress parade and Charles wrote a letter home to his mother. He was disappointed that he received no letters from home that day and also disappointed he had not heard anything regarding his latest request for a furlough home for a few days. That evening he went into town and played two games of billiards betting fifty cents a game; he lost both games. While in town, he had a ***"peck of steamed oysters"*** with cider, one of his favorite meals. Charles notes that the oysters cost him sixty cents.

On the afternoon of March 29, Charles received the furlough to visit home that he had been hoping for. Not wasting any time, that evening he went to Washington where he got current with his pay, and got on the first train that was headed north west. He missed a connection at Baltimore and spent the night there. He left Baltimore at 9:30 the next morning and arrived in Elmira, New York, at 2 a.m. the next day. Spending the rest of the night at the American Hotel, he missed the morning train to Penn Yan so he visited his old Captain, Bennett Munger, now Inspector of the prisoner of war camp at Elmira. Charles commented that Captain Munger appeared to be in fine health. On the evening of April 1, 1864, Charles arrived in Penn Yan.

Charles spent his time at home in similar fashion to his Christmas visit, seeing friends and catching up on business affairs. He attended church on Sunday April 2, and spent Monday getting his old brewery equipment ready to move. With help from friends, he had everything moved out by Tuesday night. With future business on his mind, he bought a piece of land for $100, with $50 put up as down payment. He noted that buying the land was a tough bargain.

Charles spent all day Wednesday visiting family and friends. That night his father was drunk and Charles had a quarrel with him about his drinking. He noted that ***"I suppose I ought to stop the thing myself."***

The morning of Thursday, April 6, Charles started back for his regiment. He had another visit with Captain Munger in Elmira and left on the 5 p.m. train for Baltimore. This time he indulged in the luxury of a sleeping car and arrived in Baltimore the next morning. He got to Washington on Friday April 7, about noon, and spent the rest of the day in the city. That evening he attended the theater and saw Edwin Forrest perform *King Lear*. Charles enjoyed the performance and noted that Forrest was ***"a splendid delineator of character".*** He spent the night at the Kirkwood House and wrote, ***"the house was not kept as good as it formerly was they are having too much Business to perform."***

Charles headed for the boat to Alexandria around noon on April 8, 1864. By the time he was in Alexandria it was raining so hard, he took a coach to camp. He arrived during a heavy storm and found ***"The officers of the camp on the drunk as much as when I Left for home."***

Monday morning, April 11, there were no trains running on the Orange and Alexandria Railroad. The storm that greeted Charles on his return to the 44th NY had completely washed out the bridge at Bull Run. Crews were frantically working to rebuild the structure. Remarkably, they had trains going again on the night of the 11th, and Charles once again went out on train guard duty.

Charles returned to camp about 10 a.m. the next morning. That night he went into Alexandria to see the play *Seven Sisters* but the performance was sold out. Charles woke the next morning to a mild sunny day in fine health. The sunshine greatly boosted his spirits and he writes about the warmth of the sun making the old young again. That night it was back to the theater to see *Ten Nights in a Bar-room and What I Saw There.* The play is based on a best-selling novel of the time by Timothy Shay Arthur and was a popular temperance melodrama. Charles says that the play was splendid. After a good night's sleep, Charles resolved to "... ***Leave off Drinking after due Reflection I have come to the conclusion that Demon drinking is the Root of all our Eviles in This Life..." That evening he wrote, "Drank some ale from Sargent Caswell of Co H Which Was all wrong for me to do."***

By April 14, Charles was again looking for letters from home. He had received no letters since returning to the regiment. He writes:

> ***"Our Sutlers shop is the worst thing in the Regt at this time it is making more Drunkards than anything else could do"***

Sutlers were not part of the Army commissary system; rather, they were independent businessmen who followed army camps, selling from the back of wagons or from tents. They sold just about anything that a soldier might buy, and were often a soldier's source of whiskey or ale.

Charles' see-saw relationship with whisky and ale continued as the weeks went by. On April 17, He notes, ***"I bought a gallon of Ale I have drank some Ale today."*** On the 18th he writes, ***"I think I shall quit using Tobacco after to day"*** and on April 19, ***"I have drunk some for the Last three or four days I do intend to stop."*** On April 20, he continues his reflection on the subject:

> ***"I have spent for the three Or four days some five Dollars for Drink but This is my last day for Drinking while in the Army and my Last day For chewing tobacco or Smoking I am satisfied That it is all stiff for a man to drink or smoke I am going to try and see If I cant Be a Gentleman In the future... I have liked to drink about ten gallons Of Ale since I came Back"***

On April 21, there are still no letters from home:

> ***"I Can't see why it is so I have Been here some ten days without a Letter From home"***

Guarding trains from the likes of Confederate Raider John Mosby, a constant threat to army trains in Virginia, was becoming more and more pleasant as the weather improved. April 22, Charles writes he ate dinner at Brandy Station, which cost him 75 cents, and had a pleasant ride back to Alexandria, arriving at half past one on Saturday morning. During the time the 44th NY was guarding the Orange and Alexandria Railroad there were no raids on the line.

Charles finally received a letter from his mother on April 24. The letter mentions the death of William Watt's wife ***"from the effects of drink"*** and goes on to say, ***"it was a sad affair for a woman to act as she had done"*** and that ***"William felt dreadful over it"***. Charles notes, ***"she was a fine Business woman and the children will feel awful after her."***

The order came on April 22 for the 44th NY to report to Division headquarters. Charles relates that the regiment is in good fighting trim and the men are in good spirits. The 44th NY left their comfortable camp at Alexandria on Sunday May 1, 1864. They rode the trains they had been guarding these past months and joined the 1st Division, now commanded by General Griffin, encamped near Beverly Ford on the Rappahannock River. From there the Division moved with the 5th Corps, under command of General Warren, to within two miles of Culpeper Court House. The regiment stopped there on the night of May 3. Charles set up his shelter tent, filled out some paperwork regarding clothing requisitions, and went to bed around half past nine that night eager for a good night's sleep. Two hours later, the bugle sounded and orders were given to strike tents. They were on the march that dark night a little after midnight and did not stop until they crossed the Rapidan River at Germanna Ford around 8:30 in the morning. After cooking breakfast, they resumed the march. General Grant's plan to attack Lee and destroy the Army of Northern Virginia was underway.

CHAPTER EIGHTEEN

Grant Goes for Lee

The Battle of the Wilderness

After crossing the Rapidan, they entered the same overgrown tangle of vines and small trees in which Joseph Hooker had been soundly defeated by Lee and Jackson one year earlier. It is also where Stonewall Jackson was mortally wounded by friendly fire, when his scouting party became silhouetted by the moon on the night of May 2, 1863. The heavy thickets measured about a dozen miles by eight miles of second growth brush and vegetation, almost impassable if one left its many roads and clearings. It was called the Wilderness.

Grant wanted to spend no more than two days passing through the Wilderness to the open ground on the other side where his superior numbers and better artillery could be used to advantage. Grant's sixty-mile train of 4,300 wagons, needed to support over 120,000 men and 56,000 horses and mules, set the pace. Crossing the Rapidan at Ely's Ford and Germanna Ford, Grant was greatly relieved that the crossings had gone unopposed. Regardless of what they encountered Grant was determined to march straight through the Wilderness between Mine Run and the junction of the Rapidan and Rappahannock Rivers. A Federal officer who once described Grant said, ***"He habitually wears an expression as if he had determined to drive his head through a brick wall, and was about to do it."*** The Wilderness was now Grant's brick wall.

Lee was well aware of the advantages the Wilderness afforded his much smaller army. He planned to let the Yankees cross the river and then hit them with everything he had before they emerged on open ground the other side of the thickets, and then drive them back across the Rapidan River. He would attack with Ewell's 2nd Corps up the Orange Turnpike and with Hill's 3rd Corps on the Orange Plank Road. Longstreet's 1st Corps would join the attack as soon as Longstreet arrived.

The 44th NY marched through the Wilderness until 5 p.m. on May 4, and halted near Wilderness Tavern. They had been marching without sleep since May 2. After riding trains for three months they were not accustomed to long marches, Charles and his men were exhausted and footsore.

The morning of May 5, was fine and sunny. Charles says it was his 30th birthday. Having a sense of what was coming that day Charles was in a reflective and somber mood. He noted in his diary,

> ***"The morning is fine We Expected to meet the enemy this forenoon This is my Birthday 30 years ago this morning I first saw Light and my Life has been somewhat Checkered I was Born in the city of Glasgow Scotland Things are not in good shape for me to die if my Property was Paid for I should feel satisfied But as it is my Father and mother will get a pension of 17 dollars per month which Will help to support them If I should get killed to I want the saloon sold and the money placed at Trust For the Benefit of my Father and mother and for them to use the principal if it should Be necessary the men are in good spirits this morning 1 year ago today We were at Chancellorsville Lying in the trenches... There is only one thing that I Regret in my Life and that is the want of a good Education I Now see the want of it and if I live to get out of this I shall improve time some and try and get a good Education"***

Interesting thoughts for a man facing his own mortality. However, there is a mystery in this entry of Charles' diary. If Charles was thirty years old on this day as he states, his birthdate would be May 5, 1834. However, Charles' military records, his baptismal records, his obituary, census records, and other documents all indicate that Charles was born in 1831. To compound the mystery, in Charles' diary entry from one year earlier, he says he was at that time 29 years old, doubling down on the 1834 year of birth. It is most likely that Charles was born in 1831, but why he twice wrote in his diaries of a birthdate three years later remains a mystery.

Saunders Field

About 1 o'clock that day, the 1st Division of the 5th Corps formed into line of battle across the Orange Turnpike, about two miles southwest of Wilderness

Tavern, in an opening in the woods called Saunders Field. The clearing covered forty acres. It would be the first engagement of the Battle of the Wilderness, and the first time Grant met Lee on the battlefield. It was probably not what Charles had in mind as a fitting celebration of his birthday.

While forming their line, infantry commanded by Confederate General Ewell could be seen on the west side of the field, dug in and waiting for the Yankees to arrive. The Union forces prepared to oblige them. The First Brigade of the 1st Division formed on the right of the Turnpike with the Second Brigade on the left. In the middle and front, regiments of the Third Brigade under command of General Joseph Bartlett formed, with the 44th NY on the road and the 83rd Pennsylvania and 18th Massachusetts to the left of the 44th NY. The right flank of the 44th NY was unsupported. Behind this front line was the 118th Pennsylvania and the 20th Maine.

General Griffin, commander of the 1st Division, was ordered to attack the Rebel position without hesitation, with the assurance that three divisions would soon join him to cover both his right and left flanks. As ordered, Griffin's three brigades charged into the center of the Confederate position commanded by General John Marshall Jones, about 2 p.m. They drove back a line of skirmishers, and then broke the first line of the enemy, sending them fleeing. The second line of Jones' Brigade ran from their positions in great confusion. Desperately trying to rally his troops and restore order, General Jones was killed.

Not long after the charge, The First Brigade, which was to the right of Charles Kelly's Third Brigade, encountered a "blizzard of lead" coming from the dense overgrowth on their right flank. They were unable to maintain their advance. They could not even see their attackers. In the Wilderness, a man would become invisible after traveling 100 feet into the brush. They pulled back to the east across Saunders Field, suffering heavy casualties as they went. The right flank of the entire Third Brigade was now exposed and found themselves far in advance of the rest of the Federal line, with the promised three divisions to cover their flanks nowhere in sight. While the 1st Division re-formed their lines the enemy counter-attacked from three directions driving the entire Division back to where they had started earlier that afternoon. During the retreat General Bartlett, commander of Charles' Third Brigade, had his horse shot out from under him and narrowly escaped becoming a Confederate prisoner.

Hampered by the infamous tangle of the Wilderness, the promised help did not begin to arrive until after 3 o'clock that afternoon. General Wright of Sedgwick's 6th Corps, who was to cover Griffin's right, got lost in the woods searching for Griffin's right flank. General Crawford commander of the 5th Corps 3rd Division, and General Wadsworth, commander of the 5th Corps 4th Division, were assigned to cover Griffin's left. Crawford, groping blindly in the dense woods, ran right into the Rebel counterattack, which panicked his entire division. In addition to heavy casualties, he lost an entire regiment when it fled in the wrong direction and was surrounded and captured. Wadsworth had gotten turned around in the dense trees and was flanked by Confederate General Gordon, who ripped into his division and sent his men running in all directions.

That afternoon, a short distance to the southeast, General Hancock's 2nd Corps fought a major engagement with General A.P. Hill's Corps on the Orange Plank Road. It started in earnest around 4 p.m.; hard fighting continued until dark. Men died by the hundreds and were wounded by the thousands.

For Charles, the day's battle was over. Charles' Third Brigade fell back to their entrenchments, counted their dead and wounded, and began to prepare for the next day. To their front, numerous fires started by artillery rounds were burning in the woods. Dead pine trees, with sap long dried, exploded into fiery pillars. Charles could hear screams of wounded soldiers from both sides, unable to run away as flames advanced toward them. There was a distinctive sound when a cartridge pouch exploded from the intense heat.

General Griffin was furious over the beating his division had taken; he felt let down by his fellow officers. Jumping the chain of command and cussing a blue streak, He rode directly to General Meade's headquarters. He entered the General's tent, still venting his rather unrestrained feelings, and verbally blasted General Meade for what had happened to his men that afternoon. After General Griffin left, General Grant, who had been sitting not far away, whittling on a stick, came into Meade's tent. He wanted to know ***"Who is this General Gregg? You ought to arrest him".*** General Meade responded by going up to Grant, buttoning up his coat for him and saying in a calm reassuring voice, ***"It's Griffin, not Gregg: and it's only his way of talking."***

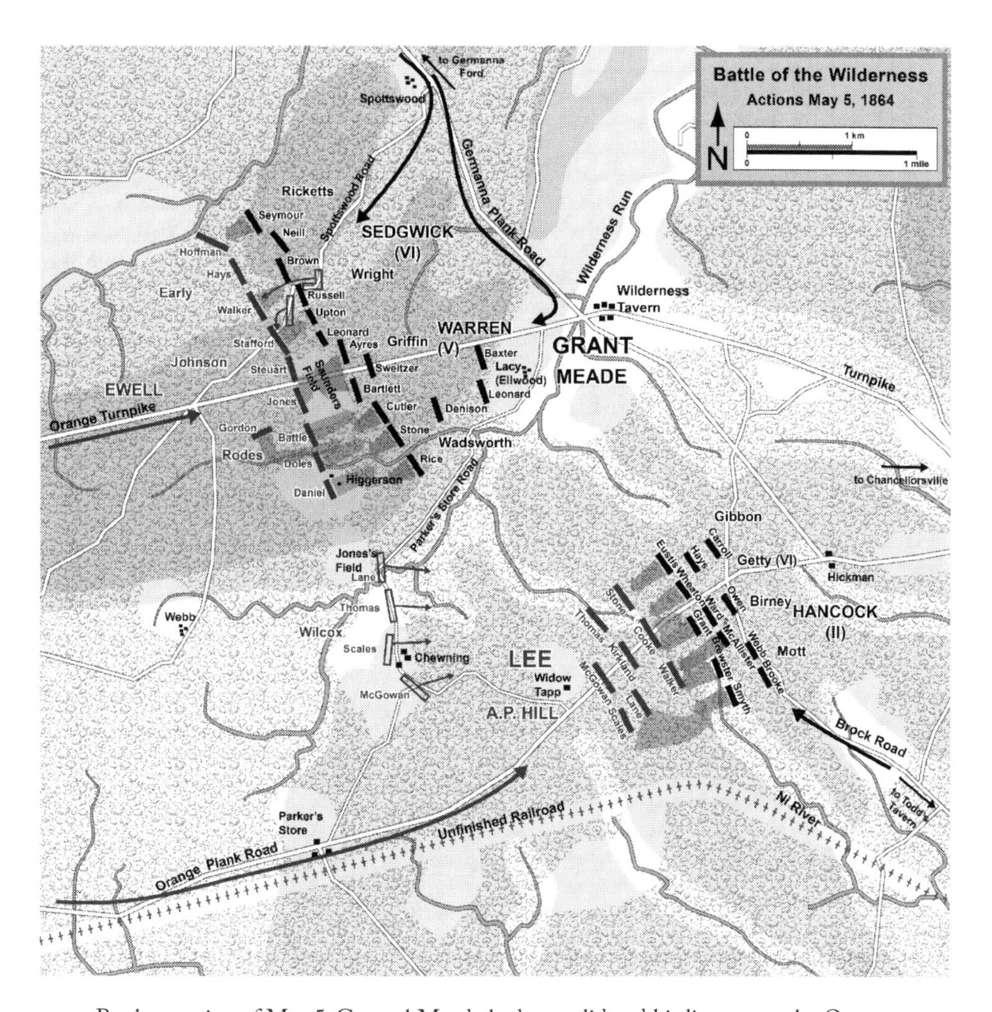

By the evening of May 5, General Meade had consolidated his line across the Orange Turnpike. Charles Kelly's brigade (commanded by Bartlett) is left of the Orange Turnpike on the east side of Saunders Field. General Sedgwick is now on Grant's right flank. Grant's HQ is at Wilderness Tavern. Lee's HQ is at the WidowTapp farm. Hancock's 2nd Corps is engaged in heavy fighting on the Orange Plank Road. The fighting would last until dark. Note the large gap between Warren's 5th Corps and Hancock's 2nd Corps. "Map by Hal Jespersen, www.cwmaps.com".

May 6, 1864

The 44th NY was quietly awakened at 4 a.m. the next morning, and moved to the front. The orders were to assault the enemy works at 5 a.m. Sedgwick's 6th Corps, on the right, was to start the assault, and when actively engaged, the 5th Corps was to attack. The 5th Corps waited all morning, taking casualties from enemy artillery shells exploding overhead, but the order to attack did not come. At noon, the order to attack was canceled.

To the east on the Orange Plank Road, General Hancock hit the enemy hard as soon as it was light. He had nearly broken the rebel line the previous evening but was stopped by darkness, and now he intended to finish the job. Lee was there that morning, filling in for A.P. Hill who was too ill to lead his men, as was often the case. A dozen Confederate guns, on the west side of a thirty-acre clearing called Tapp Field, desperately tried to hold the Yankees back with canister shot. The Confederate lines were beginning to crumble and Lee rode among the fleeing men trying to rally them. When a Texas brigade recognized Lee and the danger he was in, a great cry went up from the men demanding that Lee move to the rear. Lee seemed in a daze, not completely aware of what he was doing, when a soldier grabbed his reins and walked him back from the front line. The Texans surged forward, losing three-quarters of their men but stabilizing the line.

It was then that Longstreet arrived. Seeing that General Lee was ***"off his balance,"*** Longstreet came up to Lee and calmly informed him, ***"[your] line would be recovered in an hour if [you] would permit me to handle the troops, but if my services were not needed I would like to ride to some place of safety, as it was not quite comfortable where we were."*** To the great relief of Longstreet and Lee's staff, Lee withdrew to the rear of the Confederate lines.

By ten a.m., Longstreet had indeed stopped the determined Yankees about a half mile from the Brock Road. With his line stabilized, Lee sent two of Hill's divisions northward to plug the large gap between Hill's 3rd Corps and Ewell's 2nd Corps. They filled the gap and dug in, giving Lee a continuous line from Ewell's left to Hill's right. Lee could now contemplate going over to the attack.

Grant's army was now in grave danger. There was a large gap between Warren's 5th Corps and Hancock's 2nd Corps, and Grant's right and left flanks were exposed; not a good position to be in when facing Robert Lee. On the Confederate left, General Gordon desperately wanted to go around Sedgwick's right flank and roll up the Federal right. So far he had been unable to get permission from General Ewell, who believed that Burnside was in the rear of Sedgwick's lines waiting for such a move.

Federal General Wadsworth had come up to help fill the gap in Hancock's right, only to have his two brigades flanked and decimated. During the attack, Wadsworth was mortally wounded and abandoned by his fleeing men. He died two days later in a Confederate field hospital.

Within three hours of his arrival, Longstreet had turned the battle from a slugfest, with both sides blindly attacking and retreating through tangled thickets, into a battle based on tactics. After thoroughly scouting out the ground, he sent his young chief of staff, Lieutenant Colonel Sorrel, with four brigades east along an unfinished railroad line, and then north straight into Hancock's left flank. At the same time, he attacked Hancock's front with eleven brigades. Hancock's left flank disintegrated. Years later Hancock addressed Longstreet, saying, ***"You rolled me up like a wet blanket."***

Longstreet did not intend to make this just one more fight. As Hancock's position crumbled, he planned to follow up with two divisions attacking the left flank of Warren's 5th Corps, followed by Ewell's 2nd Corps driving straight ahead, cutting off Grant's retreat across the Rapidan. He then would destroy Grant's panicked army and capture miles of supply wagons, as the Yankees fled toward Fredericksburg.

The gods of war must have been angry with the Confederate cause that day. As the rebels continued advancing on the right, two Confederate brigades got turned at angles and mistakenly began firing on each other. Longstreet rode with his staff to put a stop to the undisciplined firing. Longstreet and three members of his staff were hit. Severely wounded, Longstreet was carried from the field. One year earlier, just four miles away, Stonewall Jackson had been mortally wounded by friendly fire a few hours after his triumphant flanking maneuver of Joseph Hooker's army at Chancellorsville.

Deeply shaken by Longstreet being wounded, Lee ordered a halt to the advance until the Confederate lines could be adjusted to avoid more friendly fire incidents. Without Longstreet in command, it took four hours to regroup his troops. The advance resumed at 4:15 p.m., but by that time Hancock had strengthened his entrenchments, shored up his flanks, and brought up reinforcements. Burnside had finally arrived and helped fill the gap between Hancock and Warren. Lee then demonstrated the futility of three Confederate divisions attacking headlong into seven Federal divisions, who were entrenched and waiting for them. Lee gave up after an hour of bloody assaults.

Throughout that day, Lee had been urging General Ewell, commanding the 2nd Corps, to go on the offensive. After giving up on the attack against Hancock, Lee rode northwest to Ewell's headquarters and arrived at half past five that evening. Ewell still believed that both Sedgwick and Burnside were in his front, and that he needed all his strength just to hold his position. Lee knew that Burnside was now with Hancock in front of the Confederate 1st and 3rd Corps. When General Gordon again put forth the plan he had been trying to sell to Ewell all day, Lee was interested. Gordon believed he could go around Sedgwick's far right and flank his entire corps. After hearing the plan, Lee, too discouraged and exhausted from the day's events to bother asking why this had not been done earlier, ordered Gordon to attack immediately.

Gordon set out at six p.m. He quickly started a wave of panic on Meade's right. He captured two generals and inflicted 600 Casualties on the Yankees, in addition to taking 600 prisoners. Gordon went all the way to Germanna Plank Road before his troops were stopped by darkness. Gordon returned to his lines having lost only 50 men. The Battle of the Wilderness was over.

That night, the two armies were about in the same positions as when the battle started on the previous day. May 6, 1864, the second day of the battle, General Grant had come dangerously close to a major disaster. If Longstreet's flanking attack on Hancock had continued under Longstreet's steady hand, and if Gordon had been allowed to attack on the Federal right earlier in the day, followed by a coordinated Confederate attack along the whole front, Lee's Army may well have routed the entire Federal Army.

Grant suffered about 17,000 casualties in two days. In the past, casualties of this magnitude would have resulted in the Army of the Potomac retreating back beyond reach of the enemy to regroup, resupply, and rethink their plan, and perhaps find a new Army commander. This process usually took months. Some of Grant's generals, visibly shaken and filled with visions of being cut off from retreat across the Rapidan, were seriously thinking such a move was necessary. Grant, in an uncharacteristic show of temper responded, ***"Oh, I am heartily tired of hearing about what Lee is going to do. Some of you always seem to think he is suddenly going to turn a double somersault, and land in our rear and on both of our flanks at the same***

time. Go back to your command, and try to think what we are going to do ourselves, instead of what Lee is going to do."

If, on that night, Grant's generals were not thinking about what Grant was going to do, Robert Lee was. Lee did not believe Grant would retreat. Considering how costly for both sides attacking entrenched positions had become, Lee reasoned with his impeccable sense of tactics, that Grant would move east of his Army of Northern Virginia and then south on the Brock Road to Spotsylvania, ten miles away. This would put Grant between Lee and Richmond, something that Lee could not allow.

Fighting in the Wilderness these past two days had also been costly for Lee. Lee suffered about 13,000 casualties, over twenty percent of the Army of Northern Virginia, and his command structure was crumbling. His 1st Corps commander, and by far his best general, James Longstreet was severely wounded. His 2nd Corps Commander Richard Ewell, had proved less than effective in the kind of fight against superior forces that Lee was engaged in. His 3rd Corps Commander, A.P. Hill, was often too sick to command his Corps. Half a dozen of Lee's generals had been killed, severely wounded or captured, and Lee's own health was declining.

Lee out-fought Grant in the Wilderness, flanking him twice and inflicting many more casualties on Grant's army than he had suffered. The problem was that Grant, even though soundly beaten, could not be convinced he was beaten. On the night of May 6, Grant commented to a reporter of the ***"sharp work General Lee had been giving us for a couple of days"*** and then went to bed. For the South, Longstreet's arithmetic calculations that he mused over after Chancellorsville, still held true. Robert Lee of course knew this but felt he had no choice but to go on.

Charles Kelly awoke on the morning of May 7, 1864, feeling well. Around daylight the Rebels attacked the center of the 5th Corps but were driven back by artillery that had been brought up to the Federal line during the night. Captain Nash of the 44th NY felt the object of the attack was to discover if the blue clad army had retreated back beyond the river during the night. Charles writes that there was no more fighting to his front that day.

At 9 o'clock that night, Charles and the entire 5th Corps left their position as quietly as possible and started a slow and tedious march in the dark toward Spotsylvania Court House. Much of the Army of the Potomac joined them. The men were exhausted after the three previous days of fighting, and still did not know if they were advancing or retreating. When they reached the junction of the Orange Turnpike and Brock Road, they knew a choice had to be made. Going straight ahead toward Chancellorsville meant they were retreating across the river or to Fredericksburg. Turing right onto the Brock Road meant that they were marching toward Richmond. They turned right. As Lee had predicted, Grant was moving his army south along the Brock Road toward the cross-roads at Spotsylvania Court House. The Army of the Potomac, greatly encouraged that they were not retreating as they had so many times in the past, got a jolt of new energy. The suffering in the Wilderness would not be in vain.

If marching to Spotsylvania was Grant's plan, Lee had no intention of losing the race to Spotsylvania, and being forced to assault an entrenched Federal army. Jeb Stuart's cavalry was already assigned the task of slowing the Federal advance along Brock Road. A division of horsemen had been battling Federal cavalry during the past two days for control of the road. Moreover, in case Lee was correct about Grant's intentions, earlier that day Lee ordered General William Pendleton, his chief of artillery, to cut a road starting at Lee's headquarters at the Tapp farmhouse on the Orange Plank Road, straight south through the trees and vines to Shady Grove Church and onto the Catharpin Road. If needed, and if the road could be finished in time, it would shorten the march to the crossroads at Spotsylvania.

Around 4 o'clock on May 7, 1864, Lee learned that Grant had pulled a number of his heavy guns from his reserve and they were now headed south down the Brock Road. Grant had begun no troop movements as of yet but moving some of his artillery was enough for Lee. He ordered General Anderson, who had taken Longstreet's place as commander of Lee's 1st Corps, to march south that night over Pendleton's newly cut road. The 1st Corps would go through the woods to Shady Grove Church, and turn east to Block House and the Brock Road, which would put them about two miles northwest of Spotsylvania.

CHAPTER NINETEEN

The Battle for Spotsylvania Courthouse

Laurel Hill

Still on the march at 8 o'clock the morning of May 8, the Federal columns finally came to a halt. It had been an exhausting night of starts and stops, poorly coordinated troop movements, and general confusion. The roads were dark and dusty, there was no moon. Everyone was tired and hungry. Up ahead federal cavalry leading the advance had encountered entrenched rebel infantry they could not brush aside. After a brief pause to let the cavalry get out of the way, the 5th Corps went into the fight. Before them, at the junction of two roads, about a half mile past the Alsop farmhouse, a clearing appeared stretching 400 yards ahead, rising to a slight ridge called Laurel Hill. It was about two miles northwest of Spotsylvania. On the ridge, dismounted Confederate cavalry were franticly constructing fieldworks. Lee knew that Laurel Hill was the last defensible position before Spotsylvania, and if it was lost Spotsylvania would probably go with it. When General Jeb Stuart saw large numbers of blue-clad infantry coming out of the trees he knew his troopers were in trouble. He sent a messenger riding hard to General Anderson, who had been marching all night through Lee's newly cut road through the thickets with the Confederate 1st Corps, and found Anderson's lead brigades near the Block House. Anderson did not hesitate; he sent two brigades north, along the Old Courthouse Road on the double quick, to cover the last mile from Block House to Laurel Hill.

General Warren, commanding Grant's 5th Corps, while examining the ridge before him, assumed he faced only dismounted cavalry. Warren sent John Robinson's 2nd Division forward on the right of Brock Road about 8:30 that morning. Warren urged them on. Robinson was given no time to scout what was ahead, and his exhausted men charged up Laurel Hill. They got within 50 yards of the Confederate works when the rebels opened up on them. This was not dismounted cavalry, but massed rifled musketry firing at them. Unknown to Warren, Anderson had arrived just minutes earlier. Anderson's worn-out rebel troops rushed into line and immediately started firing at the Yankees a few dozen feet away. All of Robinson's mounted officers were killed or wounded. Robinson was shot from his horse, and would lose a leg, He later was awarded the Congressional Medal of Honor. Robinson's division was decimated. The advance stopped. The Union troops fled across the field back to the Federal lines. The next day Robinson's division was disbanded due to loss of officers and men in the Wilderness and at Laurel Hill.

At the same time Union General Bartlett, commanding the Third Brigade of Griffin's 1st Division of Warren's 5th Corps, was marching south, past the Alsop farm on the right-hand fork of Brock Road, about a quarter of a mile short of where the two forks joined. Bartlett was followed by the First and Second Brigades of the 1st Division. Lt Colonel Conner, commanding the 44th NY, requested that his men be allowed to stack their knapsacks before becoming engaged. Bartlett told Connor's messenger, ***"No, tell Colonel Conner there is no force in front but cavalry and to march right up the road in fours."*** As they marched, the fields on their right opened to expose the Confederate position up the slope of Laurel Hill. Coming under fire from rebel cannon and musketry, Bartlett formed his brigade into a line of battle.

On the left of the road was the 83rd Pennsylvania, and on the right was the 44th NY. Behind them was the 1st Michigan and the 18th Massachusetts. An aide of General Bartlett rode up and told them to hurry or ***"you won't get a shot at them"***. After marching all night with no food, the four regiments advanced toward the rebels, a little over a quarter mile up the hill.

The 44th NY got within fifty feet of the rebel line where log and brush entanglements stopped them. They stood firing at close range. The officers were firing their pistols. Charles Kelly was hit in the thigh with a spent bullet. Fortunately for him, the bullet did not penetrate into his leg. The 83rd Pennsylvania reached the enemy lines and vicious hand to hand fighting was underway. One soldier wrote ***"for the first and last time in my warring, I saw two hostile lines lock bayonets."***

At that point, a Confederate regiment chasing the fleeing remnants of Robinson's Division a few hundred yards to the left, flanked the 44th NY from their left. Three officers and 36 men of the 44th NY were taken prisoner. Incurring heavy losses from two directions, the 44th NY and the 83rd Pennsylvania dissolved into a mob of fleeing men. The Color Guards for both regiments were obliterated. The 83rd lost 150 men. Just behind them, the 1st Michigan was reduced to 27 officers and men. The 44th NY lost their commander Freeman Connor, who was severely wounded. The regiment's Major, Edward Knox, while reforming the men, was also severely wounded by a bursting cannon shell. Captain Eugene Nash assumed command.

By 9:45 a.m., Generals Ayres and Bartlett, joined by General Griffin, managed to halt the retreat. The Third Brigade moved to the rear and formed a line near Alsop farm; for them their fighting for the day was over. Both North and South continued to pour newly arrived men into the battle for Laurel Hill; many died, but the South held their line. Around noon there was a lull in the fighting. Later that afternoon Grant ordered a new assault on the enemy line. The fighting finally diminished around dark with both sides holding the same ground they held when the battle began.

That evening Charles Kelly wrote in his diary,

> ***"...I was Hit in the thigh With a spent Ball Which makes me quite Lame I have not had nothing to eat since yesterday at noon up to this night it has Been the hardest day I ever spent in the service I had a Very good supper to Night"***

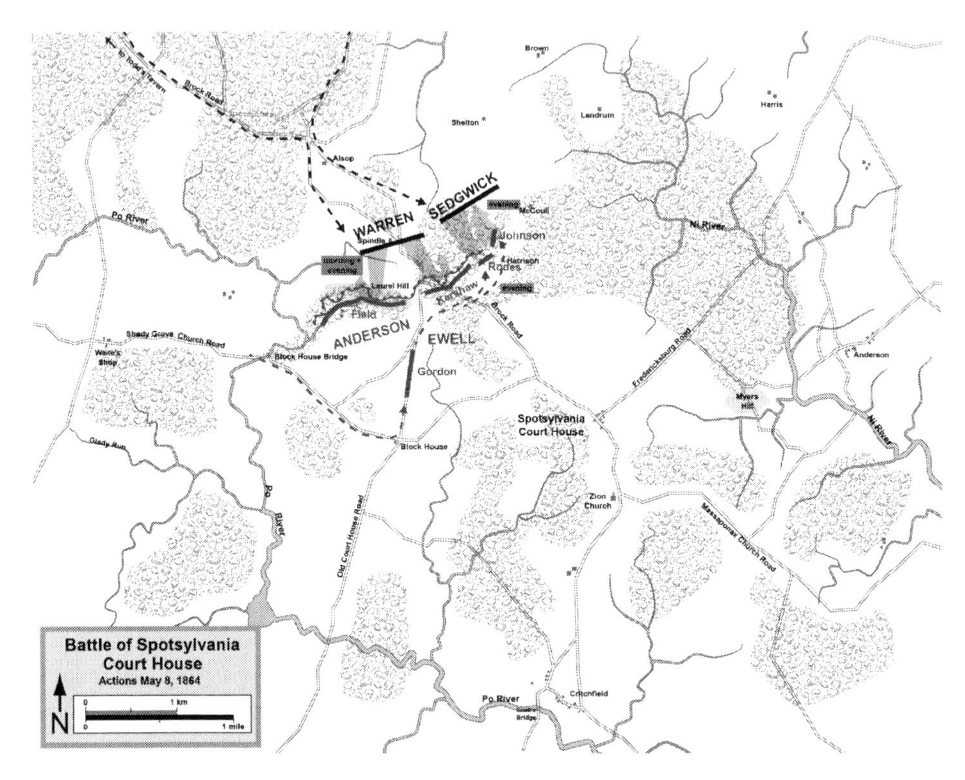

On the morning of May 8, General Warren ordered General Robinson's 2nd Division to attack the crest of Laurel Hill just as Confederate General Anderson arrived to reinforce Jeb Stuart's dismounted cavalry. At the same time General Bartlett's 3rd Brigade attacked Laurel Hill from the west fork of Brock Road. Both attacks failed, with Union forces experiencing heavy casualties. Charles Kelly is wounded when the 44th NY is flanked by rebel troops; Charles would recover. "Map by Hal Jespersen, www.cwmaps.com".

Charles Kelly slept quietly that night; it was too warm for blankets. Charles writes in his diary the following day, May 9,

> ***"We have not been engaged as yet The Rebs has got a strong position and it will Be Hard to Drive them out of it in my opinion We will move tonight from here We have got to drive the Rebs out of here or flank them if possible We have not been engaged today our brigade was placed in position the fornoon and have staid there all day We are now within 2 miles of Spotsylvania Court House the Brigade was under arms all night and we were attacked 3 times During the Night"***

The same day, May 9, General Sedgwick, commander of Grant's 6th Corps, was with his staff on the left flank of the Federal line, directing artillery placements. It was 9 o'clock in the morning. About a thousand yards away, rebel sharpshooters were occasionally firing at Federal troops as targets appeared. The General's staff and the artillerymen would duck for cover when the distinct sound of a Whitworth Rifle broke the air. When he saw what was happening, General Sedgwick berated his men: ***"What? Men dodging this way for single bullets? What will you do when they open fire along the whole line?"*** His men continued to flinch at the rebel fire. Sedgwick was reported as saying, "***Why are you dodging like this? They couldn't hit an elephant at this distance.***" Just then, he was hit under his left eye. He died a couple of minutes later. He was the senior ranking Union officer to die during the war.

General Sedgwick's staff had good reason to flinch at the sound of a Whitworth rifle firing from a mere 1,000 yards away. It was considered the most accurate sniper rife used in the war. A favorite of Confederate sharpshooters, the Whitworth, made in England, was a single shot muzzle-loading rifle that propelled a .451-inch diameter bullet, considerably smaller than Springfield or Enfield rifles. When handled by an expert marksman, the Whitworth rifle, fitted with a 4X scope, was deadly at up to 2,000 yards. Rebel sharpshooters with Whitworth rifles considered Federal officers and Federal artillery crews to be their most desirable targets.

When word of Sedgwick's death reached headquarters, Meade wept and Grant was shaken. Meanwhile the strength of Lee's entrenchments continued to grow. By this time in the war, the Army of Northern Virginia had learned to construct very effective entrenchments as a way of compensating for the larger numbers arrayed against them. Interlinking trenches with zigzag patterns, use of natural terrain, protected ports for firing from under head logs, clearing the area to the front for at least two hundred yards, and when that was not possible, constructing barriers with sharpened poles called abatis to slow an enemy attack, and interlacing fields of cannon fire were now all part of an entrenchment. The Confederate army became remarkably efficient at construction of these fortifications and by May 10, at Spotsylvania, their line extended over four miles.

General Warren now faced stronger Confederate lines than he had ever faced before but believed he could punch through the defenses and, with enough support, rout Lee's entire army. Always wanting to encourage initiative, Grant thought it was worth a try.

Charles Kelly's regiment remained at the rear in reserve until noon on May 10. Charles remarks that it was a pleasant morning, but also remarks that the regiment now had only eight officers; the field officers and the staff officers were all gone. A full regiment, prior to depletion by disease and battle, might have 34 or 35 officers.

General Warren's 5th Corps, which included the depleted 44th NY, attacked the rebel line about 4 p.m. on May 10. Sedgwick's 6th Corps, now commanded by General Horatio Wright, was on Warren's left and parts of General Hancock's 2nd Corps was on his right. In spite of having lots of support from Wright and Hancock the attack failed. Some of the men made it across the prepared ground in front of Lee's men, passed the barricades and abatis, went through massed musket fire and artillery firing canister shot from both flanks and the front, all the way to the rebel entrenchments before being cut down. Warren repeated the attack with the same result.

Charles wrote briefly about the attack that evening:

> ***"Tuesday May 10th 1864...We were ordered to move to the front this is the hardest days fighting I ever saw since I have Been in the service"***

Despite heavy losses, Grant was not done for the day. General Hancock arrived around 5 p.m., and being senior to Warren, took command of the 2nd and 5th Corps. Not having a better plan Grant ordered General Hancock to prepare for another assault at 6:30 p.m.

There was a 24 year-old colonel in the 6th Corps who believed that he had a better plan. His name was Emory Upton. After getting a close up look at the enemy's fortifications that afternoon, he explained to his commanding officer and then to his Corps Commander, General Wright, that a fast-advancing narrow formation could breach the enemy line if they did not stop to fire until they were in the rebel trenches. From there they could fan out in both directions and increase the width of the breakthrough, allowing more troops to follow.

Upton was given a dozen regiments to prove the worth of his idea, despite his plan being in conflict with a century of military doctrine. The young Colonel carefully planned the details of his attack. His target was a U shaped bulge in the rebel line called the Mule Shoe, one of the strongest points along Lee's very strong line. The Mule Shoe was a mile in depth and two-thirds of a mile wide, with the blunted point of the bulge making up the northern extent of Lee's entrenchments. Mostly wooded, with numerous paths cut through the trees, the bulge contained a second line of entrenchments on the west side about two hundred yards back from the north face of the fortification. After breaching the front of the bulge, Colonel Upton would be supported by General Mott's division from the 2nd Corps, whose job it was to exploit any breakthrough. Wanting to see what this young Colonel could do, Grant cancelled the general attack planned for 6:30 p.m.

After getting the go-ahead, Colonel Upton walked with the commanders of his twelve regiments to the edge of the woods and showed them their departure point just two hundred yards from the rebel line. He carefully explained his plan with maps, and showed each commander what was expected. Federal Corps commanders could have learned much by observing the level of preparation made by Upton.

Charles Kelly welcomed the cancelation of the general attack that evening, even though he did not know the reason for the decision. He writes:

> ***"We expected to have to charge the Rebs works this Evening But the order was Countermanded The men did not want to go up in the charge They would went up if necessary to do it... the fifth Corps is suffering Terrible in this Action our Brigade has suffered most of all I can't tell how things are going But we are holding our Lines all Right"***

Colonel Upton, with his twelve regiments consisting of 5,000 men, attacked on the west side of the Mule Shoe shortly after 6 p.m. They came in a single compact column. In spite of the rebel guns, Upton's first three regiments were mounting the enemy parapets within five minutes. The first to arrive were shot or bayoneted. There was hand-to-hand fighting in the trenches, as the gray coats put up a stubborn resistance. Then Upton's second wave arrived and the rebels turned and ran for their secondary line 200 yards to the rear. Just as planned, Upton's men fanned out and widened the breach. Things were going well. As anticipated, Confederate reinforcements began charging toward the gap in their line. Then General Mott's relief division failed to show up.

As soon as Mott's two brigades emerged from a wooded area, not far from the rebel entrenchments and formed up on the left of Upton's charge, they were raked with fire from 22 rebel guns and started taking heavy casualties. In minutes, both of Mott's brigades fell apart. They got no closer than a quarter mile from the enemy works before those who could, fled toward the safety of the trees. Still shaken from heavy casualties in the Wilderness, Mott's men were in no condition to do what they were asked to do that day.

Without support, Upton could not hold his position in the Mule Shoe. The young Colonel was wounded, but would recover. His men fought their way back to the Federal lines suffering about a thousand casualties. Darkness ended the fighting.

General Grant was impressed. With proper support, he believed the tactic would be successful. He commented, ***"We will try a corps tomorrow."*** General Grant promoted Upton to Brigadier General, and the remnants of Mott's two brigades were reassigned to another division. Their reputation could not be salvaged. It would take a day to get ready, but Grant planned a new assault, based on Upton's tactic, for the morning of May 12.

On May 11, General Grant reported his thoughts on progress since crossing the Rapidan, to the Secretary of War back in Washington. Robert Lee was now facing a general that would not quit regardless of the cost.

"Head Qrs. in the Field, Va

8 am May 11th 1864.

Hon. E. M. Stanton, Sec. of War. Washington D. C.
We have now entered the sixth day of very hard fighting. The result to this time is much in our favor. Our losses have been heavy as well as those of the enemy. I think the loss of the enemy must be greater. We have taken over five thousand prisoners, in battle, while he has taken from us but few except stragglers. I propose to fight it out on this line if it takes all summer.

U. S. Grant
Lieut. Gen. Comdg Armies"

Charles notes on May 11,

"Things are Looking good this morning No fighting as yet I slept Very Well During the Night I slept good the Night Before I had a Dream of home last night..."

After a night of heavy rain, General Hancock scheduled the attack on the Mule Shoe for 4 a.m., May 12. It was so dark the infantry did not get started until 4:35 a.m. Coming out of thick fog Hancock's men smashed through the Rebel lines. This time Lee's luck failed him. Believing Grant was retreating to Fredericksburg, Lee had withdrawn the 22 guns that on May 10, had destroyed Mott's Division. The guns were frantically returning when they were surrounded by blue-clad troops and taken.

As the Yankees poured over the log defenses, the rebels learned that the heavy rain had soaked much of their powder, and they were left to fight with bayonets, and rifles used as clubs. In the first half hour, 5,000 rebels were shot or captured. Two of Lee's Generals became Federal prisoners.

Robert Lee started his day at 3 a.m. that morning and after a brief breakfast mounted his favorite horse, Traveller. He heard the opening sounds of Hancock's assault and headed toward the gunfire where he encountered fleeing infantrymen.

General Gordon, whose men had flanked Sedgwick's 6th Corps in the Wilderness a week earlier, managed to stop the Federal advance. Gordon's division was at the base of the Mule Shoe and held in reserve, should they be needed. Once again, Lee's troops had to compel Robert Lee to withdraw from the front to prevent him from being shot from his horse.

There were now more than 15,000 Federal troops packed inside the ½-mile wide toe of the Mule Shoe. Men were pushing from the rear, with no idea what was happening in the front, and the crowded blue coats began to lose unit cohesion. The Federal officers tried to get the men to go south along the western interior of the fortification. Lacking the careful planning of Upton's assault, no coherent orders to capitalize on a breach of the Mule Shoe had been issued.

When Gordon's troops began to arrive, the Yankees' forward motion stalled. After a half hour, Lee's troops had secured most of the eastern edge of the Mule Shoe. Hancock's men could not go forward or back. As Gordon's men came up, they fired into the blue mass, unable to miss. The fighting continued in the heavy rain, back and forth, hand-to-hand, with bayonets and rifles used as clubs. Hancock's troops were pushed harder and harder against the inside toe of the Mule Shoe. They finally found shelter by climbing the log parapet, which made up the north face of the Mule Shoe, and taking positions on the outside of the logs.

General Burnside attacked the east side of the Mule Shoe at the same time as Hancock's attack, around 4:30 a.m., but was unable to reach the rebel entrenchments. Taking heavy fire, his men took cover and began firing into the rebel fortifications, but did not go forward. Burnside's attack lost momentum. Grant's plan was beginning to falter.

At 6:30 a.m., Grant sent General Wright's 6th Corps into the western leg of the Mule Shoe just where it turned south from the blunt north end, the men called it the Bloody Angle. They were stopped at the top of the log entrenchments and joined Hancock's troops huddled on the outside of the logs.

Since Upton's breach of the Confederate defenses on May 10, Lee's men had been constructing a new line of entrenchments across the base of the Mule Shoe. Lee knew his men had to hold on until the works were complete so they would have a place to withdraw to that would not endanger the rest of his line. Around 7:30 a.m., Lee was at the head of a column near the Harrison House, rushing men to support Gordon, when Lee and his staff came under Federal artillery fire. Struggling to control his mount, Lee's horse reared up, kicking the air just as a solid round shot bounced underneath both Lee and his horse. A close thing; a hit may well have altered the outcome of the battle and perhaps changed the course of the war.

General Warren, in an attempt to take pressure off Hancock's assault, was ordered forward. At 8:15 a.m., Warren once again attacked Laurel Hill. For many of Warren's men, this was the fourth or fifth time they had assaulted Laurel Hill; the only difference was that this time it had much better defenses. After 30 minutes, the attack failed. Warren reported back to Meade who, along with Grant, was losing confidence in Warren. Warren was promptly ordered to attack ***"at once at all hazards with your whole force".*** Warren ordered his division commanders ***"Do it.Don't mind the consequences."*** Th e renewed attack also failed.

Meanwhile, the fighting at the Bloody Angle continued. Men would poke their rifles through slits in the logs and fire without having any idea what was on the other side. Large trees were cut in two from musket fire. Men became frantic and climbed to the top of the logs, firing muskets as fast as their fellow soldiers could hand them loaded weapons, only to be shot minutes later. Rifles with bayonets fixed were tossed over the logs in hope of spearing an enemy, just an arm's length away. Dead and dying soldiers began to pile up four and five deep. The men on both sides of the logs lost touch with the outside world, almost in a trance, unable to imagine anything but killing and being killed. This macabre scene went on hour after hour in the rain and sleet. It grew dark, and still the killing continued. Finally, after midnight, it ended. Lee's new entrenchments were complete and by 4 a.m., of May 13, his troops had withdrawn to the base of the Mule Shoe.

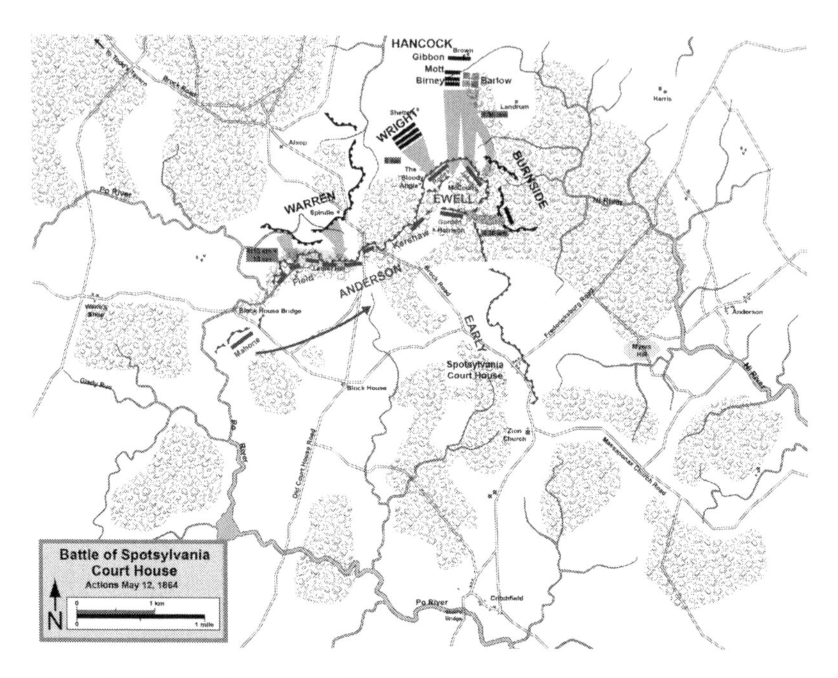

The attack on the salient in Lee's line on May 12. General Hancock attacks the northern tip of the "Mule Shoe". General Burnside is on his left and General Wright is on his right. Charles Kelly is with General Warren, who once again attacks Laurel Hill. Lee's HQ is at the Harrison House. Confederate General Gordon is frantically working to finish the line of defense at the base of the "Mule Shoe". "Map by Hal Jespersen, www.cwmaps.com".

The men who fought at the Battle of Spotsylvania Courthouse experienced a level of intensity and savagery not previously seen in the war. The reliance on trench works, which gave the defender a great advantage, pushed the use of the bayonet, canister shot, and close up killing to new levels. Federal casualties at the Mule Shoe were about 9,000. Grant stripped the defenders of Washington, as much as Lincoln would allow, to replace his losses. The South lost about 8,000, which included 3,000 men taken prisoner. Lee's army was shrinking and replacements were not to be had. Since the fight with Grant had started eight days earlier, the Army of Northern Virginia lost a third of its corps, division, and brigade commanders: 20 out of 57 killed, captured, or severely wounded. Perhaps the greatest single blow to Robert Lee, besides losing Longstreet, was on May 12, when Lee was desperately holding the Mule Shoe. It was then that Lee learned

Jeb Stuart had been mortally wounded the previous day. Attempting to stop Phil Sheridan's cavalry ten miles north of Richmond at Yellow Tavern, Stuart was shot in the stomach and would die on May 12. He was 31 years old. Lee's command structure was shattering.

General Grant's Army had lost 10 corps, division, and brigade commanders out of the 69 that started into the Wilderness. They would be replaced. Regardless, Grant was not done at the Mule Shoe. On May 13 and 14, in heavy rain, Grant began shifting his army to the east. Charles Kelly reports that the 44th left their lines at 10 p.m. on May 13, and marched all night on muddy roads. Charles writes:

> ***"...it Was the hardest marching I Ever Experienced in my campaigning... the regt Arrived at its destination about the break of day the men Were completely faged out not fit to fight today"***

Charles made an interesting observation in his diary entry of Monday, May 16. Three of the men of Company C had returned to camp the night before, probably lost or hiding from the awful carnage all around them. Charles notes, ***"in my opinion they all had the shell Fever pretty Badly."*** PTSD, and shell shock are only modern names for the same affliction of soldiers in combat throughout the ages. It was that same Monday that Charles reports seeing General Grant, General Meade, General Warren, and General Humphreys. Charles writes, ***"They were all together consulting."***

The reason behind the most recent forced marches at night in the mud and the rain was that crossing the Ni River, and reaching the Fredericksburg Road would put Grant's army behind the Army of Northern Virginia. Believing that Lee had shifted his army to counter the Federal movement, Grant saw an opportunity to break the stalemate. He ordered the 2nd and 6th Corps to once again attack Lee's line at the Mule Shoe. During the night of May 17, and morning of May 18, the two corps crossed over the log parapets at the north end of the bulge and moved 500 yards south, through the now empty Mule Shoe, to attack Lee's new line of entrenchments at the base of the bulge. The attack, planned for dawn, did not get underway until about 8 a.m. Grant's men soon learned the rebel trenches were fully occupied by Lee's 2nd Corps, who destroyed the assault with close range cannon fire. The artillery gave the rebels little chance to use their rifles before the Yankees withdrew with heavy casualties.

CHAPTER TWENTY

The March to Cold Harbor and the Siege of Petersburg

The North Anna River

Grant now had enough of Lee's entrenchments near Spotsylvania Court House. The Army of the Potomac moved to the southeast toward Hanover Junction and Richmond. The 44th NY passed through Guiney's Station (Guinea Station), located on the Richmond to Fredericksburg Railroad on the morning of May 21, and marched until 11 p.m. that night. The march resumed the next day, with enemy skirmishers and rebel artillery slowing their advance. They marched until dark and stopped for the night. That night a flock of sheep happened to wander near their camp, by morning all that was left was ***"a pile of pelts and refuse"***. One of the men commented, ***"it was the most decisive victory since the beginning of the campaign."***

By 9 o'clock the next morning, May 23, the 44th NY was again underway with the rest of their brigade headed toward Hanover Junction. When General Warren found the North Anna River at Jericho Ford unprotected, he ordered General Griffin's division to wade across and establish a beachhead. Charles Kelly forded the North Anna River at Jericho Ford around 2 p.m. The Virginia Central Railroad, a vital supply line for Richmond and a direct route to Hanover Junction, was less than two miles on the other side. The North Anna River had steep muddy banks and the crossing was slow. Engineers began erecting a pontoon bridge for the remainder of the 5th Corps, who crossed around 4:30 p.m.

The Second Brigade, who crossed ahead of Charles' Third Brigade, came under a fierce attack and the Third Brigade was divided and sent to protect each of the Second Brigade's flanks. Meanwhile, more units of the 5th Corps crossed the river and joined the battle. Heavy fighting continued until dark, first one side pushing back the enemy and then the other side doing the same. Both Yankees and Rebels

Jericho Mills, Va. Canvas pontoon bridge across the North Anna, constructed by the 50th New York Engineers; the 5th Corps under Gen. Warren crossed here on May 23rd, 1864. View from the north bank. (Library of Congress)

threw up breastworks. Charles remained near the river with three companies to guard against Rebel cavalry. He returned to his regiment at 2 a.m. the next day. The beachhead across the North Anna had held.

The next morning the expected attack from Lee's infantry did not come. Grant continued to send men across the river, and by 11 a.m., General Warren had advanced to the Virginia Central Railroad. General Lee was not running away. Lee had devised a trap for the advancing bluecoats. He formed his army into an inverted V shape with the point of the formation at Ox Ford on the North Anna River. Lee's left flank was manned by General A.P. Hill, while the right flank, extending all the way to Hanover Junction, was manned by General Anderson and

General Ewell. Lee's plan was to split the Federal Army into two parts, one part on each side of the V. This would allow one wing to be defeated without access to help from the other wing before it was too late. Lee would use his interior lines within the heavily fortified works that made up the inverted V to support the attack at whatever point was needed.

At first the plan worked. Grant now believed he had the Confederate army on the run. On May 24, General Ledlie, commanding a brigade in Burnside's 9th Corps, crossed the North Anna at Ox Ford. He had been drinking heavily that day. Instead of waiting as ordered for the rest of the division to cross and get into place, he attacked the tip of the V with a single regiment, thinking it was lightly defended. The regiment was thrown back and he sent for three more regiments to renew the assault. By the time orders came, telling him to wait until the entire division had crossed the River, General Ledlie was completely drunk. He ordered another attack. Lee's men waited until the Yankees where within close range and then cut them to pieces. General Hancock's 2nd Corps attacked Lee's entrenchments from the Federal right wing of the V but got nowhere. They pulled back and started digging their own trenches. Grant realized the situation he was in and stopped the assault. Lee's plan had worked perfectly, but that day Lee was seriously ill, unable to leave his tent. No one in his depleted command had sufficient skill or authority to launch a coordinated counter attack on Grant. Lee felt an excellent opportunity had been lost.

The 5th Corps was back across the North Anna River around 9 p.m. on May 25, and continued marching south until sundown on May 27. The weather was extremely hot and long marches with little or no sleep, and poor quality food, were wearing on Charles and his men. After marching 35 miles Charles writes he was ***"about beat out my shoes are worn out My feet are sore"***. The 44th NY, along with the rest of the 5th Corps, was now in the Federal right wing on the west side of the V, facing Lee's entrenchments. Not wanting another protracted siege Grant decided to withdraw from the V and go around Hanover Junction. He set his sights on the little town of Cold Harbor.

Charles was again on the march by five o'clock the next morning. The march was so exhausting that Charles had to get on a horse to keep up with his men. There were many stragglers that day. Charles notes that one of the stragglers in his company was Noah Shultz, a man who had enlisted with Charles back in the fall of 1862. Noah, wounded at Spotsylvania, fell out before they crossed the river, he could go no further that day. Noah was 26 years old and strong; he would recover and rejoin the regiment.

They crossed over to the south side of the Pamunkey River near Hanover Town before noon on May 28. The march continued for two miles, when the order came to stop and build breastworks so the crossing at the Pamunkey could be held for the rest of the army. The 44th resumed marching on May 29, under increasing fire from enemy skirmishers, and stopped for the night on Totopotomoy Creek around 9 p.m. The next day, enemy fire forced the 44th NY to hastily dig breastworks near Bethesda Church. When the order came to change positions, Captain Eugene Nash, then second in command of the 44th NY, was wounded. It was the end of Captain Nash's active service but he would go on the write the definitive history of the 44th NY Regiment.

Cold Harbor

In the afternoon of June 1, 1864, the rebels drove back 44th NY skirmishers and attempted to rout the regiment. The southerners were forced back with considerable losses. The 44th NY lost one man killed and five wounded.

The object of Grant's maneuvering, Cold Harbor, was actually two places, the first called Cold Harbor Tavern, or Old Cold Harbor, and the second called New Cold Harbor. They were about a mile apart and ten miles northeast of Richmond. New Cold Harbor was the sight of Gaines' Mill where so many men of the 44th NY had died two years earlier.

General Lee got to Cold Harbor first. By June 3, Lee's Army had constructed seven miles of fortifications between Old Cold Harbor and the Chickahominy River. The village of New Cold Harbor was in the middle, between Lee's army and the river. The two armies were poised to meet head on. That morning at dawn, Grant attacked with three corps. The assault on the southern end of Lee's entrenchments was driven back. Grant attempted to assault the north end of the fortifications and also renewed the assault on the south end. These attacks also failed. Grant's troops suffered massive casualties.

The 44th NY avoided much of the heaviest fighting that day but did have one man killed and three wounded by friendly fire from Burnside's Corps which was engaged in heavy fighting to the right of the 44th NY. Losses for the 44th that day totaled four killed and fourteen wounded.

Once again, the two armies stalled, each side unable to find any advantage in attacking well-entrenched enemy fortifications. By now, Grant's casualties since entering the Wilderness were about 52,000, and Lee's were about 33,000. The Northern papers began calling Grant the "fumbling butcher" for his allegedly poor decisions. Grant's plan to follow Lee's army wherever it went and destroy it was not working out. Still, Richmond was just a few miles away, the Army of Northern Virginia was growing weaker both in numbers and in leadership, and Grant had no intention of making all of the bloodshed and sacrifice his army had endured since entering the Wilderness come to nothing. He decided to march his army around Richmond, cross the James River, and take the Confederate held city of Petersburg. Richmond would then be isolated and both Grant and Lee knew there could be only one outcome of a siege of Richmond.

Petersburg, about twenty miles directly south of Richmond, was a major supply center for Richmond and was a crossroads of three railroads from the south and west. It was a prosperous city with a population of about 18,000. Going north from Petersburg, was a direct rail line to Richmond and another direct line to City Point on the James River. City Point would become a major supply depot for Grant's army, the location of Grant's headquarters, and a large field hospital, during the coming siege. For several months, it was the busiest port in the world.

The night of June 5, General Warren's 5th Corps moved out and headed for the James River, with Charles' Third Brigade acting as rear guard. On June 7, Charles notes that their baggage train finally reached them and ***"I has a clean shirt and a fine wash the first Wash and shirt in one month I of course enjoyed the change Very much"***. Later that day Charles wrote ***"there was a Mail came to the Regt this morning But no letters for this child I expect to get one soon from home."***

The 44th NY crossed the Chickahominy River on the morning of June 13, 1864. Around this time, Charles is beginning to write about getting out of the army should his efforts at promotion fail. The long marches, constant violence, and brutal conditions were taking a toll. They halted on the north side of the James River on June 15 and made camp, waiting their turn to be transported across. The 44th NY was the last of the 5th Corps to cross.

Charles had been ill the last few days, but was feeling better this morning than he had in the past week. He had a fine wash in the River that evening. Always appreciative of the beauty around him, Charles writes of the James River:

> ***"..it is a Noble stream and a splendid place the Rebs chose for their Capital With the enterprise of the North it Would soon equal the far famed Hudson with its booming commerce the farther that I travel south the more I am convinced that it is a splendid country all that it Wants is the curse of slavery Removed and some yankey thrift it would make a perfect Garden in a short time the Crops Look magnificent Wheat oats and Corn in abundance".***

Despite heavy criticism in the north of Grant's ability as a commander, Charles did not see it that way. He writes on June 16,

> ***"Grant has done splendid in all his flank movements this being the Last flank movement Was Executed finely without the loss of a man or any of our train."***

The Long Siege

Charles' division was transported across the James River by boat starting at 10:30 a.m., June 16, 1864. They left from Wilson's Wharf, and were all across in about an hour. The march continued as soon as they arrived on the south bank. It was hot, and the dusty roads made it a hard tramp. The 5th Corps marched to within seven miles of Petersburg and advanced to supporting distance of the 2nd and 9th Corps. That morning Grant had attacked the Confederate works defending Petersburg with three corps, totaling 50,000 men. Confederate General Beauregard was able to hold the rebel line with his force of 14,000.

On June 17, the 5th Corps moved to the front but was not engaged. They were still to the rear of the 2nd and 9th Corps. There was heavy fighting, and a great many wounded were now coming in from the front. Charles believed that Beauregard would be forced to abandon the city within 24 hours. Charles also notes of the fighting on the previous day ***"I learn that the Negros take the first line of works on the right."***

At Petersburg, slaves did much of the work of digging entrenchments for Lee's army. For the North, Black Americans were playing a growing role as soldiers. The United States Colored Troops, or USCT, consisted of primarily Black Americans with some other minority groups included. By the end of the war, 166 USCT regiments made up one tenth of the Union Army. About 187,000 Black Americans served as Federal soldiers. Sixteen of these men would be awarded the Congressional Medal of Honor.

The next day, General Meade, furious at the failure of his commanders to break through the Confederate lines, ordered a general assault. The 2nd and 18th Corps attacked at dawn. They came at Beauregard's left flank which was the north end of the Confederate defenses. Things were going well until they hit Beauregard's second line of defense. The Federal attackers died by the hundreds and were stopped. They remained under heavy fire for hours.

Meade renewed the attack at noon, but by then Beauregard had received reinforcements and Lee had arrived to take overall command of the Confederate forces. The Union 9th Corps, and General Warren's 5th Corps attacked Beauregard's right flank, which extended to the Jerusalem Plank Road. They were stopped with heavy losses. Along with many others, Joshua Chamberlain of Little Round Top fame, received a severe wound and was carried from the field. Meade continued the attack. Some commanders simply refused to advance. Tempers among the officers flared. As with many assaults since entering the Wilderness, Meade ordered his commanders to attack without support, regardless of what other commanders were doing. A final assault ordered around 6:30 p.m. failed with horrendous losses. The 1st Maine Heavy Artillery Regiment lost 632 out of 900 men in the assault. The morale of Grant's exhausted army sank to a new low. General Warren, now more and more at odds with General Meade was heard to say, ***"For 30 days it has been one funeral procession past me, and it has been too much!"***

Charles Kelly's Brigade, part of the 1st Division of the 5th Corps, was held in reserve, and missed much of the June 18 fighting. That night the 44th NY was ordered to the front, and placed on picket within musket range of enemy lines. In four days, the attempt to capture Petersburg had cost the north about 11,300 casualties. The toll for Lee's army was about 4,000.

General Meade expressed his regret to General Grant for the behavior of his men, noting how tired they were and that they lacked the vigor and force they had shown at the beginning of the campaign. Grant replied that he was satisfied that

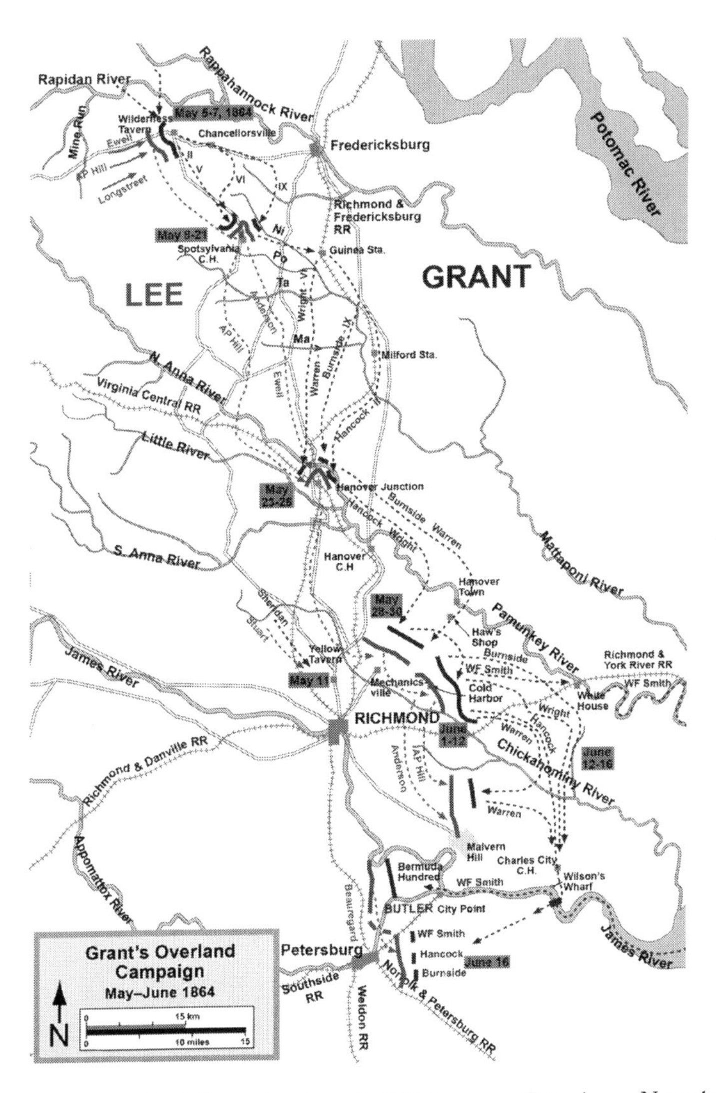

A view of Grant's Overland Campaign from the Wilderness to Petersburg. Note that General Warren crossed the North Anna River on May 23. The battle at Hanover Junction, May 23 to May 26, and Lee's inverted V formation is shown. Charles Kelly is with Warren on the west side of the V. From there, Charles crosses the James River at Wilson's Wharf on June 16, and joins in the long siege of Petersburg. "Map by Hal Jespersen, www.cwmaps.com".

everything that could be done was done. Grant told Meade, ***"Now we will rest the men and use the spade for their protection until a new plan can be struck."***

General Grant did not realize just how long it would take to strike that new plan. When Grant crossed the Rapidan and entered the Wilderness six weeks ago, the one thing he did not want was to become mired down in an extended siege. Lee felt the same way. He wanted to crush Grant's army in the way he knew best, by maneuvering in order to isolate parts of the northern invader's force and destroy each part before reinforcements could arrive from the other parts. Lee knew a prolonged siege would allow the industrial might of the north to come crashing down on his army. The only possible outcome would be the destruction of the Army of Northern Virginia, the loss of Richmond, and the defeat of the South. Now both Generals were exactly in the position they had worked so hard to avoid. The siege of Petersburg would go on for many months.

Charles Kelly was growing weary with the war. The tedium of lying flat on the ground all night in a picket line, and then spending the day huddled in a dirt trench, with the occasional crack of a sniper's rifle or the sound of a mortar shell arching its way toward his position, was affecting him. The day after the big assault, three men in his regiment had been instantly killed by snipers when, while waking from sleep, they exposed their heads above the breastworks. On June 21, 1864, he writes,

> ***"it is the Wish of my heart to see this War at an End it being a great destruction of human life and no particular Benefit to the people my opinion is that We Will be a great people When once united again United We Will Be in the End."***

General Grant was now determined to stop all supplies from getting into Petersburg and from there on to Richmond. On June 21, Grant's 2nd and 6th Corps attempted to cut the Weldon Railroad Line at Globe Tavern. They were driven back to the Jerusalem Plank Road, where they dug in. Before the attack, Charles writes,

> ***"The Enemy has a Very strong Work in our front 2 corps also 6 are on our left perhaps the 5 6 and 2 intend to charge the Enemies Works We must do something of that kind or We Will not clean the rascals out"***

As the summer days passed, Charles now had time on his hands, which was always hard for him. He started to get resentful when mail did not arrive from home. High tension went hand in hand with the tedium. Almost daily, one or two men of the regiment were killed or wounded from sniper fire or bursting cannon shells. On June 23, there was a bright spot. The regiment received a shipment of soft bread and pickles.

On June 27, Charles writes of his concern for sanitation in the trenches:

> ***"We are still in the trenches this Army must adopt some sanitary measures in Reguard to the health of Troops or our sikc List Will Role up to a Large thing before Long."***

Another factor affecting health of the troops was availability of water, which did not seem to be a concern of the higher-ranking officers. Finally, some innovative men of the 44th NY dug wells, which supplied their needs.

On July 4, 1864, Charles notes that the regimental band was playing *"Yankee Doodle"* and *"Hail Columbia"* that day. The hot summer days were drifting by with no rain. Charles remained focused on letters from home, but observed, ***"The Enemy throws over a shell about once in fifteen minutes, just Enough to give to understand we are not in cival Life".*** As the summer continued, Lee's army was showing signs of the siege. On July 15, Charles writes,

> ***"Johnnies are coming in Every day saying they have nothing to eat and that the Whole thing is played out they are tired of fighting and if the Traitors of the North would only Keep still the government Would soon get along with this whole thing".***

During the siege of Petersburg soldiers in the Federal army began building bomb shelters, basically a dugout covered by logs and several feet of earth. It was a relatively safe place to sleep as the mortar and artillery shells continued to come out of the sky.

This bomb shelter was within a strong point in the Federal lines at Petersburg called Fort Sedgwick, also known as Fort Hell. Note the woven baskets filled with earth, called gabions. Modern gabions are made using wire baskets filled with stones. The roof of the shelter, at the front is made with grain sacks filled with dirt, placed over logs. The rest of the roof is packed earth over logs. There is a substantial homemade fireplace and chimney. Quite a high-end shelter, probably for officers. This shelter is about a half mile from Confederate lines. (Library of Congress)

When not on picket duty, the men would often read to each other to help get through the nights. For example, Charles listened to a book read called *A Strange Story* by Sir Edward Bulwer. The leading character is young Doctor Allen Fenwick, who fights to counteract the sinister influence the mesmerist Margrave has over Fenwick's beloved Lilian. Will the doctor's scientific methods prevail or will he be forced to put aside the rational, and embrace the unknown? Charles writes, ***"I sat up until one o'clock hearing it Read."***

The Battle of the Crater

Well before dawn on the morning of July 30, 1864, the 44th NY received orders to prepare to attack. A large explosion was planned, meant to destroy Elliot's Salient near the Blandford Church, east of Petersburg, about 400 feet west of the Federal entrenchments. A salient is a section of fortification that juts out from a line of the entrenchments to form an angle. Less than two miles from the heart of Petersburg, destroying this strong point in the Confederate line might open a gateway to attack, and break the Rebel defense of the city.

It was a month earlier that Lieutenant Colonel Henry Pleasants, a mining engineer in command of a brigade in Burnside's 9th Corps, suggested that a tunnel be dug from behind the Federal lines to beneath Elliot's Salient. The shaft would then be filled with gunpowder and exploded, causing an opening in the Rebel lines and allowing a breakthrough. Burnside brought the idea to General Meade who was skeptical but allowed Pleasants to begin the work. Pleasants chose a hundred coal miners from the 48th Pennsylvania Regiment and began digging on June 25. By the night of July 28, the tunnel was ready.

Extending over 500 feet straight into the Rebel line, and then turning a right angle in both directions for 75 feet, the tunnel formed a T shape, with the top of the T running directly under the Confederate fortifications. As the miners dug, they shored up the shaft with scrap lumber, and sloped the tunnel gradually upward to prevent water from accumulating in the tunnel. A wood duct ran the length of the three-feet-wide and four-feet-high tunnel, which joined into a vertical shaft behind the Federal lines. A fire, kept continually burning, heated the vertical shaft and drew stale air from the tunnel and up the vertical shaft just like a chimney. No other ventilation was needed. The T was twenty feet below the Confederate soldiers in the salient. Pleasants' men filled the T with 320 kegs or about 8,000 pounds of gunpowder, and filled in the junction of the T with packed earth. The entrance to the tunnel was also filled, extending about 30 feet into the tunnel.

Everything was ready. Previously, General Burnside had ordered his 4th Division, made up of Black American troops, to receive two weeks of special training to lead the attack following the explosion. There were two brigades in the Black American Division, one would go right, around the site of the explosion, and the other would go left. They would advance to the Jerusalem Plank Road and hold that position as more troops flowed into the breach. Hopes were high for a breakthrough.

At the last minute, General Meade, fearing political repercussions should the attack fail and the Black Division be decimated, ordered Burnside to replace the 4th Division with one of his other Divisions for the lead position in the attack. Burnside, frustrated beyond words with Meade's interference, took the matter to Grant, who sided with Meade. Tired of dealing with the whole thing Burnside ordered his remaining three Division Commanders to draw straws. General James Ledlie, commanding Burnside's 1st Division, got the short straw. The 1st Division would lead the attack. General Ledlie, usually in a state of inebriation, failed to brief his men on what was expected.

After some delay igniting the charges, the gunpowder exploded at 4:44 a.m., on July 30. Earth, men, and guns shot into the air instantly killing 300 Confederate soldiers. The explosion ripped a crater in the earth 170 feet long, 100 feet wide and 30 feet deep. For a quarter of an hour, the Confederate troops to the sides and back of the crater were so stunned they did nothing. General Ledlie's troops were also stunned. Not sure what was going on or what to do, they waited about ten minutes and advanced, many of them climbing down into the crater. General Ledlie was in a bombproof bunker to the rear, drinking. Descending into the crater, the men of Ledlie's 1st Division got to the far side and discovered the walls were too steep to climb. As more troops arrived from the Federal lines, they became packed in tighter and tighter at the bottom of the giant hole. Within an hour Confederate troops counterattacked and poured musket fire into the crater from the west rim. Men in the bottom, unable to move forward or back, died by the hundreds.

Instead of cutting his losses, Burnside sent in his 4th Division of Black American troops commanded by General Edward Ferrero. The Confederates were now on both flanks of the crater in force so Ferrero's men were ordered forward, straight into the crater. For several hours the killing continued. Burnside lost almost half of the 9th Corps, of which about 1,400 were taken prisoner. The fate of the Black soldiers was particularly gruesome. For many Confederate soldiers this was the first time they had met Black Americans armed and in battle. Angered by their presence, many Black troops were shot or bayoneted while trying to surrender. Some Federal troops killed the Black troops around them, trying to avoid being killed by the rebels for fighting alongside Black Americans. Confederate generals finally were able to stop Black prisoners from being murdered. By the end of the day, both sides controlled the same ground they started the morning with.

Grant, crushed by what had happened, wrote to Washington, *"It was the saddest affair I have witnessed in this war… Such an opportunity for carrying fortifications I have never seen and do not expect again to have."*

After the war, Congress placed the blame for the fiasco on General Meade. His decision to withdraw the USCT (United States Colored Troops) and replace them with men not trained for the mission was found to be a key factor in failure of the plan. The finding of Congress provided General Burnside with little comfort. Not long after July 30, Burnside was removed from command of the 9th Corps, never to command troops again. General Ledlie was also removed from command. General Ferrero was strongly criticized for sitting in a bunker sharing a bottle of rum with General Ledlie during the attack. As far as Grant's part in the affair, he testified to Congress,

> *"General Burnside wanted to put his colored division in front, and I believe if he had done so it would have been a success. Still I agreed with General Meade as to his objections to that plan. General Meade said that if we put the colored troops in front (we had only one division) and it should prove a failure, it would then be said and very properly, that we were shoving these people ahead to get killed because we did not care anything about them. But that could not be said if we put white troops in front."*

Charles Kelly, whose regiment was standing by, never got the order to join in the fight that day. Having little knowledge of what had happened, Charles wrote,

> *"There must have Been some mistake or carelessness somewhere to think after having taken the work to Be driven out of them the men and officers feel awful about the Result of the whole thing"*

The Siege of Petersburg Goes On

For now, the siege of Petersburg continued. The days grew hotter. Charles writes of the high cost of everything in the north. He notes that *"the flies are a great pest, and they get a good Living of us poor soldiers."* Among the officers in the regiment, there was growing talk of wanting to get out of the army in the fall when the three-year enlistment of the original 44th NY was up. Charles did not join the regiment until one year after the original formation of the 44th NY and was unsure if he would be able to muster out that fall with the rest of the men. As the days of August roll on, Charles becomes more and more concerned about his chances of going home in the fall. His Colonel asked him if he would sign up for three more years if promoted to Captain. After thinking it over, Charles writes, ***"I will not muster for three years Longer I shall get out if I possibly can as I am Wanted at home."***

Reconciled to the fact that his army could not breach the massive Confederate fortifications of Petersburg, General Grant continued to close his grip on the city. On August 18, 1864, Grant ordered General Warren's 5th Corps to cut the Weldon & Petersburg Railroad, one of two remaining railroad lines supplying Petersburg. Grant had tried this before, on June 21, without success.

That afternoon, the 2nd and 3rd Divisions of the 5th Corps attacked the Confederate lines between Globe Tavern and Ream's Station while Charles Kelly's 1st Division destroyed as much of the railroad line as they could, burning ties, twisting rails, and destroying culverts. Charles writes,

> ***"We marched this morning at daylight towards the Right of our Line marched in Line of Battle all forenoon We Layed the Weldon Railroad at Ream's Station We attacked the Rebs at that front the 2 and 3 Div of our Corps was engaged the second they had a Brisk fight and Lost from Two hundred to 300 men our Div in Reserve heavy firing on our right our men Destroying the Railroad it has rained hard all day stoped at night threw up some Works the Report is that the Rebs attacked the 9 Corps in the night and Lost heavy."***

As Charles says, the 2nd and 3rd Divisions had a hard fight, suffering over eight hundred casualties that day. The following afternoon, as destruction of the rail-line continued, the rebels counterattacked Warren's infantry with four brigades, inflicting heavy losses, and taking 2,700 prisoners. By nightfall, Warren was driven back to his headquarters at Globe Tavern. A new attack was launched by the gray coats on August 21, but General Warren's troops had been given time to dig in near Globe Tavern. Driving the first line of Federal troops from their trenches, the Rebels charged into a murderous fire from Yankee artillery stationed a half mile back. The Confederate attack failed.

Charles writes of that day,

> ***"was detailed for Picket this morning Went with 32 men was stationed on the right of our Div Line We were on the Line about one hour when the enemy Drove in our Lines of Picket The fighting was on the front of the Maryland brigade also in front of the 2 Brigade of our Div The Rebels thought that they had us flanked but we only fixed a trap for them they must have Lost about one thousand men Killed wounded and Prisoners"***

By the end of the day, Lee knew that the upper portion of the Weldon Railroad line had been lost. He wrote to Confederate President Jefferson Davis on August 22, ***"Our supply of corn is exhausted today and I am informed that the small reserve in Richmond is consumed."*** For a time, supplies continued up the Weldon Railroad to Stony Creek Station, 20 miles south of Petersburg. From there the supplies were off loaded to wagons for a thirty mile haul up the Boydton Plank Road to Petersburg, and then on to Richmond. Grant's iron grip on Petersburg was getting tighter.

Charles was growing weary of endless killing with little results. Charles writes about the action of August 19:

> ***"our generals are caught Knapping too often We obtained our position without any Loss But after getting the R.R. we allowed the Enemy to flank us on the Right this was the 19th of the month and as Near as I can Learn We lost about 1700 men taken Prisoners which was all Carelessness on our part if we would only hang some of our Generals for Neglecting their Duty we would gain more Victories by it as our men fight"***

Charles continues to write of being on picket, looking for letters from home, drinking bad water, and his hope to be mustered out in the fall.

Four hundred and sixty miles to the southwest, on September 1, 1864, the Confederate army, under Command of John Bell Hood, was forced to abandon Atlanta, Georgia, a major source of supply for the South. Taking Atlanta was the task of General Grant's chief lieutenant, Tecumseh Sherman. General Sherman set out from Chattanooga about the same time Grant entered the Wilderness, and fought a series of hard battles with General Hood throughout the summer. General Hood was a fiery commander who had lost the use of his left arm, when wounded near Little Round Top at Gettysburg. General Hood was again severely wounded at the Battle of Chickamauga, which resulted in the loss of his right leg, but he kept on fighting. The fall of Atlanta caused a huge boost to morale in the north, and all but assured the victory of Abraham Lincoln in the November elections. For the South, the re-election of Lincoln was the final deathblow to hopes of reaching a compromise with the North that would allow the Confederate States of America to survive.

CHAPTER TWENTY ONE

Charles Goes Home

Back to Albany

At last, on September 23, 1864, Charles learned that he would be headed home the next morning. On the 24th, those men of the regiment who would be leaving the army, marched for City Point and boarded a steamer on the James River. They stopped at Fortress Monroe and from there continued on to Washington, arriving the morning of September 26, 1864. During the trip, Charles mentions that the officers were drinking probably more than they should. Charles spent the night with the other officers in a hotel in Washington; the celebration continued. They left Washington the afternoon of September 27 and arrived in Baltimore about 6 p.m. That night, they loaded onto freight cars and headed north to Philadelphia, arriving about 9 o'clock, the morning of September 28. From there it was back in the cars for the ride to New York City, where they boarded another train and arrived in Albany on September 29, about 4 p.m.

This is a photo of the Officers of the 44th NY Regiment who mustered out in October of 1864. Charles Kelly is in the first row, seated, on the left side of the photo. (Library of Congress)

The 44th NY received a splendid reception in Albany, with speeches from the Governor and Mayor, a march through the streets, and lots of good food. The men slept in City Hall that night, and the next day moved to the city arsenal to begin the process of mustering out of the army. Charles spent the next few days working on his muster out rolls, his final task as a soldier.

Muster out rolls were an official record containing each soldier's name, age, rank, unit, regiment, and company. The rolls included the date and place each soldier mustered in, the date the soldier mustered out, the period of enlistment, and the name of the commanding officer of the soldier's unit. They often had information such as level of pay for the soldier, the last time the soldier was paid, whether the soldier owed money to the army on his clothing account, or arms and equipment account, if the soldier had received a bounty for joining the army, and if any additional bounty or pay was now due. For example, Charles' muster out roll shows that he had been promoted to 1st Lieutenant January 31, 1863, that he was entitled to pay for commanding Company C during the months of July, August, and September of 1864, and had received pay up to June 30, 1864. These important documents would determine entitlement to pensions, and establish such thing as whether the soldier had been a prisoner of war, wounded in battle, left the army for medical reasons, or even if the soldier had deserted the army.

Charles submitted his muster out rolls for Company C, and they were rejected. For whatever reason he had to do them over. Charles comments in his diary on October 7, 1864, ***"Still in Albany I have to make out my Rolls over again which is a Damn shame."***

Charles' diary entries end on October 9, and 10, 1864, with Charles still in Albany working on his rolls. His military records indicate that his last day in the Army was October 11, 1864.

The dairies of Charles Kelly consisted of five hand written volumes, each small enough to carry with him on his journey through the war. The small size, spelling, lack of punctuation, lack of capitalization and penmanship make them at times, difficult to read.

War's End

Lasting several more months, Robert Lee's defense of Petersburg finally collapsed, and the city surrendered the morning of April 3, 1865. Richmond surrendered that evening. Lee fled with his army southwest, hoping to join with the army of Joe Johnston. Within days, Lee's army was surrounded and cut off from all source of food and other supplies, and hopelessly outnumbered. Lee surrendered the Army of Northern Virginia to General Grant on Palm Sunday, April 9, 1865, at around 1 PM. On April 14, 1865, President Abraham Lincoln was assassinated while attending a production of *Our American Cousin* at Ford's Theater, in Washington.

Over two million men served in the Union Army during the War of the Rebellion. About a quarter of them were immigrants and about 180,000 were Black Americans. Each of these men had a story to tell. Charles Kelly's service in the Army of the Potomac is but one example among millions of what men experienced during the war.

Charles started army life camped on Antietam Creek next to ground where just weeks earlier so many had died. He marched to Warrenton and saw General McClellan on his flamboyant farewell ride, when McClellan was replaced by General Burnside. He marched to Fredericksburg and was in the last Federal assault on the stonewall. He was knocked unconscious in that attack by an exploding artillery shell, but recovered and was among the last of Union troops to leave Fredericksburg, and abandon the city to the Rebels. He was in the infamous "Mud March" when Burnside's army and career sank into the winter roads of Virginia. He was part of the rear guard at Chancellorsville when Joseph Hooker fled before Robert Lee's much smaller army. He fought against Jeb Stuart's cavalry at Goose Creek, and from there made forced marches to Gettysburg, arriving on Little Round Top moments before it could be overrun by James Longstreet's gray coats. He was part of the pursuit of Robert Lee after Gettysburg when Lee crossed the Potomac with the Federal army in his front, and broke Abraham Lincoln's heart. He watched the grim execution of Federal soldiers for desertion. He camped at Alexandria for three months guarding trains and attending theater. During that time, he saw Abraham Lincoln as they were both attending a production of *"Richard the III"* at Grover's Theater in Washington. Charles travelled with Grant and Meade into the Wilderness where he lived through even greater levels of savagery and killing than he had previously experienced. He charged Laurel Hill, was wounded, and fought at Spotsylvania Courthouse. He ended his army life in the trenches outside of Petersburg, which heralded a new kind of warfare.

Army life consisted of endless marches with little food or sleep, living on hardtack and coffee, hoping for a letter from home, and enduring times of tedium and monotony. In between the monotony were periods of extreme violence, and day after day of sleeping on the ground during the cold, muddy, and wet winters of Virginia, often without even a tent. Charles shared all of these things with hundreds of thousands of others. His diaries give us a glimpse of what it was like to be a soldier in the Army of the Potomac during the War of the Rebellion. This country, and our world, was forever changed by this war. We cannot afford to forget what men did in this war, or how it shaped the nation we now live in.

Life After the War

After leaving Albany, Charles returned to Penn Yan and resumed his pursuit of various business opportunities. He opened an office over J. Brown's Clothing Store on Main Street, and offered a service finding substitutes for those wanting to avoid the draft. After the war, he formed a painting and glazing company in partnership with his younger brother Neil. The partnership ended in December of 1867, due to the poor health of Neil. Neil had contracted consumption (tuberculosis) during his time with the 126th NY Infantry during the war. Neil died of tuberculosis in January of 1874, at the age of thirty- five.

In April of 1866, Charles rented his property on Jacob Street, the location of his *Farmers Saloon*, to John Shearman who remodeled the property and opened a hotel. John named the hotel the *Central House*. In 1870, Charles purchased a license for $85 and took over as proprietor of the Central House. In June of 1870, Charles purchased livery barns adjacent to his hotel from Albert Tuell, for the convenience of his hotel guests.

On Tuesday, April 30, 1872, a fire started at the iron works of Whitaker & Bryan in the business district of Penn Yan. Over forty buildings, including the Central House and its barn and other out buildings, were burned. According to the Yates County Chronicle, Charles' loss amounted to $8,000. His insurance coverage was $4,800.

Charles was among the first to rebuild. By July of 1872, the foundation walls for his new hotel were complete. On January 1, 1873, The Penn Yan Express announced that Charles' new *Central House* was to be formally opened today. It commented that *"It is a magnificent building, complete in all of its appointments."* The new Central House accommodated forty guests, and received glowing reviews. In 1875, one correspondent wrote:

September 1, 1875:

"The Central House.—A correspondent of the Seneca Falls Reveille thus compliments the Central House in this village, and its popular proprietor, Mr. Charles Kelly:

> ***"I do your readers visiting Penn Yan a favor in recommending to favorable consideration the Central House, kept by that excellent hotel man and provider Charles Kelly, and who has not heard of "Charlie." The house is comparatively new, large, and commodious and well arranged, the rooms are airy and comfortable, well-furnished throughout. Its sleeping apartments, beds and bedding are of the very first order, clean, neat and every way enjoyable. His table is supplied with not only the substantials of life in abundance well prepared, but also with many of its luxuries in their season. The "Central" is conveniently located nearest to the railroad station of any other in the village and also in the midst of the business portion of the town."***

In 1876, Charles married Margaret A. Graham. They had a son and three daughters. Charles' son died in infancy. Charles, who always regretted his own lack of education, sent each of his three daughters to college, which was quite unusual for the time.

Charles retired from a successful business life in 1892. He was said to be a loving indulgent husband and father, and a staunch supporter of his church. Charles was well esteemed in his community and noted for his exceptionally retentive memory. In the time after the war Charles was known for his great breadth of reading, especially in his retirement years.

Charles died, 8 p.m., May 1, 1907, at the age of 76, in Penn Yan, New York.

Acknowledgements

My wife Gael made the diaries of Charles Kelly available, and thus made this book possible. She spent many hours transcribing the diaries into an easily readable form, and helped me greatly with editing and proofreading.

Ari Koontz edited my manuscript. Quite simply, Ari's attention to detail and command of the English language made this a better book.

Alison Tutton Robins took my rough manuscript and turned it into a professionally designed, attractive book, which included designing a cover that I am proud to have for my book.

I also wish to thank John Hoffmann for sharing his article, "Robert Todd Lincoln's Gettysburg Story."

A special thanks goes to Hal Jespersen for generously sharing his wonderful maps.

Bibliography

Magazines, Webpages, Articles

Hoffmann, John. (Summer 2017). Robert Todd Lincoln's Gettysburg Story. Journal of the Abraham Lincoln Association, *V. 38, No. 1*, pp. 1-13. University of Illinois Press.

Lackey, Rodney. (no date) Notes on Civil War Logistics: Facts & Stories. U.S. Army Transportation Corps. Retrieved October 2019 from https://transportation.army.mil/.

Webb, Ashley. (no date) Coffee and the Civil War. Retrieved January, 2020, from https://www.battlefields.org/learn/articles/coffee-and-civil-war

The Battle of Gettysburg, A Battle Animation Like You've Never Seen Before. Retrieved from: civilwaranimatedbattles.com/ (2022). TVM Enterprises, LLC.

Books

Arthur, Billy & Ballard, Ted. Gettysburg Staff Ride; Briefing Book. Fort Leavenworth: Army University Press

Ballard, Ted (2008) Staff Ride Guide, Battle of Antietam. Washington D.C.: Center of Military History

Billings, John. (1887) Hardtack and Coffee or The Unwritten Story of Army Life. Boston: George M. Smith & Co.

Early, Jubal. (1912) Lieutenant General Jubal Anderson Early, C.S.A., Autobiographical Sketch and Narrative of the War Between the States, With Notes by R.H. Early. Philadelphia: J.
B. Lippincott Company

Catton, Bruce. (1984). Bruce Catton's Civil War. New York: The Fairfax Press.

Doubleday, Abner. (1882). Volume VI. Chancellorsville and Gettysburg. New York: Charles Scribner's Sons

Foote, Shelby. (1974). The Civil War a Narrative, Volumes I, II, and III: Vintage Books.

Gordon, John. (1903) Reminiscences of the Civil War by General John B. Gordon of the Confederate Army. New York: Charles Scribner's Son's

Hennessy, John. (1993). Return to Bull Run, The Campaign and Battle of Second Manassas. New York: Simon and Schuster.

Johnson, Robert & Buel, Clarence; editors. (1887). Battles and Leaders of the Civil War, Volume 3: New York. The Century Co.

Katcher, Philip. (1975). Army of the Potomac. New York: Osprey Publishing Ltd.

Kesterson, Brian. (2017). Soldier of Courage, Soldier of Compassion, The Story of Captain Bennett L. Munger, Company C, 44th New York State Infantry. Washington, West Virginia: Night Hawk Press.

Matter, William. (1988). If It Takes All Summer, The Battle of Spotsylvania. Chapel Hill: The University of North Carolina Press.

McClellan, H.B. (1885) The Life and Campaigns of Major-General J.E.B. Stuart, Commander of the Cavalry of the Army of Northern Virginia. Cambridge: The Riverside Press

McCurry, Stephanie. (2010). Confederate Reckoning, Power and Politics in the Civil War South. Cambridge: Harvard University Press.

Murray, R.L. (1999) "Nothing Could Exceed Their Bravery", New Yorkers in Defense of Little Round Top. Wolcott: Benedum Books.

Nash, Eugene, Captain. (1911). A History of the Forty-forth Regiment New York Volunteer Infantry in the Civil War, 1861-1865, Chicago: The Lakeside Press.

Nevins, Allan. Editor. (1962). A Diary of Battle, The Personal Journals of Colonel Charles S. Wainwright 1861-1865. New York: Harcourt, Brace & World Inc.

Norton, Oliver. (1909) Strong Vincent and His Brigade at Gettysburg, July 2, 1863. Chicago: Oliver Willcox Norton

Norton, Oliver. (1913, reprinted 1992) The Attack and Defense of Little Round Top, Gettysburg, July 2, 1863. Gettysburg: Stan Clark Military Books.

Rhea, Gordon. (1994) The Battle of the Wilderness, May 5-6, 1864. Baton Rouge: Louisiana State University Press.

Sawyer, Franklin. (1881) A Military History of the 8th Ohio Vol. Inf'y:. Cleveland: Fairbanks & Co. Printers

Smith, John. (1905). History of the 118th Pennsylvania Volunteers, Corn Exchange Regiment. Philadelphia: J.L. Smith, Map Publisher.

Smithurst, Peter. (2011). The Pattern 1853 Enfield Rifle. New York: Osprey Publishing Ltd.

Sowell, Thomas. (1981). Ethnic America A History: Basic Books, Inc.

Swinton, William. (1882) Campaigns of the Army of the Potomac. New York: Charles Scribner's Sons

Wilson, Mark. (2001). The Extensive Side of Nineteenth-Century Military Economy: The Tent Industry in the Northern United States during the Civil War. Charlotte: University of North Carolina.

Battle Reports, Congressional Reports

Army of the Potomac, History of Its Campaigns, The Peninsula, Maryland, Fredericksburg. (1863). Testimony of Its Three Commanders, Before the Congressional Committee on the Conduct of the War. New York: Tribune Association.

Narrative of Events and Observations Connected with the Wounding of General T.J. (Stonewall) Jackson by Major Marcellus N. Moorman, Stuart Horse Artillery, Cavalry Corps, Army of Northern Virginia. Collated from his diary and memory. Lynchburg, Va., November 15th 1902.

Note: OR, refers to, *The War of the Rebellion: A Compilation of the Official Records of the Union and Confederate Armies*, published by The Government Printing Office between 1881 and 1901. The Compilation contains 127 Volumes (over 130,000 pages), plus a General Index and accompanying Atlas.

OR, Chap. XXXIII. Page 411. Battle of Fredericksburg. Report of Col. Thomas B. Stockton, Sixteenth Michigan Infantry, commanding Third Brigade. Headquarters Third Brigade, Camp near Potomac Creek, Va., December 17, 1862.

OR, Chap. XXXVII. Page 384. Reports of Maj. Gen. Daniel E. Sickles, U.S. Army; commanding Third Army Corps. Headquarters Third Army Corps, May 20, 1863.

OR, Chap. XXXVII. Page 849. Reports of Maj. Gen. Richard H. Anderson, C.S. Army, Commanding Division. April 27-May 6, 1863.—The Chancellorsville Campaign. Near Fredericksburg, Va., June 6, 1863

OR, Chap XXXIX. Page 140. Itinerary of the Army of the Potomac and co-operating forces, June 5-July 31, 1863.

OR, Chap XXXIX. Page 459. Report of Maj. Gen. Jubal A. Early, C.S. Army, commanding division. June 3-August 1, 1863.—The Gettysburg Campaign.

OR, Chap XXXIX. Page 615. Report of Colonel Strong Vincent, 83rd Pennsylvania Infantry, commanding 3rd Brigade. HQ 3rd Brigade. 1st Div., 5th Corp, Camp near Aldie VA, June 22nd 1863.

OR, Chap XXXIX. Page 622. Report of Col. Joshua L. Chamberlain, Twentieth Maine Infantry. Field Near Emmitsburg, July 6, 1863.

OR, Chap. XLVIII. Page 539. Journal of Maj. Gen. Gouverneur K. Warren, U.S. Army, commanding Fifth Army Corps

Newspapers

The Penn Yan Democrat

The Penn Yan Express

Yates County Chronicle

Diaries

Diaries of Charles Kelly. October, 1862 to October, 1864. Five handwritten volumes. Unpublished.

Made in United States
Troutdale, OR
01/14/2024

16937201R00166